"The field of mental health has be
integrative explanation for positive
Dr. Francis L. Stevens's *Affective Neuroscience in Psych...*
Guide for Working with Emotions explains what we have been missing
along."

Karin Maria Hodges, *Psychologist, Private Practice, Concord, MA*

"Cognitive approaches to psychotherapy have come to dominate the
field in recent decades, in part because of their solid scientific foundation.
They typically view emotional distress as a symptom to be reduced.
Psychotherapy approaches that emphasize experiencing and processing
emotional distress are effective but less well validated. This excellent
book aims to restore the balance and does more to link recent advances
in basic affective neuroscience and psychotherapy practice than any
other. Recommended for beginning psychotherapists as well as any
clinician who takes emotional processing in psychotherapy seriously and
wants to know how and why it works."

Richard D. Lane, M.D., Ph.D., *Professor of Psychiatry,*
Psychology and Neuroscience, University of Arizona;
Editor (with Lynn Nadel) of Neuroscience of Enduring Change:
Implications for Psychotherapy *(Oxford University Press)*

"Dr. Stevens has done a fine job of compiling recent information on
affective neuroscience and its application to therapy. His clinical
examples help to illustrate key concepts. This book provides a helpful
introduction to these topics."

Alexis D. Abernethy, Ph.D., *Professor of Clinical Psychology,*
School of Psychology & Marriage and Family Therapy,
Fuller Theological Seminary

Affective Neuroscience in Psychotherapy

Most psychological disorders involve distressful emotions, yet emotions are often regarded as secondary in the etiology and treatment of psychopathology. This book offers an alternative model of psychotherapy, using the patient's emotions as the focal point of treatment. This unique text approaches emotions as the primary source of intervention, where emotions are appreciated, experienced, and learned from as opposed to being regulated solely.

Based on the latest developments in affective neuroscience, Dr. Stevens applies science-based interventions with a sequential approach for helping patients with psychological disorders. Chapters focus on how to use emotional awareness, emotional validation, self-compassion, and affect reconsolidation in therapeutic practice. Interventions for specific emotions such as anger, abandonment, jealousy, and desire are also addressed.

This book is essential reading for clinicians practicing psychotherapy, social workers and licensed mental health counselors, as well as anyone interested in the emotional science behind the brain.

Dr. Francis L. Stevens works as a psychologist in Worcester, MA. He has taught a variety of classes in psychology and neuroscience. His research focuses on affective neuroscience applications to psychotherapy.

Affective Neuroscience in Psychotherapy

A Clinician's Guide for Working with Emotions

Francis L. Stevens

Routledge
Taylor & Francis Group

NEW YORK AND LONDON

First published 2022
by Routledge
605 Third Avenue, New York, NY 10158

and by Routledge
2 Park Square, Milton Park, Abingdon, Oxon, OX14 4RN

Routledge is an imprint of the Taylor & Francis Group, an informa business

Library of Congress Cataloging-in-Publication Data
A catalog record has been requested for this book

ISBN: 978-0-367-71442-0 (hbk)
ISBN: 978-0-367-71440-6 (pbk)
ISBN: 978-1-003-15089-3 (ebk)

DOI: 10.4324/9781003150893

Typeset in Bembo
by MPS Limited, Dehradun

Contents

PART II The Practice of Clinical Affective Neuroscience: Emotion-Based Interventions

Part I

Introduction and Scientific Background

How to Read This Book and Contents Outline

The goal of the book is to make better use of emotion in psychotherapy. The first chapter is on why I believe this book is needed. The next two chapters provide the background and foundations of affective science and affective neuroscience. The book then shifts to the practice of clinical affective neuroscience. Starting with the section on emotional awareness and mindfulness, the book explains how to apply these techniques in using emotion effectively in therapy. I start with the topic of mindfulness because a patient must be aware of what they are feeling before taking steps to work with feelings. Once aware of feeling(s), it's often important to validate the feeling(s) and provide self-compassion for them. After this, the focus is often on regulating emotions to a moderate level of arousal, which is most effective for change. In the next chapters, I cover individual emotions, and finally, the technique of affect reconsolidation is introduced. The book presents these topics in a sequential format from the basic first steps moving towards deeper, more holistic change approaches. However, readers are encouraged to apply the techniques in the order that is most useful to them or their patients. Different individuals need different things. Some patients may be quite aware of what they are feeling, others may be strong at emotional regulation, while some may need help with self-compassion. For this reason, the reader is encouraged to refer to each chapter or section as it may be helpful for them or their patients.

You can read the book from start to finish, as some explanations build upon previously presented material, but it is by no means necessary to go in order. The book can also be used as a reference guide or manual when working with a certain emotion or trying to understand the neurobiological background of a certain phenomenon. Feel free to skip around; additionally, some sections refer to other sections in the book, because just like the brain, the concepts in the book are not linear. Readers may find it useful to move from section to section in addressing some overarching psychological concepts. Some parts have a scientific orientation; other parts are more practitioner orientated, and these perspectives change

DOI: 10.4324/9781003150893-101

throughout the text. Some readers may be interested in fundamental science, while other readers may prefer the more practical concepts. The reader is encouraged to skim through parts that are less relevant for them. In blending the science with my personal experience as a psychologist, I tried to make it clear when I am offering my perspective and when the perspective is based in science. Citations exist throughout the text supporting the science when presented; these can be used for further reference as well. A challenge in writing a book like this is blending the science with the art of psychotherapy. Psychotherapy itself is a nebulous practice. Whenever I help a patient, I often think I know why they got better, but of course, this is only my assumption: not wrong, but not empirically proven. However, if I were to write this book without my subjective voice, I think I would miss a lot of what has worked for me in therapy and could help other clinicians. In focusing on emotion within psychotherapy I am offering a new perspective, so many of the ideas presented have yet to be empirically tested. It doesn't mean they are wrong; it just means I cannot definitively say they are correct. The rationale is based in part on my subjective experience and in part on an educated understanding of where the science is leading, albeit not yet at the point of empirical certainty. In psychotherapy, unlike other scientific disciplines (say physics or chemistry), empirical certainty is often harder to reach. Affective neuroscience is easier, but in translating it into its therapeutic significance, certainty is harder to establish. In the text, I will often say, "What I've done," or "What works for me," and generalizations are made based on this. That means this likely works in most cases but will not always work for all patients. I think we should approach psychotherapy with the best scientific information, while recognizing that humans are complicated and we shouldn't overly aggregate them. For example, self-compassion seems to be of high therapeutic value, but I've had patients tell me "Don't try that garbage on me." I listen and try not to argue. Perhaps they experienced extreme condescension as a child and self-compassion feels like a reenactment to them. So, while I will say self-compassion works for many of my patients, in psychotherapy there is probably an exception to every rule. I tell my patients, "We are going to try different things until we find something that works." From a therapeutic perspective, be open to failure or changing tactics for the benefit of the patient. What is probably most important is that we treat our patients like human beings. So, start from that point. Beyond that, we are going to need some treatment interventions and a strong understanding of what is happening in the brain when a patient struggles with psychopathology. I have had much success with this form of therapy, and I hope you can learn for yourself a new emotional approach to psychotherapy. At this point, you may be thinking, "How did I get here? There are so many therapy books; why write one more?"

1 The Need for a New Approach to Therapy

There are a variety of modalities of psychotherapy to choose from in treating psychological disorders. However, in my experience, I've found that many of these modalities are helpful to treatment in some regards, but are never comprehensive. Worse, I've felt that many of these modalities have a single approach to treatment, which lack flexibility when they don't work. Research supports the idea that for many people, psychotherapy remains ineffective (Driessen, Hollon, Bockting, Cuijpers, & Turner, 2015; Dragioti, Karathanos, Gerdle, & Evangelou, 2017), with little explanation as to why. Although this book is not written with the intention of being based solely upon my experience, I think it's important to share my background, as much of it has influenced my thinking and clinical work. In my master's program, like many students, I was trained in Cognitive Behavioral Therapy (CBT). CBT has a wealth of evidence demonstrating its effectiveness as a modality of psychotherapy (Hofmann, Asnaani, Vonk, Sawyer, & Fang, 2012), so it makes sense that so many programs train students according to its principles. While CBT offered some benefits to me as a therapist, I found that many of the patients I saw were not improving much from my Socratic questioning, and at times they felt misunderstood or patronized. I found myself leaning back on the "basic" clinical skills I was taught, like open-ended questioning or active listening as a way to help patients. Upon entering my Ph.D. program, I was excited to focus on a different modality of therapy. My Ph.D. program was organized around psychodynamic therapy for the most part, with a specific focus on object relations theory. Many of my professors in this program looked down upon CBT and saw it as a beginner's type of therapy. The program's psychodynamic focus greatly improved my understanding of the human psyche, and my ability for case conceptualization vastly improved under my professors. However, as a clinician during this time I still felt I lacked the tools to fully help my patients. While I now had a much better understanding of why my patients were suffering from mental illness, I still felt I lacked strong interventions to improve their condition. In many ways, I felt stuck. I'm not sure if it was because of this or some other related interest, but I started studying the neuroscience of the human brain.

DOI: 10.4324/9781003150893-1

Perhaps I felt I could find the answers I was looking for if I just went back to a more basic level. It was during this time I read Lou Cozolino's *The Neuroscience of Psychotherapy* (Cozolino, 2002) and Alan Schore's *Affect Regulation and the Origin of Self* (Schore, 2015). These books provided a grounding for all the theoretical concepts I had learned and inspired me to study neuroscience during my post-doctoral fellowship. At this point, I was interested in affective neuroscience: how the brain responds to and processes emotion. I studied the anterior cingulate cortex — an area I've found to be important in the conscious awareness of emotion (Stevens, 2016). Affective neuroscience helped me place in context all the various modalities of psychotherapy I had previously learned. After my post-doc, I continued practicing and training in the different modalities of psychotherapy. I was trying to understand how to optimize psychotherapy, long considered a black box treatment that is poorly understood as a science. I studied psychoanalytic treatment for a year at the Boston Psychoanalytic Society and Institute. I learned from some excellent teachers who had tremendous insight into patients' pathologies. However, when it came down to the mechanism of change, it was typically assumed that improved patient insight would solve their problems. This was not something I agreed with, nor could I find any empirical support for the matter. It seemed to be a holdover from Freud's original theory that making the unconscious conscious solves problems. I've seen many people both personally and professionally who have great insight into their psychopathology, but are still depressed or anxious. Needless to say, I was disappointed by this approach, but I found the more contemporary approach of CBT inadequate as well. Behavioral therapy worked well for phobias and other psychological problems with a clear external stimulus, like avoiding a party for someone with social phobia. However, what is the avoided stimulus for someone with depression or post-traumatic stress disorder (PTSD)? Moreover, interventions that gave positive rewards for eating to someone with anorexia or for not using in a substance abuse disorder never seemed to work. Cognitive therapy presumes that changing faulty beliefs will ameliorate the problem; the assumption here is that if the patient can examine their thinking, identify irrational beliefs, and change them, the psychopathology would be solved. This method also lacked effectiveness in my experience. For example, I found that individuals who were afraid to fly understood it was a perfectly safe way to travel, yet still felt afraid. Depressed individuals recognized they were not bad people, yet still felt bad about themselves. I quickly saw that changing negative thoughts about one's self typically did not directly affect one's feelings. Cognitive therapy helped many of my patients from an ensuing cascade of negative thoughts about themselves, so the problem didn't get worse, but the original negative feelings towards themselves never changed. Furthermore, I found no evidence for the tenet behind cognitive therapy — that you can change your feelings through your thoughts. I found that you can't mitigate future negative feelings by stopping negative self-talk; however, if one's self-concept is deemed to be negative, that evaluation of self doesn't respond to rational thought proving otherwise. CBT offered some good tools but never appeared to be fully effective. It somehow seemed inadequate when the concept of emotion was introduced.

During my internship as a psychologist, I had seen some positive outcomes with interpersonal therapy, but the lack of a coherent treatment approach did not appeal to me. However, it did get me started in following the work of clinicians like Diane Fosha and Leslie Greenberg. They were publishing work on novel therapeutic modalities that focused on emotion and the experiential process of therapy. They identified a corrective emotional experience that changes previous negative emotional memories into neutral or positive emotional valences. After my training, I continued to practice as a psychologist, while teaching courses in clinical psychology. It was during this time I learned about memory reconsolidation. Memory reconsolidation comes out of the neuroscience literature and shows that when a memory is retrieved it is subject to change or reconsolidation; thus when it is stored again it is different than the original memory. It struck me that the therapeutic processes Fosha and Greenberg were describing were very consistent with memory reconsolidation. This is all explained and summarized nicely in Lane, Lee, Nadel, and Greenberg's (2015) paper, which identifies memory reconsolidation as the common pathway to therapeutic change. Here I started to see a new way to think about psychotherapy; this has greatly shaped my clinical work and thinking about psychopathology. Yet, if there is one mechanism for therapeutic change, it begs the question, "Why do so many different modalities of therapy exist?" I addressed this question in a paper I published in 2019 (Stevens, 2019): for memory reconsolidation to occur, one must be able both to access the emotion and have some ability to regulate the emotion. In this capacity, there are a variety of ways to increase the emotional experience and to regulate emotion, around which many of the different psychotherapies center. In general, psychodynamic interventions are often based on increasing emotional awareness through recalled emotionally-laden childhood memories. Cognitive therapy interventions involve developing skills to regulate emotion, while exposure or behavioral therapies are designed both to increase arousal and manage the response. It seems the many therapeutic modalities indirectly address emotion, through old memories, thoughts, and behaviors, but don't address directly the concept of emotion. I think if we reframe psychotherapy from a perspective of emotion, things start to make much more sense.

1.1 Emotion in Psychotherapy

There is an assumption in an article I wrote (Stevens, 2019) that psychotherapy should focus on emotional states, as opposed to behaviors or

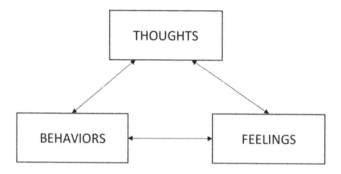

Figure 1.1 Cognitive triangle.

cognitions that modalities like CBT focus on. There is much evidence throughout the psychological literature that emotions, cognitions, and behaviors all influence one another (Pessoa, 2019). This is sometimes referred to as the cognitive triangle (see Figure 1.1). Any psychological problem can be approached from any of the three components: behavioral; cognitive; or emotional. The first two components have been addressed extensively throughout the psychotherapy literature. Yet, little psychotherapy literature exists on approaching problems from an emotions-based perspective. There are two reasons I focus on emotion in psychotherapy, the first being my experience as a therapist. When the therapy session was more focused on the patient's emotions, I recognized greater improvement in my patients than when the session was focused on their thinking or behavior. Secondly, my emphasis on emotion in psychotherapy was also consistent with the literature on affective neuroscience and brain plasticity. Increasingly, studies in neuroscience identify specific biomarkers related to emotion's role in psychopathology, from which targeted interventions can be developed to address brain dysfunction in mitigating mental illness. We are learning that emotion can drive thought and behavior. Evidence increasingly demonstrates that we can react to emotionally threatening stimuli without conscious awareness (Garrido, Barnes, Sahani, & Dolan, 2012; Garvert, Friston, Dolan, & Garrido, 2014). The textbook example of this is the hiker who quickly jumps to the side of the trail thinking they have seen a snake, then after just a moment realizes it was clearly only a stick on the trail. Information entering the eye makes a stop at the brain's thalamus before being fully processed in the visual cortex. Here at the thalamus, when a possible threat exists, the amygdala gets activated, signaling a fear response, which causes the body to jump before the conscious mind ever realizes what is happening. Once the neocortex catches up, the image of a stick is obvious, and the hiker may even feel silly for having such a strong reaction. In this example, the brain's emotional response preceded any conscious cognitive response. Given this, I saw a need for more emotion-based interventions in psychotherapy. This especially seemed important if the primary goal was the eventual reconsolidation of negatively-valenced emotional memories.

Much of CBT is built on the ABC model, an acronym that stands for activating event, belief, and consequence. The model proposes that if you can change your thinking or belief, the consequence or emotional response will also change. There is some evidence to support the intervention of cognitive reappraisal in psychopathology; however, this varies by psychological disorder and often shows a low-to-medium effect size across studies (Hofmann et al., 2012). This indicates cognition interventions can have some effect on emotion and psychopathology in general, but if psychopathology is a disease, cognitive therapy may be only a small part of the cure. Going back to the basic cognitive triangle and its concept that thoughts, emotions, and behaviors all affect one another, a CBT model uses only a unidirectional approach to emotions. That is, we can change emotions through thought and behavior, but we cannot change thought and behavior with emotion. It would seem on a surface level that addressing emotions as an agent of change could also be a useful approach to psychotherapy.

Interventions designed to affect emotion directly have been shown to be efficacious in treating psychopathology (Pascual-Leone & Greenberg, 2007; Wilson, Mackintosh, Power, & Chan, 2019). Although research in this area is still growing, the results are promising. This work demonstrates that interventions designed to address emotion directly may have important consequences on behavior, cognition, and subsequent emotions, thus offering a new treatment focus for psychopathology.

References

Cozolino, L. (2002). *The neuroscience of psychotherapy: Building and rebuilding the human brain (Norton series on interpersonal neurobiology)*. New York, NY: WW Norton & Company.

Dragioti, E., Karathanos, V., Gerdle, B., & Evangelou, E. (2017). Does psychotherapy work? An umbrella review of meta-analyses of randomized controlled trials. *Acta Psychiatrica Scandinavica, 136*(3), 236–246.

Driessen, E., Hollon, S. D., Bockting, C. L., Cuijpers, P., & Turner, E. H. (2015). Does publication bias inflate the apparent efficacy of psychological treatment for major depressive disorder? A systematic review and meta-analysis of US National Institutes of Health-funded trials. *PloS one, 10*(9), e0137864.

Garrido, M. I., Barnes, G. R., Sahani, M., & Dolan, R. J. (2012). Functional evidence for a dual route to amygdala. *Current Biology, 22*(2), 129–134.

Garvert, M. M., Friston, K. J., Dolan, R. J., & Garrido, M. I. (2014). Subcortical amygdala pathways enable rapid face processing. *Neuroimage, 102*, 309–316.

Hofmann, S. G., Asnaani, A., Vonk, I. J., Sawyer, A. T., & Fang, A. (2012). The efficacy of cognitive behavioral therapy: A review of meta-analyses. *Cognitive Therapy and Research, 36*(5), 427–440.

Lane, R. D., Ryan, L., Nadel, L., & Greenberg, L. (2015). Memory reconsolidation, emotional arousal, and the process of change in psychotherapy: New insights from brain science. *Behavioral and Brain Sciences, 38.*

Pascual-Leone, A., & Greenberg, L. S. (2007). Emotional processing in experiential therapy: Why "the only way out is through.". *Journal of Consulting and Clinical Psychology, 75*(6), 875.

Pessoa, L. (2019). Embracing integration and complexity: Placing emotion within a science of brain and behaviour. *Cognition and Emotion, 33*(1), 55–60.

Schore, A. N. (2015). *Affect regulation and the origin of the self: The neurobiology of emotional development.* New York, NY: Routledge.

Stevens, F. L. (2016). The anterior cingulate cortex in psychopathology and psychotherapy: Effects on awareness and repression of affect. *Neuropsychoanalysis, 18*(1), 53–68.

Stevens, F. L. (2019). Affect regulation and affect reconsolidation as organizing principles in psychotherapy. *Journal of Psychotherapy Integration, 29*(3), 277.

Wilson, A. C., Mackintosh, K., Power, K., & Chan, S. W. (2019). Effectiveness of self-compassion related therapies: A systematic review and meta-analysis. *Mindfulness, 10*(6), 979–995.

2 Affective Science

Werner and Gross (2010) estimate that 80–85% of psychological disorders involve impairments in emotion. Most psychological disorders, other than a few like dementia, learning disabilities, and ADHD, primarily involve difficulties with emotion. In my experience meeting individuals reporting mental health problems, they are typically most concerned with how they feel. Individuals with depression are more troubled by their decreased mood (the way they feel) than their lack of motivation, or negative cognitions. Patients with anxiety typically come to psychotherapy because they feel anxious; they are less concerned with irrational thoughts or anxious behaviors. Consistently, patients reported to me what that they most wanted was to feel better. Even individuals with substance abuse disorders more often than not wanted help to improve their feelings and seemed less concerned about the negative behavior surrounding the continued use of the substance(s). All this provided evidence to me that psychological interventions were too focused on thoughts and behaviors and not enough on emotions. This could be due to a historical distrust of emotion and the view that emotion is more primitive in nature, considered to be something of an evolutionary leftover (Fox, 2018). Emotions are also more much elusive to study than behaviors, which are more demonstrable and thus easier to measure. As psychology looked to establish itself as a science in the early twentieth century, it tried to become more empirical in nature, leading to an emphasis on studying demonstrable behavior over more nebulous emotions. B.F. Skinner believed in a behavioral approach that could reduce all behavior to a series of reinforcements (Clapano, 2007).

Historically, in research, cognition has been prioritized over emotion. Researchers focusing on intelligence testing and cognitive ability published the first IQ test, Simon-Binet, in 1916, while emotional intelligence did not gain notoriety till Daniel Goleman's (1995) book *Emotional Intelligence*. In schools, there is currently an increased emphasis on socio-emotional learning, but historically the focus was solely on cognitive development. A historical bias may exist in psychology focusing on behavior and cold cognitive processes over affective ones. These "cold" cognitive processes, such as executive function, memory, attention, and processing speed, are

DOI: 10.4324/9781003150893-2

more stable across time, as opposed to emotional or "hot" cognitive processes, which are influenced by mood and can vary throughout the day (Roiser & Sahakian, 2013). Since these "cold" cognitive processes were easier to study, the science of psychology focused on them, creating a bias against emotional processes.

Affect is an encompassing term that includes emotion, feeling, and mood (Fox, 2018). Although debate exists around the terms, emotions are considered to be more ephemeral in nature, arising from body experiences. Feelings are considered to arise after emotions and involve the experience of the emotion. For example, some individuals may feel empowered by their anger, while others feel shame in relation to their anger (Damasio, 1999). Feelings are more conscious experiences of emotion. Moods are considered to be longer-lasting states of affect, not linked to certain events. The disorder of depression can be seen as a consistent altered state of mood. It is important to note that in the literature, the terms emotions, feelings, and moods are often used interchangeably.

A large amount of evidence suggests that emotion does have a sizable influence on cognition and behavior. Individuals often misattribute their emotional state (Gawronski & Ye, 2014; Schachter & Singer, 1962) and emotion drives implicit attitudes (Dasgupta, DeSteno, Williams, & Hunsinger, 2009), suggesting that emotion does influence cognition. A substantial amount of research also exists demonstrating the deficits in cognitive functioning and behavior, which result from mental illness (Veiel, 1997). Again, this signals influences of emotional processes on thinking and behavior. The following sections review the effects of emotion on behavior, memory, attention, and judgment, to highlight the importance of emotion's role in psychological processes.

2.1 Emotion Influences Behavior

There is much evidence demonstrating that emotion affects behavior (Baumeister, Vohs, Nathan DeWall, & Zhang, 2007). The Iowa Gambling Task is a common neuropsychological test demonstrating the unconscious influence of emotion on behavior. In this task, subjects are presented with several decks of cards and asked to choose a card from one of the decks, which then results in monetary gains or losses over time. The decks are loaded, with certain decks of cards offering a higher likelihood of a positive outcome than others. Healthy individuals will typically switch to choosing higher-rewarding decks before they consciously recognize that they are making better financial choices. This is evidenced by measuring skin conductance responses, which occur before any cognitive recognition of choice. Comparably, individuals with brain damage to the ventromedial prefrontal cortex (vmPFC) show no skin conductance response and do not switch to higher-reward decks (Bechara, Damasio, Tranel, & Damasio, 1997; Dunn, Dalgleish, & Lawrence, 2006). Bechara et al. (1997) point to data from the Iowa Gambling Task to support their somatic marker hypothesis, that the felt sense of emotion precedes behavior, marked by the skin conductance changes prior to consciousness recognition of the behavior change. The somatic marker hypothesis has fallen under criticism; namely, that the psychological mechanisms through which the body influences decision making are not as clear as first proposed (Dunn et al., 2006). However, more recent data doesn't falsify the somatic marker hypothesis, but does question the findings and interpretation of some of the data supporting the somatic marker hypothesis (Wright & Rakow, 2017). One important question related to the somatic marker hypothesis, which will also be examined later, is, "Does the somatic influence always product better decisions?" Some work also suggests emotions can impact decision making negatively (Shiv, Loewenstein, & Bechara, 2005). New research also indicates that emotional intelligence moderates the relationship between somatic markers and decision making (Yip, Stein, Côté, & Carney, 2020). This indicates that although emotion can influence behavior, the mechanisms through which it occurs are complex and may be affected by many other factors before determining a final behavior.

Winkielman, Berridge, and Wilbarger (2005) did a series of experiments to demonstrate the role of unconscious affect on behavior. Participants were exposed subliminally to happy, neutral, and sad expressions. Participants were queried about their conscious feelings on a multi-item scale. Next, researchers examined participants' ratings of a beverage, how much of it they poured for themselves and drank, and how much they were willing to pay for the beverage. All of these behaviors were influenced by unconscious emotional primes that participants were not even aware of. Unconscious emotional cues have also been shown to affect altruistic behavior (Zemack-Rugar, Bettman, & Fitzsimons, 2007).

This research offers an additional reason emotions may be important to focus on in psychotherapy: the unconscious influence of emotion. Thoughts and behaviors can be considered more conscious processes. Behaviors are actions, which are measurable and can be seen. Thoughts, although sometimes perhaps not fully formed, are considered to be conscious cognitions. Freudians would say that we can push thoughts outside of conscious awareness, but once the "thought" is no longer conscious, is it still a "thought"? This is probably a matter of philosophical debate. We do know from neuroscience research that when someone is thinking, neocortical or higher brain regions are activated; participants of these studies report being aware of their thoughts. Alternately, when experiencing emotion, subcortical or lower brain regions are activated, and participants are not always aware of what they are feeling. A growing set of research is developing which shows the non-conscious effects of emotion on cortical activity. Thinking is one aspect of cortical activity (Diano, Celeghin, Bagnis, & Tamietto, 2017;Tamietto & De Gelder, 2010).

2.2 Emotion Influences Memory

The brain acts as series of neural networks, like a large three-dimensional spider web, where you could think of each concept being its own node. For example, writing, which I am doing now, is a concept in my brain and is associated with other nodes. In making the choice to write today, other nearby nodes may have been activated. Maybe I associate writing with boring high school homework assignments, which might make me less apt to write. Perhaps I'm associating writing with positive feedback, from journal reviewers (unlikely), or which I assume to be true, I associate writing with expressing my ideas which I think can be beneficial to fellow clinicians and patients. Depending on our conceptualization of writing, different individuals may have different ideas or feelings associated with writing, like whether it's enjoyable or boring. Not only does the concept of writing activate the nodes around it, the nodes, depending on which are activated, can in turn affect my ideas and attitudes about writing. If I recently have been recounting boring homework assignments from high school, my writing node will be quicker to connect writing with boredom. Perhaps, too, if I'm in a state of boredom, I may be quicker to recall boring homework assignments, which would also influence my thinking about writing. We have many past memories, and the more emotional the memory, the better we remember it (Block, Greenberg, & Goodman, 2009; Houston, Clifford, Phillips, & Memon, 2013). All of these past memories create our neural webs, making it easier or more difficult to connect certain thoughts and ideas. One reader might be thinking "Who would ever enjoy writing?" while a second may think, "How could anyone not like writing?" Our different experiences create the neural networks around how writing is perceived. Something outside our network is hard for us to understand. Our emotional states influence these networks too, making it more like or less likely to associate two concepts (Eich, Macaulay, & Ryan, 1994).

It may be no coincidence that the amygdala, highly important for emotion, and the hippocampus, important for the consolidation and recall of memories, are adjacent to one another in the brain (Richter-Levin & Akirav, 2000; Phelps, 2004). If we think about our most salient memories, they are often those which have the strongest emotions. Events like getting married, having a child, or a major car accident tend to be remembered long after the event transpires. There are obvious benefits to remembering the good and bad events in our lives. If we remember these events, we can try to recreate conditions to have another positive experience, or avoid conditions that may have led to bad outcomes. While emotion can enhance certain memories, it could affect others negatively. MacKay et al. (2004) show that including emotional taboo words on a Stroop test made subjects demonstrate impaired recall for the neutral words, suggesting the salience of the emotional words may inhibit recall of the neutral material. Kensinger, Addis, and Atapattu (2011) found that for emotional memories which are correlated with amygdala activity, participants showed increased subjective vividness of the event, but decreased recall for episodic details of the event. Research on participants with amygdala damage also shows that they struggle to learn conditioned fear responses while having unimpaired declarative memory (Bechara et al., 1995). It seems emotion can enhance certain aspects of memory, but perhaps impair others.

We "woke up on the wrong side of the bed" is a common saying: some days everything seems to go wrong. There is some evidence in mood-congruent memory to support this. Research shows that when we are feeling down, we are more likely to remember other bad events (Bower, 1981). When we wake up on the wrong side of the bed, our negative mindset influences our future thinking to recall more negative examples from the past and perhaps even biasing our attention towards negative environmental information. More recent research on mood-congruent memory shows that depressed individuals exhibited a preferential recall of negative information; however, the effect varies through several modifiers, like age, the severity of depression, and self-relevance of the information (Gaddy & Ingram, 2014). Indicating that mood does affect memory recall, but a lot of other variables affect memory recall too. Mood-congruent memory can also lead individuals to believe false memories. Ruci, Tomes, and Zelenski (2009) suggested that when patients present with disorders of negative affect, they may not even realize they are giving their clinician a biased self-report history, due to their low mood.

When trying to recall information from memory, it is better to be in the mood state in which you encoded the information when recalling it. If you are happy while you are studying for a test, you are more likely to recall that information if you are happy when taking the test; this is referred to as mood-state-dependent memory. The effects of mood-state-dependent memory are likely stronger for significant autobiographical memories than mere recall of semantic information (Eich et al., 1994), which means that effect is stronger for recalling emotional events than just information. I have seen something similar in my therapeutic practice, especially when working in emergency crisis situations. Patients will arrive distressed and will recount a litany of events that led to this emotional crisis. We'll regulate the patient's emotions and make a plan for them to come back so we can work through this chronic problem. However, upon our second meeting the patient reports that the crisis from previous meeting was a singular occurrence. The patient typically thanks me for my help and time but declines future therapy. I find myself questioning which was the real history: the crisis episode where the patient recounted a series of past problems that needed attention, or the second meeting where the patient felt calm, noting there have been some stressful past events, but nothing to the level that would warrant therapy? My guess is that the patient doesn't even know. The large variations in the patient's mood between the two sessions affected their memory recall and subsequent judgment of whether they need therapy. Does the patient need therapy? It seems to depend on their mood that day.

Research on implicit memory also suggests emotion, which is linked with implicit learning, can affect behavior unknowingly. The historically significant study by the psychiatrist Edouard Claparede demonstrates this. Claparede hid a pin in his hand before shaking hands with one of his patients who had Korsakoff's syndrome, a disorder caused by thiamine deficiency, often as a result of alcoholism. Korsakoff's syndrome often results in anterograde amnesia, a condition where the patient can no longer form new memories. Claparede would prick the patient with the needle. She would leave and upon returning would refuse to shake Claparede's hand, although she had no recollection of the previous event. The patient demonstrated an implicit memory by refusing to shake Claparede's hand, but had no explicit memory for the event. The patient would also confabulate some reason for not shaking Claparede's hand (Kihlstrom, Mulvaney, Tobias, & Tobis, 2000). The painful feeling of having your hand pricked likely helped solidify an implicit memory in avoiding handshakes, providing evidence that emotion can influence memory in the absence of conscious thought. I personally have a strong aversion to olives, though I have no conscious memory as to why I would dislike olives so much. I can't help but wonder if some event in my childhood occurred where I was disgusted by olives. Today, while the explicit memory no longer exists (or is accessible), the implicit memory has direct implications when debating pizza toppings with friends and family. The psychology of repressed memories is surrounded by controversy and debate, with some therapists swearing by the existence of repressed memories. They offer anecdotal evidence of patients with PTSD who experience emotional triggers in the absence of direct recollection of the traumatic event. Other psychologists point to evidence for false memories, which suggests that repressed memories may actually be just fabricated memories (Loftus & Bernstein, 2005). The phenomenon of repressed memories, which cannot be empirically demonstrated, creates obvious challenges in trying to resolve this debate. While the evidence for implicit memory is strong, whether an individual can repress a memory or just fail to recall it will likely continue as a matter of debate.

2.3 Emotion Influences Attention

Objects with emotional significance or salience draw our attention. A specific salience network exists in the brain, consisting of the dorsal anterior cingulate cortex (dACC) and anterior insula (AI), which is designed to draw our attention to salient environmental stimuli (see Section 3.4). A common example of this is the cocktail party effect where we can be at a large cocktail party with lots of noise, yet still perceive when our name is heard from afar. This phenomenon has also been shown to be present in infants as young as five months old (Newman & Jusczyk, 1996). Research shows that attention can be captured even when information is presented subliminally. Williams, Morris, McGlone, Abbott, and Mattingley (2004) demonstrated differential patterns in amygdala activation in reference to fearful, happy, and neutral faces, even when the stimuli were not perceived consciously. In fact, it appears the effects of emotion on attention are stronger when information is presented suboptimally or in a less conscious format (Rotteveel, de Groot, Geutskens, & Phaf, 2001). It seems our brains are uniquely wired to attend to emotional salience stimuli, especially fearful stimuli (Öhman, Flykt, & Esteves, 2001). Attention is tricky because in some ways we can control it and in others, we cannot. The direction of our attention appears to be influenced by two simultaneous brain processes: a "bottom-up" emotional salience detection, where if a tiger walks in the door we can't but help let it capture our attention; and a "top-down" cognitively-directed attention, such as focusing on a difficult task (Compton, 2003). Patients who are overwhelmed with strong emotions may struggle to focus their attention on school or work-related tasks. Emotions can unwillingly control our attention, and this could be a challenge for people who experience chronic distressful emotions. Evidence demonstrates that individuals with anxiety attend more to threat-related objects (Bar-Haim, Lamy, Pergamin, Bakermans-Kranenburg, & Van Ijzendoorn, 2007; Fox, Russo, Bowles, & Dutton, 2001), likely creating a circular feedback loop, where individuals become more anxious, and in turn attend to fearful stimuli, increasing their anxiety. Emotion also affects our field of attention; in high-intensity emotional states, such as with enthusiasm or disgust, attention is narrowed, while in low-intensity emotional states, such as sadness or amusement, attention focus is broader (Harmon-Jones, Gable, & Price, 2012). It may be important to keep in mind that when patients are emotionally overwhelmed, it is likely not a good time to try and solve problems. The ability for creative solutions will be decreased. As we will learn later, a moderate state of arousal is optimal for psychotherapy.

2.4 Emotion Influences Judgment

Psychological research provides many examples of how emotion can influence cognitive processes (Winkielman, Knutson, Paulus, & Trujillo, 2007). One of the first major papers by Schwarz and Clore (1983) demonstrated that participants' mood influenced their judgments about their lives; these judgments were also influenced by the type of mood they were in. When in bad moods, participants looked to attribute their bad mood to the environment, but this did not occur during happy moods. We want to explain away our bad moods, but we prefer to think of our good moods as our natural disposition. Another prominent example of emotion influencing judgment is the mere exposure effect. Evidence shows that when individuals are unconsciously exposed to faces, paintings, objects, or other stimuli, they will develop a preference for those stimuli (Bornstein, 1989). Phenomena like the mere exposure effect have been studied subliminally, so the subject is not consciously aware of the stimuli that they are exposed to. Findings show that after repeated exposure towards a stimulus, one's affinity for that stimulus increases, leading one to prefer stimuli with repeated exposure, without any conscious or cognitive understanding of these preferences (Harmon-Jones & Allen, 2001). The theory is the familiarity with the person or object creates an affinity, which then further draws individuals to that person or object. Harrison (1968) theorized that all novel stimuli induce negative affect. In an evolutionary sense, novel objects could be dangerous, but with repeated exposure and no negative consequences, negative affect reduces, and positive affect increases. More recent research on the mere exposure effect shows that affinity initially increases, but then decreases over time, creating an inverted U curve between exposure and liking (Montoya, Horton, Vevea, Citkowicz, & Lauber, 2017). Authors believe this is due to a habituation brain response. Initially and on subsequent new exposures when the stimulus is not well learned, neural activation in parahippocampal regions increases. However, after continued exposure, neural activation decreases in these regions, which reduces the amount of information that goes into long-term memory and subsequently liking reduces due to this reduction in neural processing and encoding. Perhaps an adaptive metaphor would be that of traveling. The traveler is initially excited and also a bit fearful of the new location. After a while, that initial fearfulness goes away but the excitement still remains. After an extended stay, the novelty wears off and the affinity for the new location decreases. What the mere exposure effect demonstrates is that we may not always be aware of the influence the feelings of novelty and habituation have on our judgments.

Furthermore, one's affect state can be influenced by subliminally presented stimuli. This subliminal exposure then affects the subsequent judgments of future unrelated stimuli, indicating that emotion can unknowingly affect later cognitive judgments (Monahan, Murphy, & Zajonc, 2000). Li, Zinbarg, Boehm, and Paller (2008) demonstrate that subliminally presented primes (pictures of emotional faces) can influence social judgments. Furthermore, this effect is moderated, showing those with greater levels of trait anxiety are more at risk for the effects of priming.

One interesting topic that is commonly researched is the influence of emotion on judgment in racial attitudes. Individuals will often express explicit egalitarian racial attitudes while having discrepant implicit attitudes (Nosek, Banaji, & Greenwald, 2002). This is measured by the implicit association test (IAT), which measures participants' reaction time between black and white faces and positive and negative words. The test shows that while we often claim to have no bias in our judgments, we often do. Moreover, these implicit attitudes are more predictive of our behavior than our explicit attitudes (Greenwald, Poehlman, Uhlmann, & Banaji, 2009; Stanley, Sokol-Hessner, Banaji, & Phelps, 2011). While the IAT has been shown to measure attitudes towards gender, political parties, and sexuality, the strongest effects are related to race (Greenwald et al., 2009). This implicit racial bias as measured by individual IAT scores is predictive of amygdala activity in the brain (Phelps et al., 2000), an area commonly activated in the experience of fear (LeDoux, 1998). Moreover, this increased amygdala activity is only seen when judging out-group individuals (Hart et al., 2000). This greater amygdala activation indicates an underlying association between black faces and fear. Individuals may unknowingly react fearfully to black individuals, contributing to the implicit bias effect, which then results in racially-biased behavior. So, even if we desire to be unprejudiced, it seems these deep emotional brain processes can affect our judgments without any conscious intention.

This chapter showed the extent to which the psychological effects of emotion can influence cognition and behavior. With this in mind, therapies like CBT where interventions are solely targeted on cognition and behavior affecting emotions are incomplete because emotion can affect behavior and cognition in the return direction. The next chapter will lay out the foundations of affective neuroscience, examining the different areas of the brain and their roles in emotion.

References

Bar-Haim, Y., Lamy, D., Pergamin, L., Bakermans-Kranenburg, M. J., & Van Ijzendoorn, M. H. (2007). Threat-related attentional bias in anxious and nonanxious individuals: A meta-analytic study. *Psychological Bulletin, 133*(1), 1.

Baumeister, R. F., Vohs, K. D., Nathan DeWall, C., & Zhang, L. (2007). How emotion shapes behavior: Feedback, anticipation, and reflection, rather than direct causation. *Personality and Social Psychology Review, 11*(2), 167–203.

Bechara, A., Damasio, H., Tranel, D., & Damasio, A. R. (1997). Deciding advantageously before knowing the advantageous strategy. *Science, 275*(5304), 1293–1295.

Bechara, A., Tranel, D., Damasio, H., Adolphs, R., Rockland, C., & Damasio, A. R. (1995). Double dissociation of conditioning and declarative knowledge relative to the amygdala and hippocampus in humans. *Science, 269*(5227), 1115–1118.

Block, S. D., Greenberg, S. N., & Goodman, G. S. (2009). Remembrance of eyewitness testimony: Effects of emotional content, self-relevance, and emotional tone 1. *Journal of Applied Social Psychology, 39*(12), 2859–2878.

Bornstein, R. F. (1989). Exposure and affect: Overview and meta-analysis of research, 1968–1987. *Psychological Bulletin, 106*(2), 265.

Bower, G. H. (1981). Mood and memory. *American Psychologist, 36*(2), 129.

Clapano, K. (2007). BF Skinner. In J. L. Kincheloe & R. A. Horn Jr (Ed.), *The Praeger handbook of education and psychology* (pp. 201–205). Praeger.

Compton, R. J. (2003). The interface between emotion and attention: A review of evidence from psychology and neuroscience. *Behavioral and Cognitive Neuroscience Reviews*, 2(2), 115–129.

Damasio, A. R. (1999). *The feeling of what happens: Body and emotion in the making of consciousness.* New York: Houghton Mifflin Harcourt.

Dasgupta, N., DeSteno, D., Williams, L. A., & Hunsinger, M. (2009). Fanning the flames of prejudice: The influence of specific incidental emotions on implicit prejudice. *Emotion*, 9(4), 585.

Diano, M., Celeghin, A., Bagnis, A., & Tamietto, M. (2017). Amygdala response to emotional stimuli without awareness: Facts and interpretations. *Frontiers in Psychology*, 7, 2029.

Dunn, B. D., Dalgleish, T., & Lawrence, A. D. (2006). The somatic marker hypothesis: A critical evaluation. *Neuroscience & Biobehavioral Reviews*, 30(2), 239–271.

Eich, E., Macaulay, D., & Ryan, L. (1994). Mood dependent memory for events of the personal past. *Journal of Experimental Psychology: General*, 123(2), 201.

Fox, E. (2018). Perspectives from affective science on understanding the nature of emotion. *Brain and Neuroscience Advances*, 2, 2398212818812628.

Fox, E., Russo, R., Bowles, R., & Dutton, K. (2001). Do threatening stimuli draw or hold visual attention in subclinical anxiety? *Journal of Experimental Psychology: General*, 130(4), 681.

Gaddy, M. A., & Ingram, R. E. (2014). A meta-analytic review of mood-congruent implicit memory in depressed mood. *Clinical Psychology Review*, 34(5), 402–416.

Gawronski, B., & Ye, Y. (2014). What drives priming effects in the affect misattribution procedure? *Personality and Social Psychology Bulletin*, 40(1), 3–15.

Goleman, D. (2005). *Emotional intelligence.* New York: Bantam Books.

Greenwald, A. G., Poehlman, T. A., Uhlmann, E. L., & Banaji, M. R. (2009). Understanding and using the Implicit Association Test: III. Meta-analysis of predictive validity. *Journal of Personality and Social Psychology*, 97(1), 17.

Harmon-Jones, E., & Allen, J. J. (2001). The role of affect in the mere exposure effect: Evidence from psychophysiological and individual differences approaches. *Personality and Social Psychology Bulletin*, 27(7), 889–898.

Harmon-Jones, E., Gable, P., & Price, T. F. (2012). The influence of affective states varying in motivational intensity on cognitive scope. *Frontiers in Integrative Neuroscience*, 6, 73.

Harrison, A. A. (1968). Response competition, frequency, exploratory behavior, and liking. *Journal of Personality and Social Psychology*, 9(4), 363.

Hart, A. J., Whalen, P. J., Shin, L. M., McInerney, S. C., Fischer, H., & Rauch, S. L. (2000). Differential response in the human amygdala to racial outgroup vs ingroup face stimuli. *Neuroreport*, 11(11), 2351–2354.

Houston, K. A., Clifford, B. R., Phillips, L. H., & Memon, A. (2013). The emotional eyewitness: The effects of emotion on specific aspects of eyewitness recall and recognition performance. *Emotion*, 13(1), 118.

Kensinger, E. A., Addis, D. R., & Atapattu, R. K. (2011). Amygdala activity at encoding corresponds with memory vividness and with memory for select episodic details. *Neuropsychologia*, 49(4), 663–673.

Kihlstrom, J. F., Mulvaney, S., Tobias, B. A., & Tobis, I. P. (2000). The emotional unconscious. *Cognition and Emotion*, 30, 86.

LeDoux, J. (1998). *The emotional brain: The mysterious underpinnings of emotional life.* Simon and Schuster.

Li, W., Zinbarg, R. E., Boehm, S. G., & Paller, K. A. (2008). Neural and behavioral evidence for affective priming from unconsciously perceived emotional facial expressions and the influence of trait anxiety. *Journal of Cognitive Neuroscience, 20*(1), 95–107.

Loftus, E. F., & Bernstein, D. M. (2005). Rich false memories: The royal road to success False Memories: The Royal Road to Success. In A. F. Healy (ed.), *Experimental cognitive psychology and its applications* (pp. 101–113). Washington, DC: American Psychological Association Press.

MacKay, D. G., Shafto, M., Taylor, J. K., Marian, D. E., Abrams, L., & Dyer, J. R. (2004). Relations between emotion, memory, and attention: Evidence from taboo Stroop, lexical decision, and immediate memory tasks. *Memory & Cognition, 32*(3), 474–488.

Monahan, J. L., Murphy, S. T., & Zajonc, R. B. (2000). Subliminal mere exposure: Specific, general, and diffuse effects. *Psychological Science, 11*(6), 462–466.

Montoya, R. M., Horton, R. S., Vevea, J. L., Citkowicz, M., & Lauber, E. A. (2017). A re-examination of the mere exposure effect: The influence of repeated exposure on recognition, familiarity, and liking. *Psychological Bulletin, 143*(5), 459.

Newman, R. S., & Jusczyk, P. W. (1996). The cocktail party effect in infants. *Perception & Psychophysics, 58*(8), 1145–1156.

Nosek, B. A., Banaji, M. R., & Greenwald, A. G. (2002). Harvesting implicit group attitudes and beliefs from a demonstration web site. *Group Dynamics: Theory, Research, and Practice, 6*(1), 101.

Öhman, A., Flykt, A., & Esteves, F. (2001). Emotion drives attention: Detecting the snake in the grass. *Journal of Experimental Psychology: General, 130*(3), 466.

Phelps, E. A. (2004). Human emotion and memory: Interactions of the amygdala and hippocampal complex. *Current Opinion in Neurobiology, 14*(2), 198–202.

Phelps, E. A., O'Connor, K. J., Cunningham, W. A., Funayama, E. S., Gatenby, J. C., Gore, J. C., & Banaji, M. R. (2000). Performance on indirect measures of race evaluation predicts amygdala activation. *Journal of Cognitive Neuroscience, 12*(5), 729–738.

Richter-Levin, G., & Akirav, I. (2000). Amygdala-hippocampus dynamic interaction in relation to memory. *Molecular Neurobiology, 22*(1–3), 11–20.

Roiser, J. P., & Sahakian, B. J. (2013). Hot and cold cognition in depression. *CNS Spectrums, 18*(3), 139–149.

Rotteveel, M., de Groot, P., Geutskens, A., & Phaf, R. H. (2001). Stronger suboptimal than optimal affective priming? *Emotion, 1*(4), 348.

Ruci, L., Tomes, J. L., & Zelenski, J. M. (2009). Mood-congruent false memories in the DRM paradigm. *Cognition and Emotion, 23*(6), 1153–1165.

Schachter, S., & Singer, J. (1962). Cognitive, social, and physiological determinants of emotional state. *Psychological Review, 69*(5), 379.

Schwarz, N., & Clore, G. L. (1983). Mood, misattribution, and judgments of well-being: Informative and directive functions of affective states. *Journal of Personality and Social Psychology, 45*(3), 513.

Shiv, B., Loewenstein, G., & Bechara, A. (2005). The dark side of emotion in decision-making: When individuals with decreased emotional reactions make more advantageous decisions. *Cognitive Brain Research, 23*(1), 85–92.

Stanley, D. A., Sokol-Hessner, P., Banaji, M. R., & Phelps, E. A. (2011). Implicit race attitudes predict trustworthiness judgments and economic trust decisions. *Proceedings of the National Academy of Sciences*, *108*(19), 7710–7715.

Tamietto, M., & De Gelder, B. (2010). Neural bases of the non-conscious perception of emotional signals. *Nature Reviews Neuroscience*, *11*(10), 697–709.

Veiel, H. O. (1997). A preliminary profile of neuropsychological deficits associated with major depression. *Journal of Clinical and Experimental Neuropsychology*, *19*(4), 587–603.

Werner, K., & Gross, J. J. (2010). Emotion regulation and psychopathology: A conceptual framework. In A. M. Kring & D. M. Sloan (Eds.), *Emotion regulation and psychopathology: A transdiagnostic approach to etiology and treatment* (pp. 13–37). New York, NY: The Guilford Press.

Williams, M. A., Morris, A. P., McGlone, F., Abbott, D. F., & Mattingley, J. B. (2004). Amygdala responses to fearful and happy facial expressions under conditions of binocular suppression. *Journal of Neuroscience*, *24*(12), 2898–2904.

Winkielman, P., Berridge, K. C., & Wilbarger, J. L. (2005). Unconscious affective reactions to masked happy versus angry faces influence consumption behavior and judgments of value. *Personality and Social Psychology Bulletin*, *31*(1), 121–135.

Winkielman, P., Knutson, B., Paulus, M., & Trujillo, J. L. (2007). Affective influence on judgments and decisions: Moving towards core mechanisms. *Review of General Psychology*, *11*(2), 179–192.

Wright, R. J., & Rakow, T. (2017). Don't sweat it: Re-examining the somatic marker hypothesis using variants of the Balloon Analogue Risk Task. *Decision*, *4*(1), 52.

Yip, J. A., Stein, D. H., Côté, S., & Carney, D. R. (2020). Follow your gut? Emotional intelligence moderates the association between physiologically measured somatic markers and risk-taking. *Emotion*, *20*(3), 462.

Zemack-Rugar, Y., Bettman, J. R., & Fitzsimons, G. J. (2007). The effects of nonconsciously priming emotion concepts on behavior. *Journal of Personality and Social Psychology*, *93*(6), 927.

3 Affective Neuroscience

3.1 Historical Background

The recent advancements in neuroimaging research have encouraged the growth of affective neuroscience. In previous research, measuring emotion was more nebulous and often assessed through self-report, which can be subjective. These more current methods allow us to identify specific brain areas that are activated when an emotion is present, helping to provide a more quantitative representation of affect. LeDoux brought interest to the emotion of fear and the activation of the amygdala in *The Emotional Brain* (1998), and in that same year, Jan Panksepp coined the term *Affective Neuroscience* (2004) in his book by the same name. Since then, affective neuroscience has mapped specific brain areas for emotions (Kragel & LaBar, 2016). The scientific scrutiny brought to emotions has helped established affective science as an important field within psychology. Affective neuroscience helps us to understand the important role emotions play in our mind and behavior. Decades ago, classical and operant conditioning helped us to understand human behavior, and with those scientific advances new treatment strategies, like positive reinforcement, were utilized to help change behavior. In a similar tone, the cognitive revolution helped us understand the effects of cognition on our mind and behaviors, which led to treatment developments in cognitive therapy. Now with the advances of affective neuroscience, we can develop further treatments to shape mind and behavior to ameliorate psychopathology. This book combines affective neuroscience with the latest developments in clinical psychology of emotion to help clinicians apply interventions for the treatment of psychopathology.

The James-Lange theory of emotion was an early attempt to understand the occurrence of emotion in the brain. The theory is this: an activating event occurs, followed by a physiological experience in the body, which is then interpreted in the brain. Based on that interpretation, an emotion occurs. The Cannon-Bard theory quickly criticized the James-Lange theory, hypothesizing that both the physiological reaction and emotion occur at the same time. The Cannon-Bard theory is also called the thalamic

DOI: 10.4324/9781003150893-3

theory of emotion because the thalamus sends an emotional message to the rest of the brain at the same time as the body's physiological experience. The Cannon-Bard theory points to evidence that an emotional response can occur, at times, much faster than the brain has time to recognize incoming nerve impulses from the body. The James-Lange theory emphasizes the role of cognition in emotion, while the Cannon-Bard theory purports the emotion is created independently. Building on the previous theories, Schachter and Singer developed the two-factor theory of emotion, so named because they believe emotion is dependent on both physiological arousal and the cognitive label. Evidence for this theory has been based on studies of misattribution of arousal, the most famous being the Dutton and Aron (1974) shaky bridge study. Researchers had male subjects interact with a female confederate after crossing a suspension bridge (high arousal) or a sturdy bridge (low arousal), or after a period of time when subjects' heart rate dropped after crossing the bridge (low arousal). Subjects were much more likely to phone the female when in a high arousal condition. Dutton and Aron believe that subjects were misattributing their arousal for interest in the female confederate and not to the actual source of arousal: the suspension bridge. This study and the two-factor theory of emotion can be looked at in two different ways. The two-factor theory believes the physiological arousal occurs, the participants recognize the female, and then concludes that they are feeling an attraction to the female—the final emotion. Yet, another interpretation is that the arousal itself is an emotion, which leads to the cognition that this female is attractive. Does the emotion occur at the initial stage of physiological arousal or does it occur when the experience is attributed? There have been many criticisms of Schachter and Singer's two-factor theory (Cotton, 1981), as it assumes that emotion has to be constructed cognitively. Which is primary—the emotion or the cognitive response? Empirical evidence exists supporting both the affective primacy hypothesis, that emotion is primary, and the cognitive primacy hypothesis, that thinking is primary. Lai, Hagoort, and Casasanto, (2012) explore both theories in an attempt to resolve the debate. She and her co-authors find that neither cognition nor affect is consistently the brain's primary response. Furthermore, emotion and cognition each affect one another, and often it is not cognition causing emotion or vice versa, but a complex interactional dynamic continually taking place between both emotion and cognition (Cunningham & Zelazo, 2007; Cunningham, Zelazo, Packer, & Van Bavel, 2007; Storbeck & Clore, 2007). Evidence indicates that the brain does not react with one single system to evaluate stimuli and send an emotional response. We tend to think of events as processes occurring along a linear timeline, but that is not how the brain works. It's more like a three-dimensional web of roads, with each road cutting through the next, affecting the traffic throughout the network.

Research examining the brain's response to faces suggests a two-pathway theory of emotional processing. Similar to the prior stick and snake example (see section 1.1), when the brain receives visual input for another individual's face, information gets processed in two directions (Garvert, Friston, Dolan, & Garrido, 2014; Garrido, Barnes, Sahani, & Dolan, 2012; Rudrauf et al., 2008). The pulvinar, a region of the thalamus, has a subcortical connection to the amygdala, which allows for rapid processing of faces before conscious awareness (Jiang et al., 2009). This pathway exists in conjunction with a primary pathway where information gets processed in the visual cortex and moves on to more cortical areas. Further evidence corroborates the two-pathway theory for rapid emotional processing, finding that even patients with lesions to their visual cortex can detect emotion in faces when no other facial characteristics can be determined (Pegna, Khateb, Lazeyras & Seghier, 2005). This condition, called affective blindsight, demonstrates that individuals can process emotional information without stimulus awareness (Morris, DeGelder, Weiskrantz, & Dolan, 2001). Research on affective blindsight also shows that non-conscious perceptions can subsequently affect conscious processes, indicating a direct effect of emotions on cognition (Tamietto & de Gelder, 2008). The two-pathway theory gives evidence that the brain can have a subconscious emotional response prior to having a cognitive evaluation. In an evolutionary context, having two systems for brain processing makes sense; one can quickly detect threatening stimuli, and the other can make more adaptive long-term judgments. However, a system designed to make rapid emotional responses may not always be adaptive in human functioning. One example is attacking a spouse in the middle of the night on the way to the bathroom, falsely assuming an intruder before full recognition of the individual can occur. Using psychotherapy interventions at a level that solely addresses the second more logical/cognitive system may miss the influence that initial emotions have on the brain and mental health in general.

Neuroimaging studies demonstrate that when stimuli are presented in a rapid fashion where individuals have no conscious perception of what they are seeing, limbic areas like the insula and amygdala are activated in response to the unconscious stimuli (Cunningham, Raye, & Johnson, 2004). This lends further evidence to the two-pathway model, that the brain may have an intuitive response to stimuli that exist outside of conscious awareness. This again has survival value, perhaps allowing the organism to react quickly to danger before stimuli can be fully recognized and understood at a more conscious level. Cunningham and Zelazo (2007) present the iterative reprocessing model, where the two systems, one more emotional (automatic) and the second more cognitive (reflective), initially react separately and then work together in forming attitudes and evaluating situations. In addition to the fMRI evidence supporting the theory, they point to the distinction between implicit and explicit attitudes, which can often vary. Implicit attitudes are considered to be instinctual emotional attitudes about a stimulus, whereas explicit attitudes are more thoughtful and reflective. A common source of discrepancy between the implicit and explicit is often seen in racial attitudes (see section 2.4). Cunningham et al. (2004) examine subjects' brain response to seeing black compared to white faces; with black faces, there is an initial evaluation of amygdala activity followed by activation of the dorsolateral prefrontal cortex (dlPFC) and anterior cingulate cortex (ACC). The authors also find the subsequent reduction of amygdala activity was consistent with an increase of dlPFC activity, suggesting the cognitive brain areas (represented by the increased dlPFC response) could be regulating the emotional areas (represented by the decreased amygdala response). Freeman, Schiller, Rule, and Ambady (2010) also examined the brain's response to black versus white faces. When responding to black faces, participants made more superficial judgments, using more basic emotional areas like the amygdala. With white faces, participants made more individuated judgments, utilizing mentalizing areas of the brain, like the left temporal parietal junction (TPJ), left inferior frontal gyrus (IFG), and left superior temporal sulcus (STS), indicating that similar stimuli can get processed in different brain areas depending on the emotional valence.

In psychology, increased evidence supports a dual systems theory for information processing (Evans & Stanovich, 2013). Most famously, Daniel Kahneman won the Nobel Prize for his research in dual processing theory, highlighted in his book *Thinking Fast and Slow* (Kahneman, 2011). However, as interest in dual systems theory has grown, it has come under criticism for its vagueness, overgeneralization, and lack of discreteness between the two systems (Evans & Stanovich, 2013; Keren & Schul, 2009). It would be an overgeneralization to say that the brain has two separate systems for processing incoming information that produce different outputs. More specifically, the brain filters information through two major pathways and then integrates information in making decisions. However, as we will examine later in the book, there can be a disconnection between thinking and emotional processes in the brain, which leads to problems in reasoning and creates psychopathology. Although initially information likely has two systems for being processed, eventually the brain works holistically in making decisions. It appears the ACC, resting above the corpus callosum, receives input from the above prefrontal cortex regions and from lower subcortical regions, like the hypothalamus, amygdala, and insula (Allman, Hakeem, Erwin, Nimchinsky, & Hof, 2001), and is in a unique position to integrate the cognitive and emotional information from these dual systems (Stevens, Hurley, & Taber, 2011). The ACC is specifically involved in error detection and conflict monitoring, functions necessary when the brain experiences discrepancies in cognition and emotion. Lieberman (2007) distinguishes the neural correlates of the two systems. He includes the dorsal anterior cingulate cortex (dACC) as part of his C system (the slower, cognitive, reflective system), and places rostral anterior cingulate cortex (rACC) as part of the X system (the faster, emotional, reflexive system). This makes the ACC (containing both the rACC and dACC) a natural connecting area for integrating information between both systems. As these two dual processing systems interact, interpretation of the information and subsequent behavioral choices is not a single choice but more likely an integration of neural systems (see section 3.4) influenced by many competing neural impulses, in what is referred to as a global neuronal workspace model (Dehaene, Changeux, Naccache, Sackur, & Sergent, 2006). In this model, there are many working influences across brain regions and the combined influence aggregates to create one conscious state of experience. In this sense, no single information pathway or brain region is responsible for the conscious experience, but a complex interaction amongst multiple brain regions gives rise to the conscious interpretation of information and behavioral choices. At a distance, generalizing between emotional and cognitive processes can provide some understanding into how the brain works; however, moving down to a smaller neuron level, generalizing between emotional and cognitive systems is no longer useful. The dual systems theory no longer acts as an adequate model. It's not a competition between the X and C systems, but a more complex dynamic reaction between various networks that gives rise to the conscious experience. We don't go actively between thinking either fast or slow; both are co-occurring and influencing each other. For example, in a simple cause and effect system, the influence of a single reward has a singular influence on behavior (Early reductionist behaviorist models believed with the correct mix of reinforcements and punishments, all behavior could be predicted (Smith, 1992).). Recent work indicates that the brain does make not decisions based solely on the immediate direct experience. During sleep, the brain integrates neural pathways, particularly between hippocampal regions (limbic) with medial PFC regions, which it then relies on for future inferential decision making, based on knowledge of assumed rewards (Barron et al., 2020). In this sense, learned emotional experiences are integrated with cognitive predictions to influence future decision making, before even being faced with a decision. Thus, brain networks like the X and C systems cannot be completely disintegrated into separate systems; they are already very much integrated in the brain. As the emotional cognitive distinction is useful in helping patients in practice, I will refer to this distinction in future sections.

3.2 Triune Brain Theory

The distinction between the emotional and cognitive brain has been theorized to be part of an evolutionary process, where phases of rapid brain development occurred from the reptile, to the mammal, to the human, each accounting for large anatomical distinctions in the brain, consisting of the cerebellum, limbic system, and neocortex respectively (MacLean, 1990). The most basic region or reptile brain consists of the brain stem and cerebellum, which is responsible for a lot of automatic motor functioning, like balancing, or even more complex motor movements like walking or riding a bicycle. Initially learning to walk or ride a bicycle is very hard and uses multiple brain regions, but once we learn the complex motor movements, the cerebellum is largely responsible for carrying out these behaviors without much conscious thought. Other autonomic nervous functions are controlled/regulated by these lower brain regions, and we don't have much conscious control over them; we cannot stop our breathing or prevent natural reflexes. Similar to a reptile, we have a central nervous system, and activities taking place in this region largely go unnoticed. Moving along the evolutionary timeline, the next region in brain development is the limbic system, which is present in mammals. Our dogs have a "limbic" brain structure; they have memory for places and people and they can express emotions, which likely help develop the human-animal bond. However, dogs have not developed the human neocortex, which is involved in making judgments, executive functioning, and critical thinking. If we leave the house, our dogs don't know if we are going away for a week's vacation or just out to get the mail. They react with the same disappointment, as they are unable to regulate emotion by comprehending the experience with neocortical thinking. Our dogs are capable of learning through reinforcement and punishment. They may learn over time a suitcase is a bad sign. Dogs are unable, however, to employ adaptive thinking strategies when conditions change. If you normally take out your suitcase to go on vacation, but this time only plan to clean out the closet, they lack the ability to understand the changes in cause and effect. Humans are unique in their evolution for development of the third layer, the neocortex region unique to complex thought and meta-cognition. Humans also seem to be unique in the animal kingdom for the presence of mental illness. This neocortical brain region, although beneficial in many respects, may outsmart itself when it comes to responding to the more primitive emotional brain. Over-reliance on cognition in the face of emotional problems may be one example.

3.3 Brain Anatomy/Neuroscience Overview

3.3.1 Basics

Neocortex—The neocortex is the most developed part of the brain and consists of four major lobes. The prefrontal cortex (PFC) is involved in complex thinking and judgment. When we go to school, we are developing our PFC. The parietal lobe rests in the back of the neocortex; it is involved in sensory and motor processing. The parietal lobe gives us a sense of where our body is in space. I can close my eyes and still determine if I'm standing, sitting, or lying down. The occipital lobe lies within the back of our brains; it is noteworthy for processing visual information. The temporal lobe is beneath the parietal lobe; it is involved in language and memory.

Limbic System—Also called the limbic lobe, it is subcortical, meaning it's beneath the neocortex. The limbic system contains the amygdala, hippo-campus, and basal ganglia. The ACC and insula are also subcortical and are sometimes considered part of the limbic system, but increasingly they are identified as their own regions (Bush, Luu, & Posner, 2000; Uddin, Nomi, Hébert-Seropian, Ghaziri, & Boucher, 2017).

Cerebellum and Brain Stem—These are at the base of the brain, the lowest part. The brain stem contains the midbrain, pons, and medulla oblongata, and rests just in front of the cerebellum. These areas are responsible for many autonomic functions—things we do without any thought, like walking, breathing, and swallowing.

3.3.2 Specific Regions

Each of the regions described below are represented in figures 3.1, 3.2, and 3.3.

3.3.3 Occipital Lobe

Visual Cortex—This receives and processes visual information. Two major pathways are used for processing incoming visual information: the dorsal stream (where) and the ventral stream (what). When we see something, our brain wants to know two important things: what something is and where in space it is. This helps us determine whether to avoid or interact with the stimuli. The dorsal stream sends information up from the visual cortex to the parietal lobe, while the ventral stream takes a lower route, sending

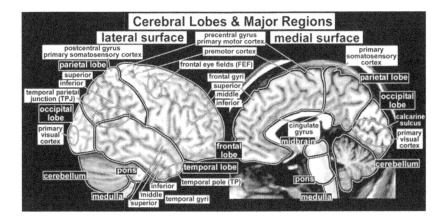

Figure 3.1 Cerebral lobes and major regions.

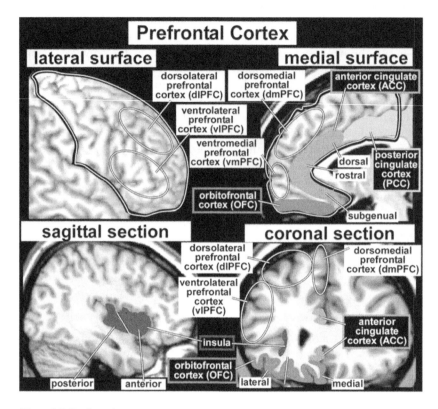

Figure 3.2 Prefrontal cortex.

information from the visual cortex to the temporal lobe for object re-cognition (Groome, 2013). The occipital lobe can be separated into two parts along the calcarine sulcus. The upper part is the cuneus and the lower is the lingual gyrus. All parts of the occipital lobe are involved in visual processing.

3.3.4 Prefrontal Cortex

Orbitofrontal Cortex (OFC)—The OFC is the lowest region of the PFC. The OFC is part of the reward/MCL circuit and has projections to the amygdala, ACC, vmPFC, CN, and VS (Rolls & Grabenhorst, 2008). The OFC is consistently overactive in obsessive-compulsive disorder (OCD) (Nakao, Okada, & Kanba, 2014; Ursu & Carter, 2009), and patients with OCD show hyperconnectivity between the OFC and areas of the MCL/reward circuit (Abe et al., 2015; Beucke et al., 2013). This suggests that the dysfunction in the OFC that contributes to OCD is perhaps part of a faulty rewarding of obsessive behaviors (see section 9.6). Research suggests that

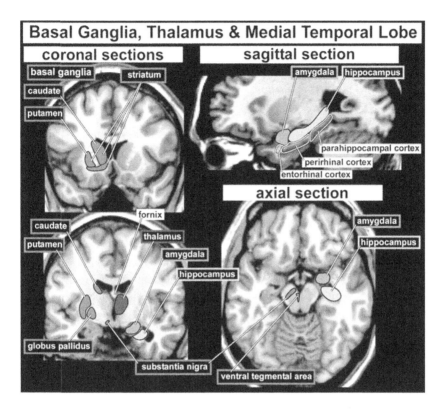

Figure 3.3 Basal ganaglia, thalamus, and medial temporal lobe.

some functional differences within the OFC exist, between the lateral orbitofrontal cortex (lOFC) and the medial orbitofrontal cortex (mOFC). The lOFC has been shown to be involved in associating choice with reward outcome, whereas mOFC (having a functional overlap with vmPFC), makes a decision amongst the possible rewarding choices (Noonan, Chau, Rushworth, & Fellows, 2017). Rolls (2019) believes that the lOFC responds to non-reward and punishment, while the mOFC responds to reward, citing evidence that in depressed individuals the lOFC has increased functional connectivity to other brain regions, while the mOFC shows decreased functional connectivity. Dysfunction in OFC has also been found in substance abuse disorders (Everitt et al., 2007), and recently it was demonstrated that neurons in the OFC fire specifically in rodents when seeking alcohol (Hernandez & Moorman, 2020).

Ventromedial Prefrontal Cortex (vmPFC)—The vmPFC is located in the middle bottom portion of the PFC. The vmPFC is involved in a number of functions involving emotional regulation (Etkin, Büchel, & Gross, 2015), episodic and semantic memory (Bertossi, Tesini, Cappelli, &

Ciaramelli, 2016; Binder, Desai, Graves, & Conant, 2009), fear conditioning and extinction learning (Phelps, Delgado, Nearing, & LeDoux, 2004), and decision making (Kahnt, Heinzle, Park, & Haynes, 2011). Rovoy, Shohamy, and Wager, (2012) take these various functions not as a sign of variable heterogeneity in the vmPFC, but as a hub area that codes conceptual information about the meaning of future outcomes. The vmPFC area allows us to use judgment in overriding habitual behavior. We may have the immediate desire to smoke a cigarette, but we can assess future outcomes, weigh affective meaning (current gratification from smoking vs. future gratification from not smoking), and make a decision. This process often involves weighing multiple competing needs (self-judgment, judgment from others, physical health, future stress, finances, etc.) and vmPFC may be uniquely suited for this complex function (also see section 3.3.8).

Dorsolateral Prefrontal Cortex(dlPFC)—If the vmPFC weighs the possibilities and potential emotional consequences in making an intuitive choice, it's the dlPFC that makes the coldly calculated pro/con list for each choice (Kahnt et al., 2011). The dlPFC may examine the choices and estimate future outcomes, while the vmPFC then decides which choice will have the most emotional benefit before executing the choice. The dlPFC is associated with self-control (Brass & Haggard, 2007) and weighs the long-term benefits to choices. The dlPFC is involved in the complicated cognitive tasks of executive functioning and working memory (Barbey, Koenigs, & Grafman, 2013). While both the vmPFC and dlPFC have been shown to be involved in emotional regulation, they regulate emotion in different ways (Etkin et al., 2015). Cognitive reappraisal, typically used in CBT, uses the dlPFC (Buhle et al., 2014). Additionally, dlPFC is the most recently evolved part of the prefrontal cortex and takes the longest to develop fully (Fuster, 2002), making dlPFC well suited to reexamining the context of things using cognitive reappraisal.

Dorsomedial Prefrontal Cortex (dmPFC)—This is located along the central midline of the brain and rests above the vmPFC and ACC. The dmPFC is involved in social cognition, especially in making self-other distinctions (Martin, Dzafic, Ramdave, & Meinzer, 2017). The dmPFC has also been found to be part of a mentalizing theory of mind system involving the TPJ and precuneus (Van Overwalle & Baetens, 2009). The dmPFC seems particularly active when trying to understand or infer the intentionality of others (Ferrari et al., 2016; Waytz, Zaki, & Mitchell, 2012).

Ventrolateral Prefrontal Cortex(vlPFC)—This is functionally and anatomically part of the IFG.

Inferior Frontal Gyrus (IFG)—The IFG varies in function and connectivity between the right and left IFG (Du et al., 2020). The left side contains Broca's area, well known for its role in the production of speech. Also, the left IFG is known for its role in semantic processing, the process by which meaning is attached to words (Devlin, Matthews, & Rushworth,

2003). The right IFG seems to play a role in response inhibition; however, it could be conceptualized as a function of selective attention, rather than inhibition (Hampshire, Chamberlain, Monti, Duncan, & Owen, 2010). Others see the right IFG role as part of a network that slows, pauses, or stops responses; the term "inhibition" alone may be too general of a word (Aron, Robbins, & Poldrack, 2014).

Middle Frontal Gyrus (MFG)—This rests just above the IFG in the brain and is often considered part of the dlPFC.

Frontal Eye Fields (FEF)—FEF is located adjacent to and just prior to the PreMC. Like the PreMC, the FEF is involved in voluntary movement, specifically movements of the eyes. The FEF would be involved in trying to find your friend in a crowd or tracking the ball during a tennis match (Muggleton, Juan, Cowey, & Walsh, 2003).

Premotor Cortex (PreMC)—PreMC is located in the dorsal rear part of the frontal lobe anterior to PriMC. The PreMC appears to play a role in directing behavior (Fornia et al., 2020), especially involving complicated multifunction motor movements. The PreMC has strong connections to and greatly influences the PriMC (Chouinard & Paus, 2006). The PreMC is involved in conscious recognition of the different parts of our own bodies (Ehrsson, Spence, & Passingham, 2004).

Primary Motor Cortex (PriMC)—The PriMC rests just behind the PreMC. Each region of the PriMC corresponds with a region of the body. However, the map is distorted because regions used more for fine motor control activities, like the hand being used for tying knots, is re-presentationally larger than other regions not typically used for fine motor skills, like our legs (Banich & Compton, 2018).

3.3.5 Parietal Lobe

Primary & Secondary Somatosensory area (S1 &S2)—The S1 (also referred to as postcentral gyrus) is located behind the PriMC, in what is the front of the parietal lobe. The S1 is involved in proprioception, the perception of body parts and their movements, and receives information from the thalamus (Zhang, Snyder, Shimony, Fox, & Raichle, 2010). The S1 is like the PriMC in that each body region corresponds with a region of the S1. S1 is also a distorted map; highly sensitive areas like the lips or genitalia occupy larger areas of the S1. Nerve impulses received in these areas are sensed in the S1. This area has achieved some notoriety for its role in phantom limb pain. Individuals that have lost limbs can sometimes feel pain in a region of the body that no longer exists, because even though that body part is not there, the corresponding region in the S1 is still active in sensing that region (Flor, 2002). The S2 is a smaller region located below the S1. The S2 is believed to provide a sensorimotor integrative function (Chen et al., 2008; Orenius et al., 2017).

Superior Parietal Lobe (SPL)—The SPL is the posterior dorsal area of the parietal lobe, and includes the precuneus. The precuneus appears to be involved in proprioception, or understanding where one's body is in space (Pisella, Havé, & Rossetti, 2019). The SPL is part of the dorsal stream and is involved in visuospatial perception (Wu et al., 2016). Damage to the SPL has caused deficits in visuospatial attention (Valdois, Lassus-Sangosse, Lallier, Moreaud, & Pisella, 2019).

Inferior Parietal Lobe (IPL)—This lobe is located below IPS. Damage to the left IPL results in apraxia, an inability to move objects (Buxbaum, Kyle, Grossman, & Coslett, 2007). A meta-analysis of hemispheric differences of the IPL showed the left side is specific for semantic aspects of memory, while the right IPL is involved in visual perception aspects of memory (Gray, Fry, & Montaldi, 2020). For example, van Elk (2014) finds evidence to suggest the left IPL may store information about hand postures, which can be used for planning one's own actions as well as predicting other's actions.

One way to think about the IPL is that it rests between the dorsal and ventral stream. If the dorsal stream is about recognizing where an object is and the ventral stream recognizing what that object is, the IPL puts the two together to understand how to react or act upon the object. For example, I recognize a tennis ball (what) coming low to my left side (where); the IPL might think this is a good position for a backhand slice (a tennis stroke associated with this position of the ball). The right IPL may play a balance between the dorsal and ventral streams in the larger picture (see section 5.3), by maintaining top-down attention while also responding to new salience objects (Singh-Curry & Husain, 2009). Hemineglect or contralateral neglect, where an individual doesn't pay attention to one side of their visual field, is common after damage to the

Figure 3.4 Clock drawing from a patient with hemineglect.

right IPL, but not the left IPL (Kleinman et al., 2007), again suggesting a potential lack of integration between the dorsal and ventral streams. Below is an example (see Figure 3.4) of a clock drawing from a patient with hemineglect. The individual is not able to attend to the left side (top-down attention) of the clock to recognize the numbers, nor are they able to recall the specific object, a clock which has numbers around its circumference (object identification), resulting in the distorted drawing.

Intraparietal Sulcus (IPS)—IPS is a major sulcus that runs through the parietal lobe. The IPS divides the SPL and IPL. The IPS is shown to be active when we process numbers or quantities of magnitude (Eger, Sterzer, Russ, Giraud, & Kleinschmidt, 2003).

3.3.6 Between the Parietal and Temporal Lobe

Temporal Parietal Junction (TPJ)—This is the area where the temporal and parietal lobes meet in the brain and the posterior of where the STS rests. Many studies use varying terminology for this area; terms such as the posterior STS or Wernicke's area referring to the left TPJ (Schurz, Tholen, Perner, Mars, & Sallet, 2017). The TPJ has been associated with several cognitive functions, like attention, language, memory, and social cognition (Cabeza, Ciaramelli, & Moscovitch, 2012; Carter & Huettel, 2013). It has been suggested these functions may be representative of a larger integrative function, possibly as a hub area for reorientating attention (Corbetta, Patel, & Shulman, 2008), social decision making (Carter & Huettel, 2013), or for purposes of mentalizing, perspective-taking, and theory of mind (Saxe & Powell, 2006; Young, Dodell-Feder, & Saxe, 2010). Eddy (2016) has suggested deficits in TPJ may account for the social impairment symptoms in disorders like schizophrenia and autism. A meta-analysis of neuroimaging studies does finds the TPJ specifically active in understanding others or what psychologists refer to as theory of mind (Van Overwalle, 2009). Other areas, including the ACC, STS, TP, and dmPFC, also contribute to this complicated process of theory of mind (Aichhorn, Perner, Kronbichler, Staffen, & Ladurner, 2006; Carrington & Bailey, 2009; Gallagher & Frith, 2003; Schurz, Radua, Aichhorn, Richlan, & Perner, 2014). In one popular study, participants made moral decisions involved in assigning blame to someone who accidentally or intentionally poisoned another. When participants received transcranial magnetic stimulation to their right TPJ, disrupting its ability to function, participants appear to be unable to apply theory of mind. As a result, participants judged the poisoning based on the outcome of an individual's actions (alive or dead) and less for their intentioned behavior (murder or manslaughter) (Young, Camprodon, Hauser, Pascual-Leone, & Saxe, 2010). Disruption of the right TPJ also disrupts the ability for cognitive empathy, also a mentalizing skill (see section 6.2) (Mai et al., 2016).

3.3.7 Temporal Lobe

Temporal Pole (TP)—The TP is located in the anterior part of the temporal lobe. The TP has strong connectivity to limbic regions (Chabardès, Kahane, Minotti, Hoffmann, & Benabid, 2002). Damage to the TP causes deficits in social and emotional processing (Olson, Plotzker, & Ezzyat, 2007). The TP is involved in the recollection of semantic and episodic memory (Dolan, Lane, Chua, & Fletcher, 2000; Lambon Ralph, Pobric, & Jefferies, 2009). The TP is also the site of frontotemporal dementia (FTD). FTD is often mistaken for Alzheimer's Disease. While both are forms of dementia and experience deficits in memory, FTD also involves deficits in social and emotional functioning (Neary, Snowden, & Mann, 2005). TP is also very much involved in theory of mind (Olson et al., 2007). Gallagher and Frith (2003), suggest that episodic and semantic memory functions of TP are useful in conjunction with tasks of theory of mind because they give humans an ability to detect discrepancies between the current behavior of others and recalled semantic and episodic information associated with others.

Superior Temporal Sulcus (STS)—The STS is located in the temporal lobe and separates the superior and middle temporal gyri of the brain. This long and deep sulcus extends across the temporal lobe from the anterior portion where TP rests, up and back to the TPJ. The STS appears to be involved in multisensory integration when paying attention to a speaker (Beauchamp, 2015). The STS is involved in reading lips (Uno et al., 2015). Overall, STS is involved in processing sensory information from voice, facial perception, human motion, language, and theory of mind; furthermore, these processes are both regionally independent and interdependent (Deen, Koldewyn, Kanwisher, & Saxe, 2015). This is probably why watching badly dubbed movies is so irritating. We expect the talker's lips to match heard speech, and when they don't our brain senses something is off. The STS is a functionally complex region that seems to be adaptive in humans for integrating sensory information to better understand the behavior and intention of others (Frith & Frith, 1999). When participants in an fMRI scanner were asked to view faces and assess trustworthiness, the right STS was found to be significantly active (Winston, Strange, O'Doherty, & Dolan, 2002). It seems the STS is examining multiple behavioral outputs of others and assessing, "Does this add up?" It might be that my STS is active when I have an intuition that a patient isn't telling me or perhaps even themselves the truth. Given what I know about brain science, I would recommend therapists pay attention to their intuitions.

Superior Temporal Gyrus (STG)—The STG is located above the STS, commonly known as Wernicke's area in the left hemisphere, which is important for language comprehension. Speech is processed in the STG, and it is well connected to other brain regions to determine the semantic meaning of words. It also responds to the distinct phonetics of words (Chang et al., 2010; Mesgarani, Cheung, Johnson, & Chang, 2014).

Medial Temporal Lobe (MTL)—MTL is an area of regions involved in memory, collectively referred to as the MTL in human and rodent brain literature. The MTL can sometimes refer to inferior regions that are also considered subcortical, including the amygdala and hippocampus. The MTL typically refers to areas that rest just outside the hippocampus, including the perirhinal cortex, parahippocampal cortex, and entorhinal cortex (Ranganath, 2010).

3.3.8 Cingulate Cortex

Cingulate Cortex—The arch-shaped cingulate cortex, which sits mostly above the corpus callosum, can be parceled into an anterior (ACC) and posterior region (PCC). The PCC is often investigated as a single structure, while the ACC is broken down into sub-regions, consisting of subgenual (sgACC), rostral (rACC), and dorsal (dACC).

Subgenual Anterior Cingulate Cortex (sgACC)—The sgACC is the beginning of the cingulate cortex; the beginning of sgACC wraps under the rest of ACC, resting below the corpus callosum. The subcallosal ACC is a similar area of the ACC that overlaps between the sgACC and rACC. Subcallosal ACC at times has been identified as being synonymous with the sgACC (Hamani et al., 2011) and at other times as its own distinct region (Asami et al., 2008). The sgACC is functionally connected to the hypothalamus, amygdala, hippocampus, VS, and OFC (Beckmann, Johansen-Berg, & Rushworth, 2009). Other studies have found connections between the sgACC and nearby PFC regions like the OFC and vmPFC (Yu et al., 2011; Torta & Cauda, 2011). The sgACC has more connections to these limbic areas than the rest of the ACC and PCC. Grey matter volume in this area is reduced in individuals with depression (Drevets, Savitz, & Trimble, 2008). Mayberg et al. (2005) have found the sgACC to be overactive in depression. They have also demonstrated that deep brain stimulation of the sgACC can be a successful treatment for depression and bipolar disorder (Holtzheimer et al., 2012; Johansen-Berg et al., 2008). Reduced activation of the sgACC in response to fearful stimuli has been associated with increased PTSD symptoms (Stevens et al., 2017). Morris et al. (2020) looked at the role of positive and negative feedback in depressed individuals with anhedonia and anxiety within the sgACC. They found depression was related to increased connectivity between the sgACC and hippocampus. They also found the higher activation of the sgACC in response to positive feedback was related to anhedonia, while higher activation of the sgACC in response to negative feedback was related to anxiety. Additionally, they showed that Ketamine can mitigate the sgACC's overactive response to positive feedback.

Rostral Anterior Cingulate Cortex (rACC)—The rACC is the next area along the cingulate continuum after the sgACC. This area has also been referred to as the pregenual ACC. Ventral ACC has also been used to refer to both the sgACC and rACC collectively (Lockwood & Wittmann, 2018). The ACC has been functionally divided into an emotional and cognitive division (Bush et al., 2000). With the rACC being part of the emotional division, it is related to emotional awareness and the ability to recognize what one is feeling (Frewen et al., 2008; Phillips, Drevets, Rauch, & Lane, 2003). The rACC is well connected to other areas of the cingulate cortex (Yu et al., 2011). Research indicates that the rACC also acts as means of emotional regulation (Etkin, Egner, Peraza, Kandel, & Hirsch, 2006; Yoshimura et al., 2010). Psychological disorders with blunted or flat affect show hypoactivity of the rACC (Stevens, 2016). When individuals experience emotional arousal, increased functional connectivity is seen between the rACC and dACC, along with other areas significant for emotion like the amygdala (Kanske & Kotz, 2011).

Dorsal Anterior Cingulate Cortex (dACC)—This area is also referred to as the anterior middle cingulate cortex. The dACC has been shown to have connections to the dlPFC, vmPFC, and insula (Yu et al., 2011; Torta & Cauda, 2011). The dACC was first identified as an area specific for conflict monitoring and inhibitory control in the brain. More recent approaches see the dACC as an area that more succinctly responds to surprise. Not only does the dACC recognize errors to override a prepotent response, it is also involved in motivated control, which involves inhibition in conjunction with weighing options for when to apply effort for prospective (not fully known) rewards (Vassena, Deraeve, & Alexander, 2020). The dACC appears to be a likelihood-monitoring model, estimating the efforts of engaging in different behavioral choices in conjunction with a likelihood estimate of future feelings or benefits. An example would be weighing the emotional effort of getting out of bed to go running vs. getting some extra sleep. The dACC is not just considering the immediate value of the choice, but additionally how one might feel later in the day if one went running vs. sleeping more. To me, this represents the challenge many patients face in giving up a behavior that was rewarding in the past, for some unknown but potentially better outcome in the future. Functional coupling between the dACC and the vmPFC, may add its role in this decision-making process (Etkin, Egner, & Kalisch, 2011).

Posterior Cingulate Cortex (PCC)—The PCC is located behind the ACC at the back of the brain. The PCC is the central hub of the DMN (default mode network), and is involved in self-referential thinking and correspondingly de-activates during meditation (Garrison, Zeffiro, Scheinost, Constable, & Brewer, 2015). The PCC is known for having significantly increased metabolic activity compared to the rest of the brain (Leech & Sharp, 2014). Consistent with its role in self-referential thinking, the PCC is activated during episodic memory retrieval with functional connections to MTL/parahippocampal brain regions (Maddock, Garrett, & Buonocore, 2001). Unlike the ACC, the PCC appears to be more functionally homogenous (Leech & Sharp, 2014), with only small regional differences existing between the dorsal PCC, more involved in spatial processing, and the ventral PCC, more involved in self-referential thinking (Yu et al., 2011).

3.3.9 Limbic or Subcortical Areas

Anterior Insula (AI) & Posterior Insula (PI)—The insula is located centrally in the brain deep past the lateral sulcus, and has connections to multiple neocortical and limbic regions, such as the amygdala, OFC, ACC, and the STG (Uddin, 2015). The insula is very much involved in the perception of bodily states; this is also called interoceptive awareness (Critchley, Wiens, Rotshtein, Öhman, & Dolan, 2004). These could be emotional in nature, like disgust, or more physiological, like pain or one's heartbeat. The insula can be further divided into the anterior insula (AI) and the posterior insula (PI). The PI may be more related to the initial perception of somatic stimuli, while AI is more involved in the sensation of the stimuli (Davis, Kwan, Crawley, & Mikulis, 1998). For example, Craig, Chen, Bandy, and Reiman, (2000) found activity in PI corresponded directly to changes in temperature. While the AI has been shown to respond to "paradoxical heat," that is, the feeling of your hand warming up even when it is at room temperature. This is also what you might experience as feeling warm coming home on a cold day; your body is not any warmer, but the temperature change gives you the illusion you're hotter (Davis, Pope, Crawley, & Mikulis, 2004). Frot, Faillenot, and Mauguière (2014) find that nociceptive input (the experience of pain), is first processed in the PI and then information is transferred on to the AI, where the emotional reaction to the pain occurs. We all know that individuals react to pain differently; sexual masochism might be at the extreme end, and this disorder could involve how AI responds to chronic pain (Kamping et al., 2016). There are also differences in connectivity between the AI and PI, with the AI connecting to more emotional regions like ACC and PI more connected to sensorimotor areas, like STG and the occipital lobe (Cauda et al., 2011, 2012; Nomi, Schettini, Broce, Dick, & Uddin, 2018). Other studies have suggested dividing the insula into three separate regions, splitting the AI into dorsal and ventral regions, with the dorsal more related to and connected with cognitive regions and the ventral more emotional (Chang, Yarkoni, Khaw, & Sanfey, 2013). Research has consistently shown decreased insula volume (Shepherd, Matheson, Laurens, Carr, & Green, 2012), connectivity (Wang et al., 2014), and activation (van der Meer et al., 2014) in individuals with schizophrenia. These insula deficits may impair interoceptive awareness, resulting in the disconnection from reality seen in schizophrenia. Overactivation of the insula has also been shown in anxiety disorders (Stein,

Simmons, Feinstein, & Paulus, 2007), as well as increased functional connectivity to the amygdala in anxiety disorders (Baur, Hänggi, Langer, & Jäncke, 2013). One theory is that individuals with anxiety have an overactive insula, increasing their salience response to overreact to events even when non-threatening (Menon & Uddin, 2010).

Basal Ganglia (BG)—The BG consist of several subcortical structures listed below, notably involving motor movement.

Substantia Nigra (SbN)—The SbN projects dopamine to the VS. Parkinson's disease is caused by the death of dopaminergic neurons in SbN, resulting in a deficit in dopamine, which leads to shaking and stiffness in motor movements. Interestingly, antipsychotic medications that typically block dopamine receptors result in side effects of involuntary and rigid motor movements, the same symptoms as Parkinson's disease.

Striatum—The striatum contains the CN, PT, and NA.

Caudate Nucleus (CN)—The CN is involved in motor processes, as well procedural learning, and other goal-directed behavior. CN projects neural pathways out to the thalamus. Limbic areas like the amygdala and hippocampus project out to the CN, which results in the physical expression of emotions (Grahn, Parkinson, & Owen, 2008).

Putamen (PT)—The PT along with CN are the major input receptors of the BG. The PT receives inputs from the motor and sensory areas of the neocortex, and projects to the thalamus, which projects back to neocortex areas, through what is referred to as the cortico-striatal-thalamic-cortical loop or nigrostriatal pathway (Rădulescu, Herron, Kennedy, & Scimemi, 2017). This loop is involved in motor reinforcement learning and habitual behavior, and could likely contribute to some of the symptoms of several psychological disorders (Maia & Frank, 2011). There are three identified basal ganglia- cortical-thalamic pathways: a motor, cortical, and limbic (see section 3.4). Sometimes the cortical and limbic pathways are combined. Some debate exists between convergence and segregation of these pathways (Banich & Compton, 2018; Simonyan, 2019).

Nucleus Accumbens (NA), which is also called the ventral striatum (VS), is part of the MCL, which receives dopamine projects from the VTA.

Globus Pallidus (GP)—Also referred to as the dorsal pallidum, the GP receives inputs from the VS, and projects out to the thalamus. The GP is also thought to be involved in motor movements, and it primarily communicates through the GABA neurotransmitter, which is involved in inhibitory behavior (Purves et al., 2018).

Ventral Tegmental Area (VTA)—The VTA is the base of the MCL network, and contains dopaminergic neurons that project to NA, along with areas in the limbic system and mPFC (Banich & Compton, 2018; Simonyan, 2019).

Thalamus—The thalamus is considered to be the relay center for the brain, often sending information from subcortical to cortical areas of the brain. Since the brain takes in a great amount of sensory information, one important role of the thalamus is to dismiss sensory input that is not useful. The pulvinar is the largest nucleus in the thalamus and has strong connections to the visual cortex (Benarroch, 2015).

Hippocampus—The hippocampus is often the area of the brain that we associate with memory. The hippocampus is active when we encode and recall memories. Much evidence demonstrates that disorders in memory are associated with damage to this region of the brain (Cipolotti & Bird, 2006). However, increasing evidence indicates that memory retrieval may be different than how many of us previously thought. Recalling a memory is not like pulling a book off the shelf: we read it and put it back, and every time we read that book, we are reading the same book. Research shows that memory can be highly biased (Schacter, 1999); for instance, we tend to remember good events more than bad events, and even for bad events we forget how bad they were (Walker, Skowronski, & Thompson, 2003). The hippocampus more likely reconstructs the memory than recalls it (Barry & Maguire, 2019). In this sense, we may never have the same memory twice, each time we recall something we are reconstructing that event again (Nadel, Samsonovich, Ryan, & Moscovitch, 2000). This will be important when we consider affect reconsolidation later (see Chapter 11). The hippocampus is not just involved in recreating past experiences; it's also involved in imagining new experiences (Hassabis, Kumaran, Vann, & Maguire, 2007). The hippocampus and regions of the PFC interact bidirectionally when recalling episodic memory, indicating that PFC may work together with the hippocampus to help reconstruct the memory (Eichenbaum, 2017). Thus, when recalling a memory, the brain uses heuristics in constructing that event. If you're trying to remember going to grandma's house for thanksgiving five years ago, the brain appears to recreate that picture from all of the times at grandma's house, making it difficult to remember if that new painting came last year or has been there for ten years. The brain would never put a live tiger in grandma's house because that scenario doesn't match any previous schema of grandma's house that you have. Research examining false memories shows that people create false memories that are conceptually similar to how things actually appear (Lyle & Johnson, 2006). This lends evidence to the theory that memories are not an exact recollection, but instead a reconstruction of the experience. Memory (affect) reconsolidation refers to a period of time that when a memory is recalled, it becomes labile and thus subject to being changed (Schwabe & Wolf, 2009). This has valuable implications for trauma and psychotherapy, indicating the emotions surrounding traumatic memories can be changed through what I call affect reconsolidation because it is not the content of the memory that is changing but the emotional nature of the memory (Stevens, 2019). The hippocampus is highly connected to the amygdala, and increased amygdala activity is associated with improved memory recall (Hamann, Ely, Grafton, & Kilts, 1999). Amygdala has a strong influence on the hippocampus in fear conditioning and emotional memories (LaBar & Cabeza, 2006), which is why our strongest memories are for emotional events good or bad.

Amygdala—The amygdala has connections to multiple brain regions including the insula, ACC, PCC, OFC, hippocampus, as well other subcortical areas (Stein et al., 2007). Perhaps the amygdala's connections through the brain make sense in light of its role in fear conditioning and survival (LeDoux, 2012). Yet, because the amygdala is so primary to survival it may also explain why variants in amygdala functioning are commonly seen in psychopathology (Schumann, Bauman, & Amaral, 2011). When we experience a threat in our environment, our amygdala reacts. It can overreact too, creating a general phobia of dogs after only a single fearful episode with a dog. We wouldn't want to prevent our fear response, but we also need to learn how to re-condition our amygdala when it influences us to engage in behaviors that are no longer helpful. Hypervigilance could have helped a child growing up in an abusive home but could be an impediment to an adult living in a different environment.

Fornix. The fornix is a large receiver of inputs from the hippocampus (Ly et al., 2016). The fornix is especially important in the formation of episodic memories as opposed to semantic memories (Hodgetts et al., 2017). So, it may not be surprising that changes in the fornix are associated with Alzheimer's Disease (Benear, Ngo, & Olson, 2020). Although not as well studied as many other brain areas, some research finds the fornix is involved in mental health disorders, like depression, eating disorders, and anxiety (Benear et al., 2020).

3.3.10 Cerebellum

Cerebellum—The cerebellum rests at the bottom of the brain, located behind the top of the brain stem, which is at the top of the spinal cord. The cerebellum traditionally has been thought to be involved mostly in movement. If you remember from childhood, walking is really hard; it requires a lot of balancing and coordinated motor movements to get everything right, so you don't fall over. Yet, with practice walking becomes second nature, and as it becomes more learned the cerebellum regulates the process without our conscious awareness. We don't think of all the micro motor movements that take place as we walk around. It occurs to me now that I don't know where any of the letters are on the keyboard; if I had to fill out a chart I'd fail. However, I somehow know how to coordinate my finger movements to correspond with the letters that I want. These rapid coordinated finger movements would be impaired with damage to the cerebellum (Miall, Reckess, & Imamizu, 2001) as would my ability to coordinate other motor movements (Morton & Bastian, 2004; Buckley, Mazzà, & McNeill, 2018). Increasing research is showing that the cerebellum has a much greater role in emotion and cognition than previously thought. Jeremy Schmahmann (2004) coined the term cerebellar cognitive affective syndrome to account for a multitude of symptoms he saw in individuals with damage to the cerebellum. Schmahmann found deficits in executive function, visuospatial cognition, speech, and language, as well as changes in emotion, and flat affect resulting from cerebellum damage. Schmahmann and colleagues theorize the cerebellum modulates emotion and cognition the same way it modulates motor movements, as an automatic unconscious process to maintain a homeostatic balance (Schmahmann, Guell, Stoodley, & Halko, 2019). Just in the same way the cerebellum may manage rote motor movements, it may regulate rote aspects of emotion and cognition.

3.3.11 Brainstem

Midbrain—The midbrain is at the top of the brain stem, which also shares some overlaps with limbic areas like the SbN. The midbrain contains the periaqueductal grey, involved in the sensation of pain and negative emotion (Buhle et al., 2013). Although not clearly understood, the periaqueductal grey seems to play a role in primal emotions (Motta, Carobrez, & Canteras, 2017). The midbrain also overlaps with the ventral tegmental area, which is closely related to the SbN; both produce dopamine, which projects throughout the brain as part of the MCL (see section 3.4).

Pons—The pons is part of the upper brain stem and connects the cerebellum to the rest of the brain. It's involved in basic regulatory functions like sleeping. While these lower areas of the brain are not typically thought to be involved in more complex functions like emotion, the pons contains the raphe nuclei and locus coeruleus, which is the basis for the synthesis and release of serotonin and norepinephrine respectively (Venkatraman, Edlow, & Immordino-Yang, 2017). These two neurotransmitters are often increased in the use of anti-depressant medication, showing that the brainstem likely does have an influence mood and emotion.

Medulla Oblongata—The medulla oblongata is typically referred to as the medulla and is located beneath the pons. It is involved in autonomic body functioning, like respiration and heart rate. Other involuntary functions like sneezing or vomiting involve the medulla as well (Banich & Compton, 2018).

3.4 Brain Networks

Historically brain areas have been studied independently, like parts of a machine, and researchers have worked to find each region's corresponding function. In 1909, Korbinian Broadmann, a German neurologist, mapped the brain into 48 areas (Jacobs, 2011). The areas are still used today and are increasingly cited as neuroimaging increases its presence as a science (Zilles, 2018). This approach, however, uses the brain as a machine metaphor, with each part having a specific function. Growing attention is now being paid to brain networks. Brain networks contain several brain areas that typically operate in tandem for a certain purpose, as opposed to a single brain area completing a task (Bressler & Menon, 2010; Gulbinaite, van Rijn, & Cohen, 2014). Brain functions don't move linearly from one region to the next, like a conveyor belt; they work interactively with multiple messages going back and forth simultaneously. If I ask you to name a city in North America, you'll name the first city that comes to mind. You don't just think of one city, you might access the names of multiple cities, and the most prominent one that you think of, you'll say first. Multiple processes are happening which then result in a single final option. Brain networks typically display both structural connectivity, physical connections between regions, and functional connectivity, marked by co-activation between regions. While functional connectivity and structural connectivity are strongly related, it's not an exact correlation; Suárez, Markello, Betzel, and Misic (2020) estimate an $r^2 = 0.5$. So, as valuable as it is to understand differing brain regions, it's also important to examine the larger networks. It has been suggested the default mode network, salience network, and central executive network make up the "triple network model" as a common framework, because they are distinct in brain structure and easily can be identified by task (Menon, 2011). First, we'll examine these networks.

Default Mode Network (DMN)—First, I think the name default mode network is confusing because it does nothing to describe what this network does. One of the first networks discovered, this area is active in the brain while the individual is in the brain scanner waiting for the experiment to begin, hence the term default mode. It was assumed at the time that this is the area of the brain that is active when nothing else is going on. If these individuals are like me or any person I know, they are not lying in the fMRI machine with their mind blank waiting for the experimenter to say something. They are thinking, and often when we think it's about ourselves. When you are waiting for the bus or driving home along the highway, you're probably thinking about what you did that day, or what you'll do when you get home. You think about all sorts of things, but mostly about yourself. This is what the DMN seems to be specialized for: self-referential thinking. The DMN contains several nodes, including the PCC, precuneus, and vmPFC (Greicius, Supekar, Menon, & Dougherty, 2009). Studies have also identified the IPL and MTL as part of the DMN (Buckner, Andrews-Hanna, & Schacter, 2008; Van Den Heuvel, Mandl, Kahn, & Hulshoff Pol, 2009). The DMN is particularly active in individuals with depression (Sheline et al., 2009), probably because they are having increased self-judgmental thoughts as is common in depression (Barcaccia et al., 2019). Further research shows that the DMN is increasingly activate in depression in comparison with other brain networks (Hamilton et al., 2011) Given its role in self-referential thinking, it may not be surprising that mindfulness meditation, a treatment that is also used for depression, reduces DMN activity (Brewer et al., 2011; Berkovich-Ohana, Glicksohn, & Goldstein, 2012).

Central Executive Network (CEN)/ Fronto-parietal Network—The CEN nodes consist of the dlPFC and SPL (Bressler & Menon, 2010). The CEN is involved in demanding cognitive tasks, like complex problem solving, working memory, and executive functioning tasks in general. One study showed children's performance on a mathematics ability test was correlated with connectivity within the CEN (Emerson & Cantlon, 2012). When the CEN is active during cognitively demanding tasks, the DMN shows a decrease in activation (Greicius, Krasnow, Reiss, & Menon, 2003). The CEN has wide functionality connectivity with other parts of the brain, especially when compared to other brain networks (Cole et al., 2013). Zanto and Gazzaley (2013) suggest that these unique connections may make the CEN a flexible hub that alters functional connectivity between other neural networks depending on task needs. Utilizing brain regions like dlPFC important for complex cognitive functioning, the CEN may act as a problem solver and recruit other brain regions as necessary to solve complex problems.

Salience network (SN)—The salience network, which is identified as the AI and dACC, gets its name from becoming active when information is salient or important enough to command our attention. Neuroimaging research demonstrates the SN switches between the DMN and CEN (Goulden et al., 2014). Sridharan, Levitin, and Menon (2008) particularly identify the right AI and its ability to activate the CEN and deactivate the DMN. Menon and Uddin (2010) believe that the AI is significant for the detection of salience stimuli, while the dACC plays a role in action selection in modulating the response to the salient stimuli. If we think of the DMN as the brain at rest or daydreaming and CEN as the brain actively working to solve problems, the SN might be the wake-up call from the DMN to CEN. When something rises to the threshold of importance, the SN alerts the CEN to start figuring out solutions to this salient problem. In fact, the CEN and the dACC have been shown to activate together in tasks requiring top-down attention (Wang et al., 2010). One study found connectivity of the SN was related to decreased negative thinking following the emotion of sadness (Lydon-Staley, Kuehner, Zamoscik, Huffziger, Kirsch, & Bassett, 2019). Another recent study found disruption between the SN and parts of the DMN and CEN in individuals with OCD (Fan et al., 2017). There are other studies showing effects within and between these networks and psychopathology. However, it is important to note that when imaging large regions of the brain, some significant effects will be found. Without a strong a priori hypothesis, we must consider issues of multicollinearity before drawing any conclusions. These studies also highlight the importance of examining interaction effects between brain networks, as opposed to examining single brain regions. AI and dACC regions of the SN are both involved in the recognition of emotion. Interestingly these two brain regions are also unique for the presence of von Economo neurons (sometimes called spindle neurons). Von Economo neurons are long straight neurons, with single extended apical and basal dendrites, that are only found in humans and great apes; no other primates have them (Watson, Jones, & Allman, 2006). These von Economo neurons may be specialized for the specific use of fast transmission of information between brain areas (Allman et al., 2001).

Dorsal and Ventral Attention Network (DAN & VAN)—If the SN represents bottom-up attention to salience stimuli, the DAN, which stretches across the top of the brain, would represent the top-down at-tentional network for spatial information, while the VAN would be the bottom-up system for salient visual information (Serences et al., 2005) (see section 4.2). The DAN has nodes in the FEF and IPS, which rests just above the IPL (Szczepanski, Pinsk, Douglas, Kastner, & Saalmann, 2013). The DAN is involved in goal-directed attention and helps orientate focus on a particular task (Corbetta et al., 2008). The VAN contains the IPL, TPJ, and a mix of centrally located areas referred to as the ventral frontal cortex (IFG & MFG) (Corbetta et al., 2008; Serences et al., 2005). The VAN also appears more localized to the right side of the brain (Corbetta et al., 2008). The VAN would typically activate when a novel or un-expected visual information enters the cortex (Kim, 2014). If one were doing a word find, the DAN would be active, not the VAN, and this is marked by activation or inactivation of the TPJ (Shulman, Astafiev, McAvoy, d'Avossa, & Corbetta, 2007). However, for many attentional tasks, the DAN and VAN work together in optimizing attention. Research demonstrates that the DAN and VAN can be correlated and anti-correlated (Vossel, Geng, & Fink, 2014; Weissman & Prado, 2012). Research suggests the DAN and VAN may work together for tasks of motor inhibition (Hsu, Yao, Hwang, & Hsieh, 2020). At times the DAN, VAN, and SN are referred to as "task-positive" networks, because of their activation during tasks that involve cognitive engagement (Kelly, Uddin, Biswal, Castellanos, & Milham, 2008), as opposed to DMN, which is active when there is no task. Yet, this discernment has some problems; first, all networks other than the DMN are task-positive; and second, it signals that the DMN does not have a useful role in brain functions by being task-negative (Spreng, 2012).

Extrinsic Mode Network (EMN)—If you were to group the task-positive networks and name them in the literature they would be referred to as the EMN. The EMN is typically active when the DMN is inactive and it is involved in tasks of focused awareness or attention (Hugdahl, Raichle, Mitra, & Specht, 2015). Studies of task activation and inactivation have supported this distinction (Hugdahl et al., 2019), and work suggests that many mental disorders may involve a disruption in switching between brain networks (Allen, Sommer, Jardri, Eysenck, & Hugdahl, 2019; Nygård et al., 2012). One theory that has been proposed is that the increased DMN activity seen in depression is related to an inability to switch between networks, and not solely a problem of an overactive DMN (Hamilton et al., 2011). If individuals with depression do struggle to activate task-positive networks like EMN, that could also explain the avolition and difficulty to initiate behavior seen in the disorder. It is also worth noting there is often overlap in the functioning and nomenclature of these various cortical networks for a review, see Witt, van Ettinger-Veenstra, Salo, Riedel, and Laird (2020).

Mesocorticolimbic Network (MCL) (reward circuit)—This has also been referred to as the pleasure network because activity in the MCL is associated with many pleasurable pursuits (Rømer Thomsen, Whybrow, & Kringelbach, 2015). Calling the MCL the pleasure network could create some confusion because the network is more specific to reinforcement learning. Whenever we engage in behavior that rewards us, it is often marked by a feeling of pleasure. The MCL releases dopamine, which reinforces the behavior that led to the dopamine release. Often initially positive or useful behaviors are reinforced. However, in the example of a drug, something that was once pleasurable can turn into being addictive and harmful, the opposite of pleasurable (see section 9.6, for a distinction between wanting and liking). So, this network is more about the reinforcement of behavior (Camara, Rodriguez-Fornells, and Münte, 2009). Sometimes divided into two separate pathways, the mesolimbic and mesocortical pathways project dopamine to limbic and neocortical areas respectively (Hauser, Eldar, & Dolan, 2017). Both pathways originate from the dopaminergic neurons in the VTA. The mesolimbic projects primarily to the NA in the basal ganglia, while the mesocortical projects to areas of the PFC (Arias-Carrión, Stamelou, Murillo-Rodríguez, Menéndez-González, & Pöppel, 2010). These cortical projections may also facilitate the learned behaviors which contribute to the reward or dopamine response. It has also been suggested the anhedonia symptoms in depression and bipolar disorder could be related to an impairment in the MCL (Abler,

Greenhouse, Ongur, Walter, & Heckers, 2008; Nestler & Carlezon, 2006; O'Sullivan, Szczepanowski, El-Deredy, Mason, & Bentall, 2011).

If you're still reading at this point you can understand that psychopathology in the brain is a complicated process. The following sections will focus on applying this knowledge to the practice of psychotherapy. Since much of psychotherapy to date has focused on addressing top-down cognitive influences on emotion, this book examines bottom-up influences of emotion and its effects. The following pages will provide a guide for how therapists can use emotion in their clinical practice.

References

Abe, Y., Sakai, Y., Nishida, S., Nakamae, T., Yamada, K., Fukui, K., & Narumoto, J. (2015). Hyper-influence of the orbitofrontal cortex over the ventral striatum in obsessive-compulsive disorder. *European Neuropsychopharmacology, 25*(11), 1898–1905.

Abler, B., Greenhouse, I., Ongur, D., Walter, H., & Heckers, S. (2008). Abnormal reward system activation in mania. *Neuropsychopharmacology, 33*(9), 2217–2227.

Aichhorn, M., Perner, J., Kronbichler, M., Staffen, W., & Ladurner, G. (2006). Do visual perspective tasks need theory of mind? *Neuroimage, 30*(3), 1059–1068.

Allen, P., Sommer, I. E., Jardri, R., Eysenck, M. W., & Hugdahl, K. (2019). Extrinsic and default mode networks in psychiatric conditions: Relationship to excitatory-inhibitory transmitter balance and early trauma. *Neuroscience & Biobehavioral Reviews, 99*, 90–100.

Allman, J. M., Hakeem, A., Erwin, J. M., Nimchinsky, E., & Hof, P. (2001). The anterior cingulate cortex: The evolution of an interface between emotion and cognition. *Annals of the New York Academy of Sciences, 935*(1), 107–117.

Arias-Carrión, O., Stamelou, M., Murillo-Rodríguez, E., Menéndez-González, M., & Pöppel, E. (2010). Dopaminergic reward system: A short integrative review. *International Archives of Medicine, 3*(1), 1–6.

Aron, A. R., Robbins, T. W., & Poldrack, R. A. (2014). Inhibition and the right inferior frontal cortex: One decade on. *Trends in Cognitive Sciences, 18*(4), 177–185.

Asami, T., Hayano, F., Nakamura, M., Yamasue, H., Uehara, K., Otsuka, T., … & Hirayasu, Y. (2008). Anterior cingulate cortex volume reduction in patients with panic disorder. *Psychiatry and Clinical Neurosciences, 62*(3), 322–330.

Banich, M. T., & Compton, R. J. (2018). *Cognitive neuroscience.* Belomont, CA: Wadsworth.

Barbey, A. K., Koenigs, M., & Grafman, J. (2013). Dorsolateral prefrontal contributions to human working memory. *Cortex, 49*(5), 1195–1205.

Barcaccia, B., Baiocco, R., Pozza, A., Pallini, S., Mancini, F., & Salvati, M. (2019). The more you judge the worse you feel. A judgemental attitude towards one's inner experience predicts depression and anxiety. *Personality and Individual Differences, 138*, 33–39.

Barron, H. C., Reeve, H. M., Koolschijn, R. S., Perestenko, P. V., Shpektor, A., Nili, H., … & Behrens, T. E. (2020). Neuronal computation underlying inferential reasoning in humans and mice. *Cell, 183*(1), 228–243.

Barry, D. N., & Maguire, E. A. (2019). Remote memory and the hippocampus: A constructive critique. *Trends in Cognitive Sciences, 23*(2), 128–142.

Baur, V., Hänggi, J., Langer, N., & Jäncke, L. (2013). Resting-state functional and structural connectivity within an insula–amygdala route specifically index state and trait anxiety. *Biological Psychiatry, 73*(1), 85–92.

Beauchamp, M. S. (2015). The social mysteries of the superior temporal sulcus. *Trends in Cognitive Sciences, 19*(9), 489–490.

Beckmann, M., Johansen-Berg, H., & Rushworth, M. F. (2009). Connectivity-based parcellation of human cingulate cortex and its relation to functional specialization. *Journal of Neuroscience, 29*(4), 1175–1190.

Benarroch, E. E. (2015). Pulvinar: Associative role in cortical function and clinical correlations. *Neurology, 84*(7), 738–747.

Benear, S. L., Ngo, C. T., & Olson, I. R. (2020). Dissecting the fornix in basic memory processes and neuropsychiatric disease: A review. *Brain Connectivity, 10*(7), 331–354.

Berkovich-Ohana, A., Glicksohn, J., & Goldstein, A. (2012). Mindfulness-induced changes in gamma band activity–implications for the default mode network, self-reference and attention. *Clinical Neurophysiology, 123*(4), 700–710.

Bertossi, E., Tesini, C., Cappelli, A., & Ciaramelli, E. (2016). Ventromedial prefrontal damage causes a pervasive impairment of episodic memory and future thinking. *Neuropsychologia, 90*, 12–24.

Beucke, J. C., Sepulcre, J., Talukdar, T., Linnman, C., Zschenderlein, K., Endrass, T., … & Kathmann, N. (2013). Abnormally high degree connectivity of the orbitofrontal cortex in obsessive-compulsive disorder. *JAMA Psychiatry, 70*(6), 619–629.

Binder, J. R., Desai, R. H., Graves, W. W., & Conant, L. L. (2009). Where is the semantic system? A critical review and meta-analysis of 120 functional neuroimaging studies. *Cerebral Cortex, 19*(12), 2767–2796.

Brass, M., & Haggard, P. (2007). To do or not to do: The neural signature of self-control. *Journal of Neuroscience, 27*(34), 9141–9145.

Bressler, S. L., & Menon, V. (2010). Large-scale brain networks in cognition: Emerging methods and principles. *Trends in Cognitive Sciences, 14*(6), 277–290.

Brewer, J. A., Worhunsky, P. D., Gray, J. R., Tang, Y. Y., Weber, J., & Kober, H. (2011). Meditation experience is associated with differences in default mode network activity and connectivity. *Proceedings of the National Academy of Sciences, 108*(50), 20254–20259.

Buckley, E., Mazzà, C., & McNeill, A. (2018). A systematic review of the gait characteristics associated with Cerebellar Ataxia. *Gait & Posture, 60*, 154–163.

Buckner, R. L., Andrews-Hanna, J. R., & Schacter, D. L. (2008). The brain's default network: Anatomy, function, and relevance to disease. *Annals of the New York Academy of Sciences, 1124*, 1–38.

Buhle, J. T., Kober, H., Ochsner, K. N., Mende-Siedlecki, P., Weber, J., Hughes, B. L., … & Wager, T. D. (2013). Common representation of pain and negative emotion in the midbrain periaqueductal gray. *Social Cognitive and Affective Neuroscience, 8*(6), 609–616.

Buhle, J. T., Silvers, J. A., Wager, T. D., Lopez, R., Onyemekwu, C., Kober, H., … & Ochsner, K. N. (2014). Cognitive reappraisal of emotion: A meta-analysis of human neuroimaging studies. *Cerebral Cortex, 24*(11), 2981–2990.

Bush, G., Luu, P., & Posner, M. I. (2000). Cognitive and emotional influences in anterior cingulate cortex. *Trends in Cognitive Sciences, 4*(6), 215–222.

Buxbaum, L. J., Kyle, K., Grossman, M., & Coslett, B. (2007). Left inferior parietal representations for skilled hand-object interactions: Evidence from stroke and corticobasal degeneration. *Cortex, 43*(3), 411–423.

Cabeza, R., Ciaramelli, E., & Moscovitch, M. (2012). Cognitive contributions of the ventral parietal cortex: An integrative theoretical account. *Trends in Cognitive Sciences, 16*(6), 338–352.

Camara, E., Rodriguez-Fornells, A., & Münte, T. F. (2009). Functional connectivity of reward processing in the brain. *Frontiers in Human Neuroscience, 2*, 19.

Carrington, S. J., & Bailey, A. J. (2009). Are there theory of mind regions in the brain? A review of the neuroimaging literature. *Human Brain Mapping, 30*(8), 2313–2335.

Carter, R. M., & Huettel, S. A. (2013). A nexus model of the temporal–parietal junction. *Trends in Cognitive Sciences, 17*(7), 328–336.

Cauda, F., Costa, T., Torta, D. M., Sacco, K., D'Agata, F., Duca, S., ... & Vercelli, A. (2012). Meta-analytic clustering of the insular cortex: Characterizing the meta-analytic connectivity of the insula when involved in active tasks. *Neuroimage, 62*(1), 343–355.

Cauda, F., D'Agata, F., Sacco, K., Duca, S., Geminiani, G., & Vercelli, A. (2011). Functional connectivity of the insula in the resting brain. *Neuroimage, 55*(1), 8–23.

Chabardès, S., Kahane, P., Minotti, L., Hoffmann, D., & Benabid, A. L. (2002). Anatomy of the temporal pole region. *Epileptic Disorders, 4*, S9–S16.

Chang, E. F., Rieger, J. W., Johnson, K., Berger, M. S., Barbaro, N. M., & Knight, R. T. (2010). Categorical speech representation in human superior temporal gyrus. *Nature nNeuroscience, 13*(11), 1428.

Chang, L. J., Yarkoni, T., Khaw, M. W., & Sanfey, A. G. (2013). Decoding the role of the insula in human cognition: Functional parcellation and large-scale reverse inference. *Cerebral Cortex, 23*(3), 739–749.

Chen, T. L., Babiloni, C., Ferretti, A., Perrucci, M. G., Romani, G. L., Rossini, P. M., ... & Del Gratta, C. (2008). Human secondary somatosensory cortex is involved in the processing of somatosensory rare stimuli: an fMRI study. *Neuroimage, 40*(4), 1765–1771.

Chouinard, P. A., & Paus, T. (2006). The primary motor and premotor areas of the human cerebral cortex. *The Neuroscientist, 12*(2), 143–152.

Cipolotti, L., & Bird, C. M. (2006). Amnesia and the hippocampus. *Current Opinion in Neurology, 19*(6), 593–598.

Cole, M. W., Reynolds, J. R., Power, J. D., Repovs, G., Anticevic, A., & Braver, T. S. (2013). Multi-task connectivity reveals flexible hubs for adaptive task control. *Nature Neuroscience, 16*(9), 1348–1355.

Corbetta, M., Patel, G., & Shulman, G. L. (2008). The reorienting system of the human brain: From environment to theory of mind. *Neuron, 58*(3), 306–324.

Cotton, J. L. (1981). A review of research on Schachter's theory of emotion and the misattribution of arousal. *European Journal of Social Psychology, 11*(4), 365–397.

Craig, A. D., Chen, K., Bandy, D., & Reiman, E. M. (2000). Thermosensory activation of insular cortex. *Nature Neuroscience, 3*(2), 184–190.

Critchley, H. D., Wiens, S., Rotshtein, P., Öhman, A., & Dolan, R. J. (2004). Neural systems supporting interoceptive awareness. *Nature Neuroscience, 7*(2), 189–195.

Cunningham, W. A., Johnson, M. K., Raye, C. L., Gatenby, J. C., Gore, J. C., & Banaji, M. R. (2004). Separable neural components in the processing of black and white faces. *Psychological Science, 15*(12), 806–813.

Cunningham, W. A., Raye, C. L., & Johnson, M. K. (2004). Implicit and explicit evaluation: fMRI correlates of valence, emotional intensity, and control in the processing of attitudes. *Journal of Cognitive Neuroscience, 16*(10), 1717–1729.

Cunningham, W. A., & Zelazo, P. D. (2007). Attitudes and evaluations: A social cognitive neuroscience perspective. *Trends in Cognitive Sciences, 11*(3), 97–104.

Cunningham, W. A., Zelazo, P. D., Packer, D. J., & Van Bavel, J. J. (2007). The iterative reprocessing model: A multilevel framework for attitudes and evaluation. *Social Cognition, 25*(5), 736–760.

Davis, K. D., Kwan, C. L., Crawley, A. P., & Mikulis, D. J. (1998). Functional MRI study of thalamic and cortical activations evoked by cutaneous heat, cold, and tactile stimuli. *Journal of Neurophysiology, 80*(3), 1533–1546.

Davis, K. D., Pope, G. E., Crawley, A. P., & Mikulis, D. J. (2004). Perceptual illusion of "paradoxical heat" engages the insular cortex. *Journal of Neurophysiology, 92*(2), 1248–1251.

Deen, B., Koldewyn, K., Kanwisher, N., & Saxe, R. (2015). Functional organization of social perception and cognition in the superior temporal sulcus. *Cerebral Cortex, 25*(11), 4596–4609.

Dehaene, S., Changeux, J. P., Naccache, L., Sackur, J., & Sergent, C. (2006). Conscious, preconscious, and subliminal processing: A testable taxonomy. *Trends in Cognitive Sciences, 10*(5), 204–211.

Devlin, J. T., Matthews, P. M., & Rushworth, M. F. (2003). Semantic processing in the left inferior prefrontal cortex: A combined functional magnetic resonance imaging and transcranial magnetic stimulation study. *Journal of Cognitive Neuroscience, 15*(1), 71–84.

Dolan, R. J., Lane, R., Chua, P., & Fletcher, P. (2000). Dissociable temporal lobe activations during emotional episodic memory retrieval. *Neuroimage, 11*(3), 203–209.

Drevets, W. C., Savitz, J., & Trimble, M. (2008). The subgenual anterior cingulate cortex in mood disorders. *CNS Spectrums, 13*(8), 663.

Du, J., Rolls, E. T., Cheng, W., Li, Y., Gong, W., Qiu, J., & Feng, J. (2020). Functional connectivity of the orbitofrontal cortex, anterior cingulate cortex, and inferior frontal gyrus in humans. *Cortex, 123*, 185–199.

Dutton, D. G., & Aron, A. P. (1974). Some evidence for heightened sexual attraction under conditions of high anxiety. *Journal of Personality and Social Psychology, 30*(4), 510.

Eddy, C. M. (2016). The junction between self and other? Temporo-parietal dysfunction in neuropsychiatry. *Neuropsychologia, 89,* 465–477. 10.1016/j.neuropsychologia. 2016.07.030.

Eger, E., Sterzer, P., Russ, M. O., Giraud, A. L., & Kleinschmidt, A. (2003). A supramodal number representation in human intraparietal cortex. *Neuron, 37*(4), 719–726.

Ehrsson, H. H., Spence, C., & Passingham, R. E. (2004). That's my hand! Activity in premotor cortex reflects feeling of ownership of a limb. *Science, 305*(5685), 875–887

Eichenbaum, H. (2017). Prefrontal–hippocampal interactions in episodic memory. *Nature Reviews Neuroscience, 18*(9), 547–558

Emerson, R. W., & Cantlon, J. F. (2012). Early math achievement and functional connectivity in the fronto-parietal network. *Developmental Cognitive Neuroscience, 2,* S139–S151.

Etkin, A., Büchel, C., & Gross, J. J. (2015). The neural bases of emotion regulation. *Nature Reviews Neuroscience, 16*(11), 693–700.

Etkin, A., Egner, T., & Kalisch, R. (2011). Emotional processing in anterior cingulate and medial prefrontal cortex. *Trends in Cognitive Sciences, 15*(2), 85–93.

Etkin, A., Egner, T., Peraza, D. M., Kandel, E. R., & Hirsch, J. (2006). Resolving emotional conflict: A role for the rostral anterior cingulate cortex in modulating activity in the amygdala. *Neuron, 51*(6), 871–882.

Evans, J. S. B., & Stanovich, K. E. (2013). Dual-process theories of higher cognition: Advancing the debate. *Perspectives on Psychological Science, 8*(3), 223–241.

Everitt, B. J., Hutcheson, D. M., Ersche, K. D., Pelloux, Y., Dalley, J. W., & Robbins, T. W. (2007). The orbital prefrontal cortex and drug addiction in laboratory animals and humans. *Annals of the New York Academy of Sciences, 1121*(1), 576–597.

Fan, J., Zhong, M., Gan, J., Liu, W., Niu, C., Liao, H., ... & Zhu, X. (2017). Altered connectivity within and between the default mode, central executive, and salience networks in obsessive-compulsive disorder. *Journal of Affective Disorders, 223*, 106–114.

Ferrari, C., Lega, C., Vernice, M., Tamietto, M., Mende-Siedlecki, P., Vecchi, T., ... & Cattaneo, Z. (2016). The dorsomedial prefrontal cortex plays a causal role in integrating social impressions from faces and verbal descriptions. *Cerebral Cortex, 26*(1), 156–165.

Flor, H. (2002). Phantom-limb pain: Characteristics, causes, and treatment. *The Lancet Neurology, 1*(3), 182--189.

Fornia, L., Puglisi, G., Leonetti, A., Bello, L., Berti, A., Cerri, G., & Garbarini, F. (2020). Direct electrical stimulation of the premotor cortex shuts down awareness of voluntary actions. *Nature Communications, 11*(1), 1–11.

Freeman, J. B., Schiller, D., Rule, N. O., & Ambady, N. (2010). The neural origins of superficial and individuated judgments about ingroup and outgroup members. *Human Brain Mapping, 31*(1), 150–159.

Frewen, P., Lane, R. D., Neufeld, R. W., Densmore, M., Stevens, T., & Lanius, R. (2008). Neural correlates of levels of emotional awareness during trauma script-imagery in posttraumatic stress disorder. *Psychosomatic Medicine, 70*(1), 27–31.

Frith, C. D., & Frith, U. (1999). Interacting minds--a biological basis. *Science, 286*(5445), 1692–1695.

Frot, M., Faillenot, I., & Mauguière, F. (2014). Processing of nociceptive input from posterior to anterior insula in humans. *Human Brain Mapping, 35*(11), 5486–5499.

Fuster, J. M. (2002). Frontal lobe and cognitive development. *Journal of Neurocytology, 31*(3–5), 373–385.

Gallagher, H. L., & Frith, C. D. (2003). Functional imaging of 'theory of mind'. *Trends in Cognitive Sciences, 7*(2), 77–83.

Garrido, M. I., Barnes, G. R., Sahani, M., & Dolan, R. J. (2012). Functional evidence for a dual route to amygdala. *Current Biology, 22*(2), 129–134.

Garrison, K. A., Zeffiro, T. A., Scheinost, D., Constable, R. T., & Brewer, J. A. (2015). Meditation leads to reduced default mode network activity beyond an active task. *Cognitive, Affective, & Behavioral Neuroscience, 15*(3), 712–720.

Garvert, M. M., Friston, K. J., Dolan, R. J., & Garrido, M. I. (2014). Subcortical amygdala pathways enable rapid face processing. *Neuroimage, 102*, 309–316.

Goulden, N., Khusnulina, A., Davis, N. J., Bracewell, R. M., Bokde, A. L., McNulty, J. P., & Mullins, P. G. (2014). The salience network is responsible for switching between the default mode network and the central executive network: Replication from DCM. *Neuroimage, 99*, 180–190.

Grahn, J. A., Parkinson, J. A., & Owen, A. M. (2008). The cognitive functions of the caudate nucleus. *Progress in Neurobiology, 86*(3), 141–155.

Gray, O., Fry, L., & Montaldi, D. (2020). Information content best characterises the hemispheric selectivity of the inferior parietal lobe: A meta-analysis. *Scientific Reports, 10*(1), 1–9.

Greicius, M. D., Krasnow, B., Reiss, A. L., & Menon, V. (2003). Functional connectivity in the resting brain: A network analysis of the default mode hypothesis. *Proceedings of the National Academy of Sciences, 100*(1), 253–258.

Greicius, M. D., Supekar, K., Menon, V., & Dougherty, R. F. (2009). Resting-state functional connectivity reflects structural connectivity in the default mode network. *Cerebral Cortex, 19*(1), 72–78.

Groome, D. (2013). *An introduction to cognitive psychology: Processes and disorders.* London, UK: Psychology Press.

Gulbinaite, R., van Rijn, H., & Cohen, M. X. (2014). Fronto-parietal network oscillations reveal relationship between working memory capacity and cognitive control. *Frontiers in Human Neuroscience, 8*, 761.

Hamani, C., Mayberg, H., Stone, S., Laxton, A., Haber, S., & Lozano, A. M. (2011). The subcallosal cingulate gyrus in the context of major depression. *Biological Psychiatry, 69*(4), 301–308.

Hamann, S. B., Ely, T. D., Grafton, S. T., & Kilts, C. D. (1999). Amygdala activity related to enhanced memory for pleasant and aversive stimuli. *Nature Neuroscience, 2*(3), 289–293.

Hamilton, J. P., Furman, D. J., Chang, C., Thomason, M. E., Dennis, E., & Gotlib, I. H. (2011). Default-mode and task-positive network activity in major depressive disorder: Implications for adaptive and maladaptive rumination. *Biological Psychiatry, 70*(4), 327–333.

Hampshire, A., Chamberlain, S. R., Monti, M. M., Duncan, J., & Owen, A. M. (2010). The role of the right inferior frontal gyrus: Inhibition and attentional control. *Neuroimage, 50*(3), 1313–1319.

Hassabis, D., Kumaran, D., Vann, S. D., & Maguire, E. A. (2007). Patients with hippocampal amnesia cannot imagine new experiences. *Proceedings of the National Academy of Sciences, 104*(5), 1726–1731.

Hauser, T. U., Eldar, E., & Dolan, R. J. (2017). Separate mesocortical and mesolimbic pathways encode effort and reward learning signals. *Proceedings of the National Academy of Sciences, 114*(35), E7395–E7404.

Hernandez, J. S., & Moorman, D. E. (2020). Orbitofrontal cortex encodes preference for alcohol. *Eneuro, 7*(4).

Hodgetts, C. J., Postans, M., Warne, N., Varnava, A., Lawrence, A. D., & Graham, K. S. (2017). Distinct contributions of the fornix and inferior longitudinal fasciculus to episodic and semantic autobiographical memory. *Cortex, 94*, 1–14.

Holtzheimer, P. E., Kelley, M. E., Gross, R. E., Filkowski, M. M., Garlow, S. J., Barrocas, A., ... & Mayberg, H. S. (2012). Subcallosal cingulate deep brain stimulation for treatment-resistant unipolar and bipolar depression. *Archives of General Psychiatry, 69*(2), 150–158.

Hsu, H. M., Yao, Z. F., Hwang, K., & Hsieh, S. (2020). Between-module functional connectivity of the salient ventral attention network and dorsal attention network is associated with motor inhibition. *Plos One, 15*(12), e0242985.

Hugdahl, K., Kazimierczak, K., Beresniewicz, J., Kompus, K., Westerhausen, R., Ersland, L., ... & Specht, K. (2019). Dynamic up-and down-regulation of the default (DMN) and extrinsic (EMN) mode networks during alternating task-on and task-off periods. *PLoS One*, *14*(9), e0218358.

Hugdahl, K., Raichle, M. E., Mitra, A., & Specht, K. (2015). On the existence of a generalized non-specific task-dependent network. *Frontiers in Human Neuroscience*, *9*, 430.

Jacobs K.M. (2011) Brodmann's areas of the cortex. In J. S. Kreutzer, J. DeLuca, & B. Caplan (Eds.), *Encyclopedia of clinical neuropsychology*. New York, NY: Springer. doi:10.1007/978-0-387-79948-3_301.

Jiang, Y. I., Shannon, R. W., Vizueta, N., Bernat, E. M., Patrick, C. J., & He, S. (2009). Dynamics of processing invisible faces in the brain: Automatic neural encoding of facial expression information. *Neuroimage*, *44*(3), 1171–1177.

Johansen-Berg, H., Gutman, D. A., Behrens, T. E. J., Matthews, P. M., Rushworth, M. F. S., Katz, E., ... & Mayberg, H. S. (2008). Anatomical connectivity of the sub-genual cingulate region targeted with deep brain stimulation for treatment-resistant depression. *Cerebral Cortex*, *18*(6), 1374–1383.

Kahneman, D. (2011). *Thinking, fast and slow*. New York, NY: Macmillan.

Kahnt, T., Heinzle, J., Park, S. Q., & Haynes, J. D. (2011). Decoding different roles for vmPFC and dlPFC in multi-attribute decision making. *Neuroimage*, *56*(2), 709–771

Kamping, S., Andoh, J., Bomba, I. C., Diers, M., Diesch, E., & Flor, H. (2016). Contextual modulation of pain in masochists: Involvement of the parietal operculum and insula. *Pain*, *157*(2), 445.

Kanske, P., & Kotz, S. A. (2011). Emotion triggers executive attention: Anterior cingulate cortex and amygdala responses to emotional words in a conflict task. *Human Brain Mapping*, *32*(2), 198–208.

Kelly, A. C., Uddin, L. Q., Biswal, B. B., Castellanos, F. X., & Milham, M. P. (2008). Competition between functional brain networks mediates behavioral variability. *Neuroimage*, *39*(1), 527–537.

Keren, G., & Schul, Y. (2009). Two is not always better than one: A critical evaluation of two-system theories. *Perspectives on Psychological Science*, *4*(6), 533–550.

Kim, H. (2014). Involvement of the dorsal and ventral attention networks in oddball stimulus processing: A meta-analysis. *Human Brain Mapping*, *35*(5), 2265–2284.

Kleinman, J. T., Newhart, M., Davis, C., Heidler-Gary, J., Gottesman, R. F., & Hillis, A. E. (2007). Right hemispatial neglect: Frequency and characterization following acute left hemisphere stroke. *Brain and Cognition*, *64*(1), 50–59.

Kragel, P. A., & LaBar, K. S. (2016). Decoding the nature of emotion in the brain. *Trends in Cognitive Sciences*, *20*(6), 444–455.

LaBar, K. S., & Cabeza, R. (2006). Cognitive neuroscience of emotional memory. *Nature Reviews Neuroscience*, *7*(1), 54–64.

Lai, V. T., Hagoort, P., & Casasanto, D. (2012). Affective primacy vs. cognitive primacy: Dissolving the debate. *Frontiers in Psychology*, *3*, 243.

Lambon Ralph, M. A., Pobric, G., & Jefferies, E. (2009). Conceptual knowledge is underpinned by the temporal pole bilaterally: Convergent evidence from rTMS. *Cerebral Cortex*, *19*(4), 832–838.

LeDoux, J. (1998). *The emotional brain: The mysterious underpinnings of emotional life*. New York, NY: Simon and Schuster.

LeDoux, J. (2012). Rethinking the emotional brain. *Neuron*, *73*(4), 653–676.

Leech, R., & Sharp, D. J. (2014). The role of the posterior cingulate cortex in cognition and disease. *Brain*, *137*(1), 12–32.

Lieberman, M. D. (2007). The X- and C-systems: The neural basis of automatic and controlled social cognition. In E. Harmon-Jones & P. Winkielman (Eds.), *Social neuroscience: Integrating biological and psychological explanations of social behavior* (pp. 290–315). New York, NY: The Guilford Press.

Lockwood, P. L., & Wittmann, M. K. (2018). Ventral anterior cingulate cortex and social decision-making. *Neuroscience & Biobehavioral Reviews*, *92*, 187–191.

Ly, M., Adluru, N., Destiche, D. J., Lu, S. Y., Oh, J. M., Hoscheidt, S. M., ... & Johnson, S. C. (2016). Fornix microstructure and memory performance is associated with altered neural connectivity during episodic recognition. *Journal of the International Neuropsychological Society*, *22*(2), 191–204.

Lydon-Staley, D. M., Kuehner, C., Zamoscik, V., Huffziger, S., Kirsch, P., & Bassett, D. S. (2019). Repetitive negative thinking in daily life and functional connectivity among default mode, fronto-parietal, and salience networks. *Translational Psychiatry*, *9*(1), 1–12.

Lyle, K., & Johnson, M. (2006). Importing perceived features into false memories. *Memory*, *14*(2), 197–213.

MacLean, P. D. (1990). *The triune brain in evolution: Role in paleocerebral functions.* New York, NY: Springer Science & Business Media.

Maddock, R. J., Garrett, A. S., & Buonocore, M. H. (2001). Remembering familiar people: The posterior cingulate cortex and autobiographical memory retrieval. *Neuroscience*, *104*(3), 667–676.

Mai, X., Zhang, W., Hu, X., Zhen, Z., Xu, Z., Zhang, J., & Liu, C. (2016). Using tDCS to explore the role of the right temporo-parietal junction in theory of mind and cognitive empathy. *Frontiers in Psychology*, *7*, 380.

Maia, T. V., & Frank, M. J. (2011). From reinforcement learning models to psychiatric and neurological disorders. *Nature Neuroscience*, *14*(2), 154–162.

Martin, A. K., Dzafic, I., Ramdave, S., & Meinzer, M. (2017). Causal evidence for task-specific involvement of the dorsomedial prefrontal cortex in human social cognition. *Social Cognitive and Affective Neuroscience*, *12*(8), 1209–1218

Mayberg, H. S., Lozano, A. M., Voon, V., McNeely, H. E., Seminowicz, D., Hamani, C., ... & Kennedy, S. H. (2005). Deep brain stimulation for treatment-resistant depression. *Neuron*, *45*(5), 651–660.

Menon, V. (2011). Large-scale brain networks and psychopathology: A unifying triple network model. *Trends in Cognitive Sciences*, *15*(10), 483–506.

Menon, V., & Uddin, L. Q. (2010). Saliency, switching, attention and control: A network model of insula function. *Brain Structure and Function*, *214*(5–6), 655–667.

Mesgarani, N., Cheung, C., Johnson, K., & Chang, E. F. (2014). Phonetic feature encoding in human superior temporal gyrus. *Science*, *343*(6174), 1006–1010.

Miall, R. C., Reckess, G. Z., & Imamizu, H. (2001). The cerebellum coordinates eye and hand tracking movements. *Nature Neuroscience*, *4*(6), 638–644.

Morris, L. S., Costi, S., Tan, A., Stern, E. R., Charney, D. S., & Murrough, J. W. (2020). Ketamine normalizes subgenual cingulate cortex hyper-activity in depression. *Neuropsychopharmacology*, *45*(6), 975–981.

Morris, J. S., DeGelder, B., Weiskrantz, L., & Dolan, R. J. (2001). Differential extra-geniculostriate and amygdala responses to presentation of emotional faces in a cortically blind field. *Brain*, *124*(6), 1241–1252.

Morton, S. M., & Bastian, A. J. (2004). Cerebellar control of balance and locomotion. *The Neuroscientist*, *10*(3), 247–259.

Motta, S. C., Carobrez, A. P., & Canteras, N. S. (2017). The periaqueductal gray and primal emotional processing critical to influence complex defensive responses, fear learning and reward seeking. *Neuroscience & Biobehavioral Reviews*, *76*, 39–47.

Muggleton, N. G., Juan, C. H., Cowey, A., & Walsh, V. (2003). Human frontal eye fields and visual search. *Journal of Neurophysiology*, *89*(6), 3340–3343.

Nadel, L., Samsonovich, A., Ryan, L., & Moscovitch, M. (2000). Multiple trace theory of human memory: Computational, neuroimaging, and neuropsychological results. *Hippocampus*, *10*(4), 352–368.

Nakao, T., Okada, K., & Kanba, S. (2014). Neurobiological model of obsessive–compulsive disorder: Evidence from recent neuropsychological and neuroimaging findings. *Psychiatry and Clinical Neurosciences*, *68*(8), 587–605.

Neary, D., Snowden, J., & Mann, D. (2005). Frontotemporal dementia. *The Lancet Neurology*, *4*(11), 771–780.

Nestler, E. J., & Carlezon Jr, W. A. (2006). The mesolimbic dopamine reward circuit in depression. *Biological Psychiatry*, *59*(12), 1151–1159.

Nomi, J. S., Schettini, E., Broce, I., Dick, A. S., & Uddin, L. Q. (2018). Structural connections of functionally defined human insular subdivisions. *Cerebral Cortex*, *28*(10), 3445–3456.

Noonan, M. P., Chau, B. K., Rushworth, M. F., & Fellows, L. K. (2017). Contrasting effects of medial and lateral orbitofrontal cortex lesions on credit assignment and decision-making in humans. *Journal of Neuroscience*, *37*(29), 7023–7035.

Nygård, M., Eichele, T., Løberg, E. M., Jørgensen, H. A., Johnsen, E., Kroken, R. A., … & Hugdahl, K. (2012). Patients with schizophrenia fail to up-regulate task-positive and down-regulate task-negative brain networks: An fMRI study using an ICA analysis approach. *Frontiers in Human Neuroscience*, *6*, 149.

Olson, I. R., Plotzker, A., & Ezzyat, Y. (2007). The enigmatic temporal pole: A review of findings on social and emotional processing. *Brain*, *130*(7), 1718–1731.

Orenius, T. I., Raij, T. T., Nuortimo, A., Näätänen, P., Lipsanen, J., & Karlsson, H. (2017). The interaction of emotion and pain in the insula and secondary somatosensory cortex. *Neuroscience*, *349*, 185–194.

O'Sullivan, N., Szczepanowski, R., El-Deredy, W., Mason, L., & Bentall, R. P. (2011). fMRI evidence of a relationship between hypomania and both increased goal-sensitivity and positive outcome-expectancy bias. *Neuropsychologia*, *49*(10), 2825–2835.

Panksepp, J. (2004). *Affective neuroscience: The foundations of human and animal emotions*. Oxford: Oxford University Press.

Pegna, A. J., Khateb, A., Lazeyras, F., & Seghier, M. L. (2005). Discriminating emotional faces without primary visual cortices involves the right amygdala. *Nature Neuroscience*, *8*(1), 24–25.

Phelps, E. A., Delgado, M. R., Nearing, K. I., & LeDoux, J. E. (2004). Extinction learning in humans: Role of the amygdala and vmPFC. *Neuron*, *43*(6), 897–905.

Phillips, M. L., Drevets, W. C., Rauch, S. L., & Lane, R. (2003). Neurobiology of emotion perception I: The neural basis of normal emotion perception. *Biological Psychiatry*, *54*(5), 504–514.

Pisella, L., Havé, L., & Rossetti, Y. (2019). Body awareness disorders: Dissociations between body-related visual and somatosensory information. *Brain, 142*(8), 2170–2173.

Purves, D., Augustine, G. J., Fitzpatrick, D., Hall, W. C., Lamantia, A. S., Mooney, R. D., ... & White L. E. (Eds.). (2018). *Neuroscience* (6th ed.). New York. Sinauer Associates.

Rădulescu, A., Herron, J., Kennedy, C., & Scimemi, A. (2017). Global and local excitation and inhibition shape the dynamics of the cortico-striatal-thalamo-cortical pathway. *Scientific Reports, 7*(1), 1–21.

Ranganath, C. (2010). A unified framework for the functional organization of the medial temporal lobes and the phenomenology of episodic memory. *Hippocampus, 20*(11), 1263–1290.

Rolls, E. T. (2019). The orbitofrontal cortex and emotion in health and disease, including depression. *Neuropsychologia, 128,* 14–43.

Rolls, E. T., & Grabenhorst, F. (2008). The orbitofrontal cortex and beyond: From affect to decision-making. *Progress in Neurobiology, 86*(3), 216–244.

Rømer Thomsen, K., Whybrow, P. C., & Kringelbach, M. L. (2015). Reconceptualizing anhedonia: Novel perspectives on balancing the pleasure networks in the human brain. *Frontiers in Behavioral Neuroscience, 9,* 49.

Rovoy, M., Shohamy, D., & Wager, T. D. (2012). Ventromedial prefrontal-subcortical systems and the generation of affective meaning. *Trends in Cognitive Sciences, 16*(3), 147–156.

Rudrauf, D., David, O., Lachaux, J. P., Kovach, C. K., Martinerie, J., Renault, B., & Damasio, A. (2008). Rapid interactions between the ventral visual stream and emotion-related structures rely on a two-pathway architecture. *Journal of Neuroscience, 28*(11), 2793–2803.

Saxe, R., & Powell, L. J. (2006). It's the thought that counts: Specific brain regions for one component of theory of mind. *Psychological Science, 17*(8), 692–699.

Schacter, D. L. (1999). The seven sins of memory: Insights from psychology and cognitive neuroscience. *American Psychologist, 54*(3), 182.

Schmahmann, J. D. (2004). Disorders of the cerebellum: Ataxia, dysmetria of thought, and the cerebellar cognitive affective syndrome. *The Journal of Neuropsychiatry and Clinical Neurosciences, 16*(3), 367–378.

Schmahmann, J. D., Guell, X., Stoodley, C. J., & Halko, M. A. (2019). The theory and neuroscience of cerebellar cognition. *Annual Review of Neuroscience, 42,* 337–364.

Schumann, C. M., Bauman, M. D., & Amaral, D. G. (2011). Abnormal structure or function of the amygdala is a common component of neurodevelopmental disorders. *Neuropsychologia, 49*(4), 745–759.

Schurz, M., Radua, J., Aichhorn, M., Richlan, F., & Perner, J. (2014). Fractionating theory of mind: A meta-analysis of functional brain imaging studies. *Neuroscience & Biobehavioral Reviews, 42,* 9–34.

Schurz, M., Tholen, M. G., Perner, J., Mars, R. B., & Sallet, J. (2017). Specifying the brain anatomy underlying temporo-parietal junction activations for theory of mind: A review using probabilistic atlases from different imaging modalities. *Human Brain Mapping, 38*(9), 4788–4805.

Schwabe, L., & Wolf, O. T. (2009). New episodic learning interferes with the reconsolidation of autobiographical memories. *PLoS One, 4*(10), e7519.

Serences, J. T., Shomstein, S., Leber, A. B., Golay, X., Egeth, H. E., & Yantis, S. (2005). Coordination of voluntary and stimulus-driven attentional control in human cortex. *Psychological Science*, *16*(2), 114–122

Sheline, Y. I., Barch, D. M., Price, J. L., Rundle, M. M., Vaishnavi, S. N., Snyder, A. Z., ... & Raichle, M. E. (2009). The default mode network and self-referential processes in depression. *Proceedings of the National Academy of Sciences*, *106*(6), 1942–1947.

Shepherd, A. M., Matheson, S. L., Laurens, K. R., Carr, V. J., & Green, M. J. (2012). Systematic meta-analysis of insula volume in schizophrenia. *Biological Psychiatry*, *72*(9), 775–784.

Shulman, G. L., Astafiev, S. V., McAvoy, M. P., d'Avossa, G., & Corbetta, M. (2007). Right TPJ deactivation during visual search: Functional significance and support for a filter hypothesis. *Cerebral Cortex*, *17*(11), 2625–2633.

Simonyan, K. (2019). Recent advances in understanding the role of the basal ganglia. *F1000Research*, *8*.

Singh-Curry, V., & Husain, M. (2009). The functional role of the inferior parietal lobe in the dorsal and ventral stream dichotomy. *Neuropsychologia*, *47*(6), 1434–1448.

Smith, L. D. (1992). On prediction and control: B. F. Skinner and the technological ideal of science. *American Psychologist*, *47*(2), 216–223.

Spreng, R. N. (2012). The fallacy of a "task-negative" network. *Frontiers in Psychology*, *3*, 145.

Sridharan, D., Levitin, D. J., & Menon, V. (2008). A critical role for the right fronto-insular cortex in switching between central-executive and default-mode networks. *Proceedings of the National Academy of Sciences*, *105*(34), 12569–12574.

Stein, M. B., Simmons, A. N., Feinstein, J. S., & Paulus, M. P. (2007). Increased amygdala and insula activation during emotion processing in anxiety-prone subjects. *American Journal of Psychiatry*, *164*(2), 318–327.

Stein, J. L., Wiedholz, L. M., Bassett, D. S., Weinberger, D. R., Zink, C. F., Mattay, V. S., & Meyer-Lindenberg, A. (2007). A validated network of effective amygdala connectivity. *Neuroimage*, *36*(3), 736–745.

Stevens, F. L. (2016). The anterior cingulate cortex in psychopathology and psychotherapy: Effects on awareness and repression of affect. *Neuropsychoanalysis*, *18*(1), 53–68.

Stevens, F. L. (2019). Affect regulation and affect reconsolidation as organizing principles in psychotherapy. *Journal of Psychotherapy Integration*, *29*(3), 277.

Stevens, F. L., Hurley, R. A., & Taber, K. H. (2011). Anterior cingulate cortex: Unique role in cognition and emotion. *The Journal of Neuropsychiatry and Clinical Neurosciences*, *23*(2), 121–125.

Stevens, J. S., Kim, Y. J., Galatzer-Levy, I. R., Reddy, R., Ely, T. D., Nemeroff, C. B., ... & Ressler, K. J. (2017). Amygdala reactivity and anterior cingulate habituation predict PTSD symptom maintenance after acute civilian trauma. *Biological Psychiatry*, *81*(12), 1023.

Storbeck, J., & Clore, G. L. (2007). On the interdependence of cognition and emotion. *Cognition and Emotion*, *21*(6), 1212–1237.

Suárez, L. E., Markello, R. D., Betzel, R. F., & Misic, B. (2020). Linking structure and function in macroscale brain networks. *Trends in Cognitive Sciences*, *24*(4), 302–315.

Szczepanski, S. M., Pinsk, M. A., Douglas, M. M., Kastner, S., & Saalmann, Y. B. (2013). Functional and structural architecture of the human dorsal frontoparietal attention network. *Proceedings of the National Academy of Sciences*, *110*(39), 15806–15811.

Tamietto, M., & de Gelder, B. (2008). Affective blindsight in the intact brain: Neural interhemispheric summation for unseen fearful expressions. *Neuropsychologia*, *46*(3), 820–828.

Torta, D. M., & Cauda, F. (2011). Different functions in the cingulate cortex, a meta-analytic connectivity modeling study. *Neuroimage*, *56*(4), 2157–2172.

Uddin, L. Q. (2015). Salience processing and insular cortical function and dysfunction. *Nature Reviews Neuroscience*, *16*(1), 55–61.

Uddin, L. Q., Nomi, J. S., Hébert-Seropian, B., Ghaziri, J., & Boucher, O. (2017). Structure and function of the human insula. *Journal of Clinical Neurophysiology*, *34*(4), 300.

Uno, T., Kawai, K., Sakai, K., Wakebe, T., Ibaraki, T., Kunii, N., ... & Saito, N. (2015). Dissociated roles of the inferior frontal gyrus and superior temporal sulcus in audiovisual processing: Top-down and bottom-up mismatch detection. *PLoS One*, *10*(3), e0122580.

Ursu, S., & Carter, C. S. (2009). An initial investigation of the orbitofrontal cortex hyperactivity in obsessive-compulsive disorder: Exaggerated representations of anticipated aversive events? *Neuropsychologia*, *47*(10), 2145–2148.

Valdois, S., Lassus-Sangosse, D., Lallier, M., Moreaud, O., & Pisella, L. (2019). What bilateral damage of the superior parietal lobes tells us about visual attention disorders in developmental dyslexia. *Neuropsychologia*, *130*, 78–91.

Van Den Heuvel, M. P., Mandl, R. C., Kahn, R. S., & Hulshoff Pol, H. E. (2009). Functionally linked resting-state networks reflect the underlying structural connectivity architecture of the human brain. *Human Brain Mapping*, *30*(10), 3127–3141.

van der Meer, L., Swart, M., van der Velde, J., Pijnenborg, G., Wiersma, D., Bruggeman, R., & Aleman, A. (2014). Neural correlates of emotion regulation in patients with schizophrenia and non-affected siblings. *PloS One*, *9*(6), e99667.

van Elk, M. (2014). The left inferior parietal lobe represents stored hand-postures for object use and action prediction. *Frontiers in Psychology*, *5*, 333.

Van Overwalle, F. (2009). Social cognition and the brain: A meta-analysis. *Human Brain Mapping*, *30*(3), 829–858.

Van Overwalle, F., & Baetens, K. (2009). Understanding others' actions and goals by mirror and mentalizing systems: A meta-analysis. *Neuroimage*, *48*(3), 564–584.

Vassena, E., Deraeve, J., & Alexander, W. H. (2020). Surprise, value and control in anterior cingulate cortex during speeded decision-making. *Nature Human Behaviour*, *4*(4), 412–422.

Venkatraman, A., Edlow, B. L., & Immordino-Yang, M. H. (2017). The brainstem in emotion: A review. *Frontiers in Neuroanatomy*, *11*, 15.

Vossel, S., Geng, J. J., & Fink, G. R. (2014). Dorsal and ventral attention systems: Distinct neural circuits but collaborative roles. *The Neuroscientist*, *20*(2), 150–159.

Walker, W. R., Skowronski, J. J., & Thompson, C. P. (2003). Life is pleasant—and memory helps to keep it that way!. *Review of General Psychology*, *7*(2), 203–210.

Wang, L., Liu, X., Guise, K. G., Knight, R. T., Ghajar, J., & Fan, J. (2010). Effective connectivity of the fronto-parietal network during attentional control. *Journal of Cognitive Neuroscience*, *22*(3), 543–553.

Wang, X., Xia, M., Lai, Y., Dai, Z., Cao, Q., Cheng, Z., ... & Li, K. (2014). Disrupted resting-state functional connectivity in minimally treated chronic schizophrenia. *Schizophrenia Research*, *156*(2–3), 150–156.

Watson, K. K., Jones, T. K., & Allman, J. M. (2006). Dendritic architecture of the von Economo neurons. *Neuroscience, 141*(3), 1107–1112.

Waytz, A., Zaki, J., & Mitchell, J. P. (2012). Response of dorsomedial prefrontal cortex predicts altruistic behavior. *Journal of Neuroscience, 32*(22), 7646–7650.

Weissman, D. H., & Prado, J. (2012). Heightened activity in a key region of the ventral attention network is linked to reduced activity in a key region of the dorsal attention network during unexpected shifts of covert visual spatial attention. *Neuroimage, 61*(4), 798–804.

Winston, J. S., Strange, B. A., O'Doherty, J., & Dolan, R. J. (2002). Automatic and intentional brain responses during evaluation of trustworthiness of faces. *Nature Neuroscience, 5*(3), 277–283.

Witt, S. T., van Ettinger-Veenstra, H., Salo, T., Riedel, M. C., & Laird, A. R. (2020). What executive function network is that? An image-based meta-analysis of network labels. *Brain Topography*, 1–10.

Wu, Y., Wang, J., Zhang, Y., Zheng, D., Zhang, J., Rong, M., ... & Jiang, T. (2016). The neuroanatomical basis for posterior superior parietal lobule control lateralization of visuospatial attention. *Frontiers in Neuroanatomy, 10*, 32.

Yoshimura, S., Okamoto, Y., Onoda, K., Matsunaga, M., Ueda, K., & Suzuki, S. I. (2010). Rostral anterior cingulate cortex activity mediates the relationship between the depressive symptoms and the medial prefrontal cortex activity. *Journal of Affective Disorders, 122*(1–2), 76–85.

Young, L., Camprodon, J. A., Hauser, M., Pascual-Leone, A., & Saxe, R. (2010). Disruption of the right temporoparietal junction with transcranial magnetic stimulation reduces the role of beliefs in moral judgments. *Proceedings of the National Academy of Sciences, 107*(15), 6753–6758.

Young, L., Dodell-Feder, D., & Saxe, R. (2010). What gets the attention of the temporo-parietal junction? An fMRI investigation of attention and theory of mind. *Neuropsychologia, 48*(9), 2658–2664.

Yu, C., Zhou, Y., Liu, Y., Jiang, T., Dong, H., Zhang, Y., & Walter, M. (2011). Functional segregation of the human cingulate cortex is confirmed by functional connectivity based neuroanatomical parcellation. *Neuroimage, 54*(4), 2571–2581.

Zanto, T. P., & Gazzaley, A. (2013). Fronto-parietal network: flexible hub of cognitive control. *Trends in Cognitive Sciences, 17*(12), 602–603.

Zhang, D., Snyder, A. Z., Shimony, J. S., Fox, M. D., & Raichle, M. E. (2010). Noninvasive functional and structural connectivity mapping of the human thalamocortical system. *Cerebral Cortex, 20*(5), 1187–1194.

Zilles, K. (2018). Brodmann: A pioneer of human brain mapping—his impact on concepts of cortical organization. *Brain, 141*(11), 3262.

Part II

The Practice of Clinical Affective Neuroscience: Emotion-Based Interventions

Overview of Interventions

This work will focus specifically on interventions clinicians can use to address their patients' emotions directly. Interventions to change thinking or alter behavior will be minimally addressed, as much practical information for those types of interventions already exists. The interventions are presented in a linear format, although different patients and problems will likely need more or less attention in the different stages presented. The work is outlined this way because each stage builds off the next in regulating and changing affect. The format outlined should help for ease of understanding, but clinicians do not need to apply this treatment in a sequential approach. Clinicians are encouraged to utilize and revisit sections as needed for patient care.

Mindfulness is presented as the first step because it allows for the awareness of the emotion(s); you cannot work with an emotion unless you first recognize it. The second stage involves validating the emotion, to increase both emotional awareness and acceptance of what a patient may be feeling. The third stage is self-compassion, which offers kindness and humanity to one's self when faced with difficult feelings. The fourth stage is about helping patients understand the nature of emotion, which can help provide context for upsetting feelings. The fifth stage involves coping with emotion. These interventions are traditional to many previous methods of therapy, but the text will focus more on direct application to emotion. Stage six addresses specific emotions, offering tools on how to work with and approach different emotions. Each section is divided by the type of emotion. Clinicians are encouraged to help their patients see their emotions as adaptive, as opposed to the presumption that emotions are solely maladaptive and need to be mitigated. In this section, patients can learn from their emotions to make better decisions and behavioral choices. The last stage, labeled affect reconsolidation, is about permanently changing negative unwanted emotions. Affect reconsolidation has shown promise as a universal mechanism of change principle in psychotherapy (Goldman & Fredrick-Keniston, 2020; Lane, Ryan, Nadel, & Greenberg, 2015).

DOI: 10.4324/9781003150893-102

4 Emotional Awareness/ Mindfulness

I often start the beginning of therapeutic interaction with a mindfulness exercise. This won't be helpful for all your patients. However, upon the first session, I find some patients present in an acute state of stress, or some patients present as lost and unsure of themselves or what to do. I find mindfulness does two important things. One, it helps us to recognize and connect with our body and feelings. Secondly, it then helps us see feelings as part of us but not all of us, an important emotion regulation skill. Patients can feel bad yet need not be defined by their feelings.

4.1 Emotional Awareness

The first step to solving any problem is to understand the problem. Mindfulness can act as a way to increase recognition of our experience. Typically, in daily life for most of us, we move from our reaction to behavior without recognizing the in-between processes. We are on the go, acting quickly to get things done. We don't stop to reflect, "Why I am I taking the trash out now?" Nor for the most part should we; usually our behaviors make sense, and don't require any self-reflection. When something doesn't feel right intuitively, that should act as a clue to stop and self-reflect. This is why most people show up to therapy: something doesn't feel right.

Typically, most individuals I see don't arrive at therapy until feelings reach a crescendo that they can no longer ignore. Too often individuals neglect to acknowledge their feelings, ignoring the difficult emotions until they can no longer manage. Furthermore, this often coincides with unhealthy behaviors as a way to cope. For some patients, slowing down to acknowledge their feelings can be a painful, but important first step. Sometimes the cause of the feelings is obvious; at other times it is not. Taking the time out to slow down and recognize our experience can help patients acknowledge something they have previously been ignoring. Sometimes a patient ·will arrive and say something like, "Give me some skills to help manage my anxiety." As a trained psychologist I have some skills I can teach, but I often find myself hesitating to give the patient what

DOI: 10.4324/9781003150893-4

they are asking for here. It's not that I don't think they can benefit from the skills; rather, I am concerned we're missing the bigger problem, such as why they feel so much anxiety to begin with. For example, a patient with OCD may seem like they just have series of uncontrollable thoughts followed by repetitious behavior. They say, "Please give me skills to reduce these obsessive behaviors." As a therapist, I might first think how I could use positive reinforcement to shape behavior in reducing obsessive behaviors. However, OCD is really about an inability to control desire and anxiety. Here mindfulness can help patients to slow down and recognize their anxiety, perhaps helping a patient see how their emotions drive their behaviors. The point is there are multiple ways to try and solve a problem (as therapists we should always be thinking about different possible solutions), but if we just go with the first thing the patient asks for, we might be missing something else. In my experience, when a patient says, "I just need to ..." they are missing the bigger picture of the problem. If a patient "just needs" some relaxation skills, a quick internet search could suffice. Likely the problem is often more complex, which why it's important that we first slow down, recognize our experience, and increase consciousness.

4.2 Bottom-up and Top-down Attention in Emotion

Dehaene, Changeux, Naccache, Sackur, and Sergent (2006) present a theoretical model for what becomes conscious. They define two influences on conscious perception: a bottom-up influence, which is based upon stimulus strength (see section 3.4, SN); and a top-down influence (see section 3.4, DAN and VAN), which is based on individual directed attention. For example, increasing the temperature one degree in a room may not be enough change for conscious perception of temperature change. However, increasing the temperature by ten degrees should provide sufficient stimulus strength to notice the temperature change consciously, a bottom-up influence. Additionally, if an individual were to be informed that the temperature of the room would be changing in the upcoming hour, they will then have an increased attentional awareness to any temperature change, a top-down influence. This top-down influence would then increase their perceptional threshold for consciously recognizing a change in temperature. Similar to how attention is moderated by top-down and bottom-up influences, Dehaene et al. (2006) theorize that a combination of sufficient bottom-up stimulus strength and top-down attention allows for the conscious perception of stimuli. These stimuli could be external, like a change in temperature, or internal, like the recognition of an upset stomach. Conscious perception is also moderated by other stimuli competing for bottom-up stimulus strength or top-down attention. Awareness of temperature change will be moderated by an extremely upset stomach, which could produce enough bottom-up stimulus strength to crowd out other competing sensory stimuli, like the feeling of becoming warmer. Similarly, someone highly engrossed in reading a gripping novel could lack the top-down attention resources to notice other competing stimuli, again such as a change in the surrounding temperature.

This model becomes important to consider when increasing emotional awareness for patients. If a patient is unaware of their emotional experience, interventions to change and/or regulate emotions will be difficult. If a patient doesn't recognize their stress, it's difficult to respond to the stress, and increasing the top-down focus to stress/ body sensations could help patients determine when relaxation skills might help them. Often individuals don't recognize their psychological concerns until there is sufficient bottom-up stimulus strength. That is, a certain threshold of intolerable negative feeling must occur before someone takes action in addressing his or her mental health. Sometimes this can be triggered by an intense emotional episode like a panic attack or suicidal feelings. Often, I'll have patients make a follow-up appointment after seeing me for a crisis, like a break-up or job loss. Then, at the time of appointment, they cancel because they are no longer in that acute state of emotional distress. For some individuals, this may be okay, yet for others even though the strength of the bottom-up stimulus is gone, the underlying emotional concerns still exist; they just haven't reached the threshold for feeling emotionally overwhelmed. In helping these patients, it can sometimes be beneficial to help them recognize that these difficult emotions still exist, even though they are not currently feeling them. The upsetting emotions become recognized when a certain event(s) emotionally activates the patient, increasing the bottom-up stimulus strength to a threshold where they become "emotionally triggered." This can sometimes be done through explaining to the patient or increasing top-down attention to these negative emotions. If done successfully, the patient will recognize that the panic attack or overwhelming suicidal feelings were not just a one-off, but part of a larger more consistent psychological problem.

4.3 Interoceptive and Feeling Awareness/Alexithymia

Research demonstrates that awareness of our internal experience can be broken down into two constructs, interoceptive awareness and feelings awareness. Interoceptive awareness is the awareness of internal body states. Examples include our heart rate, internal temperature, or sensations such hunger or thirst (Craig, 2009). Feeling awareness involves your ability to understand and think about emotion (Suchy, 2011). For example, our interoceptive awareness would notice when we are tired, while our feeling awareness would recognize that we are grumpy likely because we are tired. Of course, tiredness and grumpiness are occurring together, but we can sometimes notice one without noticing the other. Some people recognize they are grouchy and that probably means they are hungry; others recognize they are hungry which is causing them to be grouchy.

Typically, it's considered that interoceptive awareness occurs first, and this is marked by activity in the insula and somatosensory cortices, followed by activity in the ACC and prefrontal cortex. As the sensation becomes more recognized, we gain awareness into our total experience (Lane, Reiman, Axelrod, Yun, Holmes, & Schwartz, 1998; Pollatos, Gramann, & Schandry, 2007). The AI and dACC, you may recall, are the regional hubs of the salience network, which makes us aware of salience information. Pollatos, Schandry, Auer, and Kaufmann (2007) show that activation of these brain areas are linked to increased interoceptive awareness. They also found that interoceptive awareness was predictive of feeling awareness and was marked by activity in the dACC, but not the insula. This suggests that interoceptive awareness, which is marked primarily by insula activity, is an important precursor to feeling awareness, which is more related to the ACC than the insula (for a more in-depth discussion, see Smith, Thayer, Khalsa, & Lane, 2017). It seems you can have interoceptive awareness without feeling awareness, but it's hard to have feeling awareness without interoceptive awareness. This lack of feeling awareness is referred to as alexithymia in the clinical literature. While alexithymia is not a psychological disorder in and of itself, alexithymia or the absence of feelings is highly correlated to many types of psychopathology (Grabe, Spitzer, & Freyberger, 2004). Some studies suggest that alexithymia occurs as a result of impaired interhemispheric transfer across the corpus callosum (Larsen, Brand, Bermond, & Hijman, 2003; Paul et al., 2006; Richter et al., 2006). fMRI studies of alexithymia demonstrate increased insula activation and decreased dACC activation (Karlsson, Näätänen, & Stenman, 2008). Moreover, alexithymia has been shown to correlate with reduced volume throughout the ACC (Borsci et al., 2009; Paradiso, Vaidya, McCormick, Jones, & Robinson, 2008). Pollatos, Traut-Mattausch, Schroeder, and Schandry (2007), find that increased interoceptive awareness increases the relationship between trait anxiety and unpleasant feelings, indicating that perhaps the more tuned in to your body you are, the more apt you might be to experience unpleasant feelings. It has also been suggested that the relationship between interoceptive awareness and feeling awareness has a limit (Suchy, 2011). De Berardis et al. (2007) find a relationship between interoceptive awareness and alexithymia, and both variables are predictive of panic disorder. This reminds me of a patient I once had who reported having a panic attack while riding in the car. The patient was baffled why she had a panic attack in such a benign environment. Only after talking for some time did the patient recall that just prior to the attack she received a phone call from her ex-boyfriend who had broken up with her. She was quite distraught over the breakup, and it took some time for her to identify the ex-boyfriend as the source of anxiety, leading to the panic attack. Panic disorder, particularly when compared with other anxiety disorders, is strongly correlated to alexithymia (Parker, Taylor, Bagby, & Acklin, 1993; Zeitlin & McNally, 1993). Given that panic attacks for most patients seemingly come out of nowhere, it is likely the patient is disconnected from their difficult feelings. However, when those feelings reach an emotional threshold, the bottom-up stimulus becomes so intense that it can no longer be ignored. This of course results in a panic attack of overwhelming anxiety. It appears that with alexithymia feelings are being ignored so greatly that they result in physical manifestations of the feelings, like panic attacks. This explains the correlations found in research among panic disorder, interoceptive awareness, and alexithymia (De Berardis et al., 2007; Palser et al., 2018). Mindfulness can act as a tool to help increase feeling awareness, while alexithymia, whether intentional or not, reduces feeling awareness. Given the high correlation between alexithymia and mental health disorders, perhaps reducing feeling awareness may be a way to reduce experience of unpleasant feelings. The unpleasant experience may still exist in the body; however, the diminished feeling awareness makes the person unaware of this experience. In fact, there is a strong correlation between alexithymia and somatoform symptoms and disorders (Duddu, Isaac, & Chaturvedi, 2003; Mattila et al., 2008), as well as dissociative symptoms (Grabe et al., 2004). In working as a therapist at a university counseling center with many international students, I noticed a trend. Students from countries that had less of a vocabulary and culture around emotions were more likely to express somatic symptoms, often referred to me from the medical end of the university health center. Often with these patients, we would practice mindfulness to help recognize feelings as well as develop a vocabulary for feelings and skills to cope with emotions. It's important to recognize that our bodies don't always naturally recognize our experiences and feelings. Before fully conceptualizing your patient's psychopathology or developing a treatment plan, increasing the patient's recognition and awareness of their experience may be valuable. Treating a foreign student for a stomach condition that is actually a depressive disorder that the student does not even have the words to describe would be a misdiagnosis. Sometimes what the therapist or patient might first think is the problem is really a misnomer, absent the emotional experience driving the mental disorder.

Often explanations for behavior are secondary in nature. Rarely do we say, "I don't know I why I did that." This would be akin to someone with OCD saying, "I wanted to clean my hands, because they were dirty" or "I was just checking to make sure it was locked," rather than saying, "I was compelled to act to reduce my anxiety." We're expected to have a reasonable explanation for our behaviors, so we typically provide ourselves with an explanation when asked or when reasoning with ourselves. However, these explanations are only a best guess for why we behave the way we do; often we actually don't know. It's very common to set an intention and not follow through. We give ourselves reasons for not following through with our intentions, but unless something in the environment clearly stopped us from completing the action, these reasons are only a best guess.

Mindfulness helps to slow down our mind in recognizing underlying emotions that drive thoughts and behaviors. This is why increasing emotional awareness is an important first step in psychotherapy to help better understand personal experience. Richard Lane created the Levels of Emotional Awareness Scale (LEAS) to assess the level by which individuals recognize and understand their internal experience (Lane, Quinlan, Schwartz, Walker, & Zeitlin, 1990). The LEAS scores range from 0 to 5. Level 0 is defined by only using thought words and no emotion words. At level 1, the individual can identify physiological cues, like sick or tired. At level 2, the individual can identify action tendencies, like "I want to scream" and can assign basic valences like "good" or "bad" to the experience. At level 3, the individual can express single word emotional responses like "I feel happy or scared." At level 4, individuals can identify mixtures of feelings like "bittersweet" or "angry and proud." At the highest level, 5, individuals can recognize the complexity of emotions both within themselves and others (Lane, Subic-Wrana, Greenberg, & Yovel, 2020). The LEAS is correlated with other scales of psychological maturity, like the sentence completion task for measuring ego development (Lane et al., 1990). Neuroimaging studies show that increased LEAS scores are related to increased activity in the rACC (Lane et al., 1998), consistent with the research presented prior. Recognizing and responding appropriately to emotions is a developmental process. When we talk to our children, we try to encourage them to express their feelings ("What happened?"), identify their feelings ("Are you upset?"), respond appropriately ("Use your words"), and respond appropriately with others ("Did you tell him/her how you feel?"). We are trying to help children to better identify feelings and healthy ways of responding to them, although at times we invalidate their experience too (Chapter 5 will cover this more). The challenge with difficult feelings is we often want to avoid or ignore the feelings rather than accept them. Mindfulness-based therapies like Acceptance and Commitment Therapy (ACT) are valuable because they encourage acceptance of all feelings (Hayes, Strosahl, & Wilson, 2009).

Recognizing feelings is often a challenging first step. As humans, we engage in many behaviors to dissociate from our feelings. Substances are commonly used to avoid one's experience, which removes one from having to experience their feelings. Addiction often happens later, as a physical dependence develops from the repeated use of substances as a coping mechanism. In this light, addiction is a secondary result of a primary problem involving an inability to cope with one's emotions. Other distracting behaviors exist too which can cause varying degrees of suffering for the individual unable to cope with emotion. Yet no behavior used to avoid an emotion changes an emotion. These behaviors result in short term fixes to alleviate one's emotional experience but provide no long-term cure.

Behaviors are not the only way we dissociate from our feelings. PTSD is the brain's natural coping response when emotionally overwhelmed.

This too provides an immediate means of coping with the environmental trauma, while creating a later problem in the form of PTSD. This coping mechanism exists across species in the form of playing dead or going numb when under severe threat (for a greater understanding of this process see, Porges, 2011). For a full resolution of PTSD, individuals must go back and reconsolidate the prior traumatic experience. PTSD has been shown to have unique effects in the ACC. Brain imaging research involving the ACC demonstrates this area can act as a gateway between thought and emotion and is important in the awareness of emotion (Smith, Ahern, & Lane, 2019; Stevens, 2016). Often the brain can be in conflict between its thoughts and emotions (see Chapter 7). The dACC region is significant for conflict monitoring, as demonstrated by one of the most common psychological tests which consistently activates the dACC: the stroop color-word test (Van Veen, Cohen, Botvinick, Stenger, & Carter, 2001). In this test, words are printed in an inconsistent color (i.e., the word "blue" is printed in red ink). Participants are asked to name the word color while ignoring the written word, creating an inconsistency in the mind of the participant. The logic of the task is simple, yet participants feel something is off when they see an inconsistency between the written word and the color in which it appears; this discrepancy slows down performance. This conflict is similar in many ways to what happens in the brain of someone with PTSD. Individuals with PTSD have repressed their emotional experience because it is too overwhelming to manage. The brain simultaneously has competing desires to recognize the uncomfortable feeling and to dissociate from this same feeling, placing the ACC in a state of conflict. The dissociative symptoms of PTSD are the brain trying to reject the feelings, while the intrusive thoughts and feelings are the brain wanting to accept the feelings. These two competing desires give patients a choice point to accept or reject the feelings surrounding past traumatic events. Now the person with PTSD must weigh the cost of continuing to repress their feelings with the cost of having to feel and they must estimate the future benefits of each. The dACC is probably active in making this choice as it is functional for outcome likelihood monitoring (see section 3.3), weighing choices concerning both future emotional benefits with immediate emotional efforts. This is a demanding task, and it is important to slow down and recognize emotions to make this judgment effectively. Many times, we are too caught up in the immediate stress and symptoms to slow down and recognize the deeper emotional struggles which are directly causing the secondary symptoms of the psychological disorder. Sometimes we don't even want to recognize this deeper emotional conflict and engage defense mechanisms to avoid our true self. A defense mechanism is the common therapeutic term used when a patient is trying to deny their emotional experience. Mindfulness may help individuals move past or recognize defense mechanisms that interfere with the ability to recognize their experience. Once awareness of the emotion occurs, it's important to accept and validate that feeling.

4.4 Separating the Feeling from the Self

Mindfulness is also important as a technique to regulate or separate from emotion. If we look at brains that practice mindfulness and their neural correlates, a common relationship is seen between the reduction of DMN activity and mindfulness (Berkovich-Ohana, Glicksohn, & Goldstein, 2012; Brewer et al., 2011; Garrison, Zeffiro, Scheinost, Constable, & Brewer, 2015). Individuals who are mindful by nature showed a reduction in connectivity between nodes of the DMN (Harrison, Zeidan, Kitsaras, Ozcelik, & Salomons, 2019). Similarly, practicing mindfulness over time leads to reduced connectivity between DMN nodes, while also showing increased connectivity between DMN and other brain regions (Doll, Hölzel, Boucard, Wohlschläger, & Sorg, 2015; King et al., 2016; Taylor et al., 2013). While on the opposite end, depression and schizophrenia show increased activation and connectivity within the DMN (Hamilton et al., 2011; Whitfield-Gabrieli & Ford, 2012). Some scientists believe the DMN is the neuroanatomical manifestation of Freud's concept of ego (Carhart-Harris & Friston, 2010) (Note: The term shrink for a psychologist comes from the concept of shrinking the ego as the job of a psychologist.) This same group of scientists finds correlation evidence between decreased DMN activity, "ego dissolution," and use of hallucinogenics (Carhart-Harris et al., 2014; Tagliazucchi et al., 2016). Carhart-Harris et al. (2014) draw a connection between the use of hallucinogenics and mindfulness, suggesting they both work similarly in letting go of self, resulting in decreased DMN activation. This connection has drawn increasing attention since the publication of Michael Pollan's book *How to Change Your Mind* (2019), which examines the increasing evidence around hallucinogenics in mental health and as a treatment for psychopathology. Either way, through hallucinogenics or mindfulness, the theory is the same: both involve letting go of self-referential thought, which is what DMN is primarily involved in. There is even some evidence that selective serotonin uptake inhibitors (SSRIs/ anti-depressants drugs) work through the same mechanism in reducing DMN activity (Dutta et al., 2019). Further research on mindfulness meditation demonstrates that it increases one's sense of nonattachment (Sahdra, Shaver, & Brown, 2010). Nonattachment involves experiencing the world without becoming overly attached to objects, ideas, thoughts, and feelings. It is this detaching from the thoughts and feelings of self that can be so helpful in not reinforcing negative ideas about the self and associating one's self with one's negative feelings.

Mindfulness allows the patient to separate their feelings from themselves. This is a helpful tool for managing emotion because it allows patients to recognize that the emotion is part of them, but not all of them. Very often when I see patients in highly distressful states of emotion, they feel overwhelmed by a feeling and it feels like the emotion will never go away. At that moment, the patient's brain is overtaken by the emotion and it is hard for the patient to recognize that this emotional state is only temporary. Furthermore, patients overwhelmed by their emotions are so distressed they lack the emotional and/or cognitive resources to consider solutions to overcome their problem.

Think back to a time when you felt emotionally overwhelmed. At the time the emotion felt inescapable. It can often feel like this feeling will last forever. At times I have validated this experience for many of my patients, saying, "Yes, if this feeling were to last forever, suicide makes sense." Who would ever want to feel this emotional dread forever? I then explain it's extremely unlikely you will continue to feel this way forever; in fact, probably in a few days your mood will improve. I talk about other patients that have come to me in the same state of distress, that after we worked through the emotion, they are completely glad they did not kill themselves. Looking back upon the time you were emotionally overwhelmed, you might feel embarrassed by your extreme behaviors or even silly for having had such a strong emotional reaction. However, the current you can't fully identify with the emotional experience of the past you. In the past when you were emotionally overwhelmed, you were doing the best you could. It is only with the perspective of time that you can recognize so much of that behavior was driven by emotions that were out of your control. When the feeling is that overwhelming it's extremely hard not to overreact. Cutting behavior, which ostensibly seems like an act of self-harm with no purpose, can actually be a way of distracting one's self from emotional pain with physical pain. These overwhelming emotional reactions tend to decrease with age, because we have developed experience with difficult feelings and we recognize these feelings will pass. Practicing mindfulness also helps build this perspective. The patients are aware of feeling awful, but it's only part of who they are and their experience. Patients can recognize that they are in an intolerable state of emotion and they do not need to react to the feeling that is driving them. One variable that greatly increases death by suicide is access to firearms (Conwell et al., 2002; Lubin et al., 2010). There are multiple ways to commit suicide. Firearms are a quick and efficient means. Other methods take more planning and or thought (some methods that are also easily accessible are just not as efficacious, like pills). This extra time needed to perform the act of suicide is valuable. It is where the patient's initial overwhelming state of emotion comes to pass. In fact, I feel more comfortable in crisis situations where the patient is overwhelmed by feelings, than when they are distant and resigned to the feelings. With these patients in an overwhelming state of emotion, I know once we can regulate their emotions, the impetus for suicide will reduce; this is not the case for those in long depressive states who have made a judgment that they no longer want to live. These individuals need immediate and ongoing help. These latter types of patients are also rarer and often do not seek out help. What mindfulness does is help the patient separate the self from an overwhelming emotional state, which helps them recognize, "Ok, at this moment I wish I were dead, but this moment will pass and in future moments I will enjoy being alive." After practicing this mindfulness, patients can recognize the emotion but not overly identify with the feeling(s). A patient might say, "Yes I feel like garbage, but I recognize that I am not garbage." This helps patients manage overwhelming feelings when they are upset or get triggered.

4.5 Practicing Mindfulness

I tell my patients that I practice mindfulness, though I'm not very good at it. This is what I think mindfulness should be: a practice, not an end state. Too often patients get discouraged by their inability to be mindful and give up trying, and it's exactly these patients that probably need it the most. Mindfulness practice also helps me control my attention. There are probably a million things a day competing for my attention. I tell my patients by practicing mindfulness I'm able to stay more attuned to the therapy session, and I am less distracted about phone calls I forgot to make or my plans for the weekend. It's not that these thoughts don't pass through my head; it's that with mindfulness practice, it is easier to let them go. Sure, there are times the intensity of the bottom-up stimulus distracts me from what I want to do, but with mindfulness that happens less often. I'm also able to let go of challenging patients and enjoy my free time. This ironically seems to put some patients at ease, as some patients will worry that their problems will burden me to a level where I will not be able to tolerate them. I also point out to my patients that they don't have to sit cross-legged on the floor for an hour straight to practice mindfulness (for many patients this is a scary thought and makes them want to avoid the whole topic). Slowing down each day to check in with yourself is part of a healthy mindfulness practice. Sometimes for a patient with stress, I have them set a timer to go off every two hours on their phone. When the timer sounds, they ask themselves, "How do I feel?" or "What is my stress level?" This helps them check in with themselves; maybe they need to practice a stress reduction exercise, or notice which behaviors they may be doing that increase their stress. This is all developing mindfulness, and after a few weeks, the patient no longer needs the timer. The patient has become mindful of the stress and learns how to respond effectively.

4.6 Mindfulness and Psychotherapy: One Last Point

One last important point I tell patients is that mindfulness can help you recognize your problems and can help you cope with your problems, but it typically doesn't solve your problems. With the current emphasis on mindfulness, it can often be seen as a panacea for any mental health concerns. I like point out to patients that the original emotion that is causing your distress is still there. The patient is now more aware of their feelings with mindfulness and can separate themselves from their feelings with mindfulness; however, typically the initial emotion is still left unchanged. I once had a friend tell me he meditates three hours a day to manage his depression. I was impressed with his ability to meditate but couldn't help but think something was lacking in the treatment for his depression. Mindfulness has probably captured the attention of the western world because for the most part we're all too self-focused. If you're in agony from depression, you probably don't need to meditate on that; you need to attend to those feelings. Meditation and mindfulness have their strengths, but they also have limitations. I tell patients that mindfulness will help them cope with the problem, making it easier to work on, but more work needs to be done in preventing the onset of distressful emotions.

4.7 Other Ways to Increase Emotional Awareness

Sometimes mindfulness just is not something some patients want to do. Patients with a lot of anxiety can sometimes find the process excruciating. It's not that these types of patients wouldn't likely benefit; it's just not a practical short-term solution for some patients. In these cases, I use alternative interventions for raising emotional awareness. I would recommend journaling about feelings as one means for these patients. I am careful to describe that the journaling should not be about the content of their day, but their experience of their day: what stood out to them and how did it make them feel? I tell them to try not to think too much, because too much subjective judgment stops the free flow of feelings. They don't have to show their writing to anyone; it's an exercise to help them get more in touch with themselves. Many of these patients will also say they forget to journal but would like to (probably just avoiding their feelings). You can set punishments and reinforcements as one approach. Another idea is to have them set an alarm to go off every few hours to go on their phones and write down their feelings or even audio record them. The goal is to get them in the practice of being aware of their emotions. Don't forget to use the therapy session; patients really struggling with accepting emotions will need your support and guidance.

Occasionally in therapy, I'll get patients with very blunted affect, maybe like an extreme dysthymia. I'll usually notice because I'll get tired of myself talking. These patients don't have much to offer up, but usually want to hear my solution for their problem. Without any emotion the therapy usually stalls. The patient will say they tried the skills I offered them, but it hasn't caused any major changes in their disposition. Sometimes they'll even console me, noting they've had several therapists that have tried to help them unsuccessfully. They say, "it's not my fault; it's theirs." If I haven't recognized the problem by now, this usually does it. Talking about it or making process comments (me saying "I notice you're reluctant to talk about feelings") usually doesn't help either. They say, "I don't know; what should I be feeling?" At this point, I have two interventions for accessing emotion. One is somatic experiencing (Payne, Levine, & Crane-Godreau, 2015). Peter Levine has a lot of good resources for this approach (somaticexperiencing.com). These therapeutic approaches have been designed for this type of blunted affect or dissociation (Ogden & Minton, 2000; Ogden & Fisher, 2015), which focuses on the body as an entry point, through increasing self-awareness of body states. The goal is through increasing self-awareness of your body, you will eventually increase emotional awareness. The second technique I use is a guided meditation, often bringing the patient back to a time when they did feel an emotion. I will create the context by asking about the environment around them, asking the patient to describe the room, whom they are with, what they think of these people, what noises and smells they experience, etc., trying to get as detailed as possible in recreating the experience. Then I ask the patients how they feel and tell them to focus on these sensations. The process should go slowly, almost hypnotically. I speak in a rhythmic tone, creating a trance-like state, and some research suggests that this changes brain patterns which could lead to insight (Hove et al., 2015). Regardless, it seems to relax the patient and can help them achieve awareness into their emotional experience. Lastly, some therapists will use other experiential techniques like psychodrama or Gestalt therapy interventions to increase emotional awareness. I have shied away from these formats because the techniques seem less controlled to me and I believe it's valuable for the patient to feel in control of the experience, but I wouldn't rule them out.

References

Berkovich-Ohana, A., Glicksohn, J., & Goldstein, A. (2012). Mindfulness-induced changes in gamma band activity–implications for the default mode network, self-reference and attention. *Clinical Neurophysiology*, *123*(4), 700–710.

Borsci, G., Boccardi, M., Rossi, R., Rossi, G., Perez, J., Bonetti, M., & Frisoni, G. B. (2009). Alexithymia in healthy women: a brain morphology study. *Journal of Affective Disorders*, 114, 208–215.

Brewer, J. A., Worhunsky, P. D., Gray, J. R., Tang, Y. Y., Weber, J., & Kober, H. (2011). Meditation experience is associated with differences in default mode network activity and connectivity. *Proceedings of the National Academy of Sciences*, *108*(50), 20254–20259.

Carhart-Harris, R. L., & Friston, K. J. (2010). The default-mode, ego-functions and free-energy: A neurobiological account of Freudian ideas. *Brain*, *133*(4), 1265–1283.

Carhart-Harris, R. L., Leech, R., Hellyer, P. J., Shanahan, M., Feilding, A., Tagliazucchi, E., … & Nutt, D. (2014). The entropic brain: A theory of conscious states informed by neuroimaging research with psychedelic drugs. *Frontiers in Human Neuroscience*, 8, 20.

Conwell, Y., Duberstein, P. R., Connor, K., Eberly, S., Cox, C., & Caine, E. D. (2002). Access to firearms and risk for suicide in middle-aged and older adults. *The American Journal of Geriatric Psychiatry*, *10*(4), 407–416.

Craig, A. D. (2009). How do you feel--now? The anterior insula and human awareness. *Nature Reviews Neuroscience, 10*(1).

De Berardis, D., Campanella, D., Gambi, F., La Rovere, R., Sepede, G., Core, L., ... & Salerno, R. M. (2007). Alexithymia, fear of bodily sensations, and somatosensory amplification in young outpatients with panic disorder. *Psychosomatics, 48*(3), 239–246.

Dehaene, S., Changeux, J. P., Naccache, L., Sackur, J., & Sergent, C. (2006). Conscious, preconscious, and subliminal processing: a testable taxonomy. *Trends in Cognitive Sciences, 10*(5), 204–211.

Doll, A., Hölzel, B. K., Boucard, C. C., Wohlschläger, A. M., & Sorg, C. (2015). Mindfulness is associated with intrinsic functional connectivity between default mode and salience networks. *Frontiers in Human Neuroscience, 9*, 461.

Duddu, V., Isaac, M. K., & Chaturvedi, S. K. (2003). Alexithymia in somatoform and depressive disorders. *Journal of Psychosomatic Research, 54*(5), 435–438.

Dutta, A., McKie, S., Downey, D., Thomas, E., Juhasz, G., Arnone, D., ... & Anderson, I. M. (2019). Regional default mode network connectivity in major depressive disorder: Modulation by acute intravenous citalopram. *Translational Psychiatry, 9*(1), 1–9.

Garrison, K. A., Zeffiro, T. A., Scheinost, D., Constable, R. T., & Brewer, J. A. (2015). Meditation leads to reduced default mode network activity beyond an active task. *Cognitive, Affective, & Behavioral Neuroscience, 15*(3), 712–720.

Goldman, R., & Fredrick-Keniston, A. (2020). Memory reconsolidation as a common change process. In R. D. Lane & L. Nadel (Eds.), *Neuroscience of enduring change: Implications for psychotherapy.* USA: Oxford University Press.

Grabe, H. J., Spitzer, C., & Freyberger, H. J. (2004). Alexithymia and personality in relation to dimensions of psychopathology. *American Journal of Psychiatry, 161*(7), 1299–1301.

Hamilton, J. P., Furman, D. J., Chang, C., Thomason, M. E., Dennis, E., & Gotlib, I. H. (2011). Default-mode and task-positive network activity in major depressive disorder: Implications for adaptive and maladaptive rumination. *Biological Psychiatry, 70*(4), 327–333.

Harrison, R., Zeidan, F., Kitsaras, G., Ozcelik, D., & Salomons, T. V. (2019). Trait mindfulness is associated with lower pain reactivity and connectivity of the default mode network. *The Journal of Pain, 20*(6), 645–654.

Hayes, S. C., Strosahl, K. D., & Wilson, K. G. (2009). *Acceptance and commitment therapy.* Washington, DC: American Psychological Association.

Hove, M. J., Stelzer, J., Nierhaus, T., Thiel, S. D., Gundlach, C., Margulies, D. S., ... & Merker, B. (2015). Brain network reconfiguration and perceptual decoupling during an absorptive state of consciousness. *Cerebral Cortex, 26*(7), 3116–3124.

Karlsson, H., Näätänen, P., & Stenman, H. (2008). Cortical activation in alexithymia as a response to emotional stimuli. *The British Journal of Psychiatry, 192*(1), 32–38.

King, A. P., Block, S. R., Sripada, R. K., Rauch, S., Giardino, N., Favorite, T., ... & Liberzon, I. (2016). Altered default mode network (DMN) resting state functional connectivity following a mindfulness-based exposure therapy for posttraumatic stress disorder (PTSD) in combat veterans of Afghanistan and Iraq. *Depression and Anxiety, 33*(4), 289–299.

Lane, R. D., Quinlan, D. M., Schwartz, G. E., Walker, P. A., & Zeitlin, S. B. (1990). The levels of emotional awareness scale: A cognitive-developmental measure of emotion. *Journal of Personality Assessment, 55*(1–2), 124–134.

Lane, R. D., Reiman, E. M., Axelrod, B., Yun, L. S., Holmes, A., & Schwartz, G. E. (1998). Neural correlates of levels of emotional awareness: Evidence of an interaction between emotion and attention in the anterior cingulate cortex. *Journal of Cognitive Neuroscience, 10*(4), 525–535.

Lane, R. D., Ryan, L., Nadel, L., & Greenberg, L. (2015). Memory reconsolidation, emotional arousal, and the process of change in psychotherapy: New insights from brain science. *Behavioral and Brain Sciences, 38.*

Lane, R. D., Subic-Wrana, C., Greenberg, L., & Yovel, I. (2020). The role of enhanced emotional awareness in promoting change across psychotherapy modalities. *Journal of Psychotherapy Integration.* https://doi.org/10.1037/int0000244.

Larsen, J. K., Brand, N., Bermond, B., & Hijman, R. (2003). Cognitive and emotional characteristics of alexithymia: A review of neurobiological studies. *Journal of Psychosomatic Research, 54*(6), 533–541.

Lubin, G., Werbeloff, N., Halperin, D., Shmushkevitch, M., Weiser, M., & Knobler, H. Y. (2010). Decrease in suicide rates after a change of policy reducing access to firearms in adolescents: A naturalistic epidemiological study. *Suicide and Life-Threatening Behavior, 40*(5), 421–424.

Mattila, A. K., Kronholm, E., Jula, A., Salminen, J. K., Koivisto, A. M., Mielonen, R. L., & Joukamaa, M. (2008). Alexithymia and somatization in general population. *Psychosomatic Medicine, 70*(6), 716–722.

Ogden, P., & Fisher, J. (2015). *Sensorimotor psychotherapy: Interventions for trauma and attachment (Norton series on interpersonal neurobiology).* New York: WW Norton & Company.

Ogden, P., & Minton, K. (2000). Sensorimotor psychotherapy: One method for processing traumatic memory. *Traumatology, 6*(3), 149–173.

Palser, E. R., Palmer, C. E., Galvez-Pol, A., Hannah, R., Fotopoulou, A., & Kilner, J. M. (2018). Alexithymia mediates the relationship between interoceptive sensibility and anxiety. *PloS One, 13*(9), e0203212.

Paradiso, S., Vaidya, J. G., McCormick, L. M., Jones, A., & Robinson, R. G. (2008). Aging and alexithymia: Association with reduced right rostral cingulate volume. *The American Journal of Geriatric Psychiatry, 16*(9), 760–769.

Parker, J. D., Taylor, G. J., Bagby, R. M., & Acklin, M. W. (1993). Alexithymia in panic disorder and simple phobia: A comparative study. *American Journal of Psychiatry, 150,* 1105-1107.

Paul, L. K., Lautzenhiser, A., Brown, W. S., Hart, A., Neumann, D., Spezio, M., & Adolphs, R. (2006). Emotional arousal in agenesis of the corpus callosum. *International Journal of Psychophysiology, 61*(1), 47–56.

Payne, P., Levine, P. A., & Crane-Godreau, M. A. (2015). Somatic experiencing: Using interoception and proprioception as core elements of trauma therapy. *Frontiers in Psychology, 6,* 93.

Pollan, M. (2019). *How to change your mind: What the new science of psychedelics teaches us about consciousness, dying, addiction, depression, and transcendence.* New York, NY: Penguin Books.

Pollatos, O., Gramann, K., & Schandry, R. (2007). Neural systems connecting interoceptive awareness and feelings. *Human Brain Mapping, 28*(1), 9–18.

Pollatos, O., Schandry, R., Auer, D. P., & Kaufmann, C. (2007). Brain structures mediating cardiovascular arousal and interoceptive awareness. *Brain Research, 1141,* 178–187.

Pollatos, O., Traut-Mattausch, E., Schroeder, H., & Schandry, R. (2007). Interoceptive awareness mediates the relationship between anxiety and the intensity of unpleasant feelings. *Journal of Anxiety Disorders, 21*(7), 931–943.

Porges, S. W. (2011). *The polyvagal theory: Neurophysiological foundations of emotions, attachment, communication, and self-regulation (Norton Series on Interpersonal Neurobiology).* New York: WW Norton & Company.

Richter, J., Möller, B., Spitzer, C., Letzel, S., Bartols, S., Barnow, S., ... & Grabe, H. J. (2006). Transcallosal inhibition in patients with and without alexithymia. *Neuropsychobiology, 53*(2), 101–107.

Sahdra, B. K., Shaver, P. R., & Brown, K. W. (2010). A scale to measure nonattachment: A Buddhist complement to Western research on attachment and adaptive functioning. *Journal of Personality Assessment, 92*(2), 116–127.

Smith, R., Ahern, G. L., & Lane, R. D. (2019). The role of anterior and midcingulate cortex in emotional awareness: A domain-general processing perspective. In B. A. Vogt (Ed.), *Handbook of clinical neurology* (Vol. 166, pp. 89–101). Elsevier.

Smith, R., Thayer, J. F., Khalsa, S. S., & Lane, R. D. (2017). The hierarchical basis of neurovisceral integration. *Neuroscience & Biobehavioral Reviews, 75*, 274–296.

Stevens, F. L. (2016). The anterior cingulate cortex in psychopathology and psychotherapy: Effects on awareness and repression of affect. *Neuropsychoanalysis, 18*(1), 53–68.

Suchy, Y. (2011). *Clinical neuropsychology of emotion.* New York, NY: Guilford Press.

Tagliazucchi, E., Roseman, L., Kaelen, M., Orban, C., Muthukumaraswamy, S. D., Murphy, K., ... & Bullmore, E. (2016). Increased global functional connectivity correlates with LSD-induced ego dissolution. *Current Biology, 26*(8), 1043–1050.

Taylor, V. A., Daneault, V., Grant, J., Scavone, G., Breton, E., Roffe-Vidal, S., ... & Beauregard, M. (2013). Impact of meditation training on the default mode network during a restful state. *Social Cognitive and Affective Neuroscience, 8*(1), 4–14.

Van Veen, V., Cohen, J. D., Botvinick, M. M., Stenger, V. A., & Carter, C. S. (2001). Anterior cingulate cortex, conflict monitoring, and levels of processing. *Neuroimage, 14*(6), 1302–1308.

Whitfield-Gabrieli, S., & Ford, J. M. (2012). Default mode network activity and connectivity in psychopathology. *Annual Review of Clinical Psychology, 8*, 49–76.

Zeitlin, S. B., & McNally, R. J. (1993). Alexithymia and anxiety sensitivity in panic disorder and obsessive-compulsive disorder. *The American Journal of Psychiatry, 150*(4), 658–660.

5   Emotional Validation

Once we recognize our feelings, the next step is to validate them. Validating is a simple act, yet often something we do not do. Validation is telling ourselves that our feelings are real and true. Many patients will often say, " I shouldn't be feeling this way." There is no right or wrong way to feel. Invalidating your feelings creates confusion because it's a movement away from self. Even worse, invalidating feelings can cause individuals to feel shame for how they are feeling. Frequently I tell my patients, "**We cannot control our feelings, only how we react to our feelings.**" Once we feel something we cannot go back in time and undo that feeling. Telling ourselves that we should not feel something that we do feel is a denial of our very own experience.

Invalidating feelings often occurs as a defense mechanism around not having to acknowledge our emotional pain. Yet, repressing or suppressing (Note: suppressing typically refers to a conscious attempt to reject feeling, whereas repressing is unconscious; since the intent in rejecting feelings is often hard to decipher, the terms are used interchangeably.) feelings take both an emotional and cognitive toll. Franchow and Suchy (2015) show that individuals who suppress their emotions show deficits in executive functioning, working memory, and processing speed. Repression is often used as a short-term coping strategy to avoid emotion, but in the long term it doesn't help to reduce emotional pathology (Geraerts, Merckelbach, Jelicic, & Smeets, 2006). Data on mental illness shows that the suppression of emotions is negatively correlated with indicators of mental health (Hu et al., 2014). Research demonstrates that individuals with mental illness are often afraid of their feelings and suppress emotions (Beblo et al., 2012) because they become too overwhelmed by them. When working with difficult feelings, is important not to encourage patients to increase awareness of emotions that patients feel unable to cope with. While the book lays out sequential steps in overcoming psychopathology, if a patient is not ready to manage stronger emotions it's important to build coping skills before moving on (see Chapter 8). For example, in the previous chapter on mindfulness, emotional awareness was discussed; however, as a

DOI: 10.4324/9781003150893-5

therapist, you would not want to increase a patient's awareness of their emotions if they are struggling to cope with the current emotions they are experiencing. Sometimes if emotions are too overwhelming for patients, they will resort to drastic coping measures to manage emotion: severe substance abuse; cutting; or even suicide. As a clinician, it's important to pay attention to how your patients manage feelings as you encourage them to access and validate stronger and potentially more uncomfortable emotions.

5.1 Feeling "Crazy"

When becoming aware of our emotions, we can be surprised by an emotional reaction that we have, and then we invalidate our feeling because the feeling doesn't seem relevant to the current situation. When we find ourselves "overreacting" or having an unexpected emotional response that doesn't appear to make sense, we often label these feelings as "crazy." Crazy is defined as "mentally deranged," which means "insane" or acting "irregular." This is exactly what can happen when our expected emotional reaction does not match the given context, and we react solely from a place of emotion. This occurs because our emotional reactions, albeit always valid, do not always match the current environmental context. Emotions can be stored like memory. We all have circumstances that we are sensitive to or get under our skin. This is a result of our life experience. We've all had intense events which leave emotional memories, both good and bad. A favorite song from childhood or trip back home may activate positive feelings for some, whereas another individual exposed to that same stimulus may have little or no reaction. Additionally, someone who has been bitten by a dog may hold a negative emotional memory towards that dog, causing them excessive unease upon meeting a new dog. When feeling "crazy," the current environmental context doesn't warrant the elicited emotion. For example, our hometown may no longer have our friends from childhood but is still able to elicit positive feelings from us. While meeting a new dog can be a completely benign experience, our emotional memory from the past causes us to respond in habitual ways to stimuli, even once the context has changed. If you've ever asked yourself, "Why I am so upset about this?" the emotion is probably not related to the current context, but the context has evoked an old emotional experience. Then is when we label ourselves as "crazy." Sometimes we recognize emotional memories and their effects; for example, we might say "I'm scared of the beach, because I almost drowned there as a child. Can we go somewhere else?" However, this is not always the case and often we don't know why certain emotions get triggered. The unexplained emotion gets activated from the environmental cues or primes that occur outside of our awareness. We may find ourselves getting angry at some small thing, and label ourselves "crazy." Our emotional response does not fit the context; we're angry for what seems to be no reason. This does not mean our emotion is invalid; it just means we don't know why we are feeling the way we do. Our anger could be triggered by subliminal stimuli; and not wanting to be angry about nothing, we find some small thing in our environment to which we can attribute our anger. However, attributing our anger to this small thing is crazy, because it doesn't at all relate to our anger. This wouldn't be so much of a problem, except that we then negatively judge ourselves and our emotions for being crazy. I believe this problem has influenced psychology to see emotions as harmful as opposed to helpful. Because we often cannot understand why we feel the way we do, we wrongly label the emotion as the problem, when instead the real problem is the lack of understanding.

Multiple studies have demonstrated that we consistently provide a rationale for our feelings even though the rationale we provide is often wrong. The psychological term for this is attribution error, and the most common example is the fundamental attribution error, where individuals tend to overattribute others' behaviors to their personality and not the situation (Forgas, 1998). For example, if we are late to work, we attribute our lateness to traffic or challenges getting out of the house, whereas if our co-worker is late, we'll assume they're not that conscious of time, which is a dimension of their personality. More current research on the effect suggests this attribution error is fueled by a self-serving bias (Malle, 2006). Our mistakes are outside of our control, while others' mistakes are a deficit of character. Multiple experiments exist demonstrating we often make false attributions for others' and our own behavior (Myers & Smith, 2015). We often assume that we should know why we feel the way we do, when in actuality few of us really understand where our feelings are coming from. So, it's common for us to not have clear explanations for our feelings; however, rarely do we say, "I don't know" when asked why we feel a certain way. The assumption is we should have a clear rationale for our feelings. So, when we have a feeling that doesn't match the current context, our response is to label ourselves "crazy" and not to be curious about our unique emotional response. If we could be less judgmental of our feelings, it would allow us to more easily validate our experience. We might say, "I'm surprised I'm feeling so sad; I wonder what this could be about?" Telling ourselves we are crazy and labeling the feeling as wrong only shames us and moves us further away from our true experience. When I see a patient invalidate their feelings, I often tell a story from when I worked at the Veterans Affairs (VA) Hospital. Veterans are a great population to work with and have many strengths as patients. However, many veterans struggle with anger, and I noticed a common pattern in male veterans with road rage. The pattern was they would come into my office apologizing saying they got carried away on the road and got in trouble with their aggressive driving. They would say something like, person X pulled out in front of me, I lost my cool, and then I tried to run them off the road. They would go on to say that their anger had gotten the better of them, they felt bad about it, and that it wouldn't happen again. The veterans would say that they just needed to control their anger better. Sometimes it would end there, but if possible, I would try to get them to notice that their anger just didn't go away; in fact, maybe this wasn't their first time seeing me. If they were open to it, we'd talk about their anger, anger often stemming from abuse as a child, or going to wars they didn't want to go, along with doing things they didn't want to do. These are all examples of events where the veterans didn't have control and their boundaries were crossed. These guys had good reason to be angry. For the most part, they got along fine in daily life, but every now and then something like someone pulling out in front of them would set them off. Granted, this makes us all a little angry, but these veterans would go into a rage state because this incident was the spark that opened up all their anger from the past. When you feel that level of rage, it's easy to misattribute your anger to the driver that pulled out in front of you. In this rage state, it makes sense that you want to knock the other driver off the road. However, their anger was an overreaction and a misattribution; it was "crazy." Of course, afterward the veterans feel shame for their actions, and they feel shame about their anger. The veterans would use this shame to invalidate their feelings of anger. They would apologize, say "Sorry it won't happen again," and "I just need to keep this anger in check," as if the anger was the problem and not the violent behavior. I understand they were blaming the anger for their behavior, but this puts the veterans in a trap because they can't erase their anger. If the anger is the problem, but you can't make the emotion disappear, you're stuck. I would try and validate their anger, the opposite of shaming it. I would also remind them, **"We cannot control our feelings only how we react to our feelings."** Their job is not to prevent the anger, but to respond effectively to it. We would then work on accepting and validating their anger, which would allow us to start working through all the past events that caused their anger to begin with (see section 9.1). This story, I find, helps patients recognize that we all have difficult emotions and how important it is to validate whatever feelings we have, even if we don't know the source of them. Not all veterans could easily link back their anger to previous trauma, but when we started validating their anger, it made it easier to connect the emotional memories. Validating emotions makes us feel better (Shenk & Fruzzetti, 2011) and allows us to understand ourselves better. We need to acknowledge our feelings if we are going to fix our mental health problems. I sometimes use the metaphor of driving a car that is falling apart to illustrate this. I have had some junk cars and at times I've known I need to get the car repaired, but I find myself pushing the car, just to get to the next place. I recognize that driving such a car when it's making noises and having problems is probably a bad idea, but I don't want to stop, go to a mechanic to have them look under the hood, and tell me how bad a shape this car is really in. I know the car needs work; I just don't want to accept it. Invalidating our feelings is often a way for us to avoid our problems; it might work for a little while in the short run, but it never fixes the problem.

Invaliding our feelings makes it hard for us to recognize our experience. If we don't validate our feelings it's hard to move on to future steps, such as providing self-compassion, understanding the feeling, and/or re-consolidating the feeling. If mindfulness helps us develop emotional awareness, validation is the next tool to help us accept those emotions. Helping patients recognize there is no right or wrong way to feel can help patients normalize and accept emotions. I will tell patients, "Nobody signs up for distressful feelings, but when you have them, they are there, and the sooner we accept the feelings, the quicker we can get towards fixing the feelings." For some of us, validating feelings is natural, while for others it can be a struggle. Let's try to understand how these differences occur, with the final goal not being for us as therapists to validate patients' feelings, but for the patients to learn to validate their own feelings.

5.2 Caregiver Attunement

Much emotional communication goes on between the child and care-taker between the ages of zero and two, well before infants can even start to express their needs through verbal communication. The non-verbal communication that occurs in early life mostly involves expressing physical and emotional needs, and the response to these needs is extremely important to the overall emotional development of the child. The PFC responsible for executive functions and expression of thoughts is still in basic stages of development at this age, while the limbic areas are more fully developed, albeit still developing synaptic connec-tions (Monk, Webb, & Nelson, 2001). How the caretaker responds to the child's needs will lay the foundations for how the child expresses and expects their emotions to be responded to, and also shapes future brain development (Fox, Levitt, & Nelson, 2010). This age also corresponds to the time period of Erik Erickson's trust vs. mistrust stage (Erikson, 1993). According to Erickson, if a child's basic needs are met, they will develop trust for the world; alternatively, if the emotional needs of the child are not met, they will develop a basic mistrust for the world. It is in these early stages that emotional problems can first start to develop. Newborn infants will direct their gaze toward caregivers in making eye contact (Farroni, Massaccesi, Pividori, & Johnson, 2004) and smile less when caregivers advert their eye contact (Hains & Muir, 1996). This is the beginning of emotional attunement, the reflective practice of recognizing another's emotions and reflecting that emotion back. When we tell a friend that we had a bad day, we don't want to get a smile or puzzled look back; we want to see that friend frowning, demonstrating that they recognize and validate our emotional experience. A great demonstration of emotional attunement with infants is Ed Tronick's still face experiment, where a mother will interact normally with her baby and then express a still face, a face with no affect. Most babies express immediate discomfort, often crying and throwing a tantrum (Weinberg & Tronick, 1996). Google Ed Tronick Still Face Experiment; there is a great video demonstrating the study. I've shown this video several times to my students when teaching developmental psychology, and it can be painful to watch the infant in distress. This is probably a good thing; it means my students and I have a normal human response to an infant in distress, which makes us want to reach out to soothe the baby. This is the natural reflex that most of us have, to attend to and validate the baby's feelings. This helps the baby to establish a sense of trust in the world, secure in the knowledge that their needs will be met. Most caregivers would react the same way, perhaps even more so given their attachment to their own child. One outcome study of the still face experiment with 6-month-old infants showed that children with depressed mothers will demonstrate higher rates of problem behaviors after a year to 18 months of age (Moore, Cohn, & Campbell, 2001). However, maternal depression was not the sole contributing factor to problem behaviors at 18 months; the infant's own temperament as measured by the still face experiment was its own unique contributor. This also provides further support for the influences of both nature and nurture on development. The still face experiment has been demonstrated multiple times across various groups. It has been shown to be both robust as a study and a stronger contributor to attachment style (see section 10.2), with securely attached infants trying to elicit an emotional response from their mother (Mesman, van IJzendoorn, & Bakermans-Kranenburg, 2009).

This reflection of emotion between the caregiver and infant is often referred to as facial or emotional mimicry, where parents and infants will mimic each other's expression as a bonding tool. This is a process too of expressing and validating emotions. Consider when a friend looks at you smiling and says, "That is great;" your facial expression in response can either validate or invalidate their feeling. If you smile back, that is a sign of agreement and validation. A blank expression or a frown is likely to get a response from your friend such as, "What, do you disagree?" Your invalidation may leave your friend feeling frustrated and confused; we expect to be validated by one another, and this starts as infants. Research shows that when presented subliminally with faces, we unconsciously mimic those facial expressions (Dimberg, Thunberg, & Elmehed, 2000), suggesting that in some ways we may be innately programed to validate each other's feelings. I've noticed in a room full of people who are laughing, it's hard not to laugh even if I don't know what the joke is. Emotional mimicry is also related to emotional contagion, with the latter being not just imitating the expression of another, but actually experiencing the same emotional state. Prochazkova and Kret (2017) suggest that emotional mimicry precedes emotional contagion, which eventually leads to affective empathy (see section 6.2). Through mimicking another's expression we can better recognize how they feel. Similar brain regions activate when feeling an emotion as when the facial expression of that emotion is made. It's been theorized that mimicry helps us empathize and understand others better (Wood, Rychlowska, Korb, & Niedenthal, 2016). Interference with mimicry through biting a pen or chewing gum impairs our ability to recognize emotions (Oberman, Winkielman, & Ramachandran, 2007). This ability to recognize the emotions of caregivers quickly and effectively may be evolutionarily adaptive for survival. Young children can look to their caregiver's expression to determine quickly what is and is not safe in their environment through a vicarious learning process (Niedenthal & Brauer, 2012). Regardless, we use emotional mimicry to build rapport and connection with others (Lakin & Chartrand, 2003). This mimicry process is extremely valuable to the emotional bonding that occurs between the child and caregiver.

5.3 Attunement and Brain Hemispheres

Therapists call this synchronous process of sharing emotion, emotional attunement, whereas in the neuroscience literature it is referred to as a neural resonance or shared neural activation. Anders, Heinzle, Weiskopf, Ethofer, and Haynes (2011) put romantic couples in fMRI machines and examined the exchange of emotional information between couples' facial expressions. They found could predict the neural activity of the perceiver's brain from the neural activity of the sender's brain. Interestingly, initially there was a lag between the perceiver's brain response and the sender's; however, over time this lag decreased, representing greater attunement between the couples. Now when people say, "We're on the same wavelength," there is some empirical evidence to support this attunement process. Emotional attunement appears to be related to a right hemisphere to hemisphere process between infant and caregiver (Borod et al., 1998; Gainotti, 2012; Krautheim et al., 2019; Schore, 2001). Studies indicate that the right hemisphere initially develops more rapidly than the left (Trevarthen, 1996), perhaps related to this early parent-infant bonding process. Ross and Monnot (2008) propose a theoretical model for these brain hemisphere differences. Through neuropsychological testing of patients with brain damage, Ross finds the right frontal/temporal lobe areas are analogous for non-verbal communication, and the left frontal/temporal lobe areas for verbal communication. If you have taken Cognitive Psychology, you'll probably remember Broca's and Wernicke's areas. In the left IFG is Brocas's area, important for language production. In the left posterior temporal lobe, also known as the STG, is Wernicke's area, involved in language comprehension. Wernicke's area receives information from the auditory cortex, decodes that information, then sends signals to Broca's area, which produces the speech in response. Recent research shows the right IFG is particularly important in emotional expression through prosody (Patel et al., 2018). Overall, there appears to be a right-hemisphere bias for emotion (Alpers, 2008; Borod, Bloom, Brickman, Nakhutina, & Curko, 2002; Wallez & Vauclair, 2011), but not all studies agree (Smith & Bulman-Fleming, 2005); others show a predominance for "negative" emotions on the right and "positive" emotions on the left (Najt, Bayer, & Hausmann, 2013). Still other studies find a hemispheric division between approach emotions/ left hemisphere vs. avoid emotions/ right hemisphere (Harmon-Jones, Gable, & Peterson, 2010). In a meta-analysis of neuroimaging studies, Costafreda, Brammer, David, and Fu (2008) find right lateralization of amygdala activity for masked emotional stimuli. Some neuroscience research supports this right lateralization for emotion, although it is inconsistent. Findings do show the emotion of anger appears to be more left-lateralized (Lindquist, Wager, Kober, Bliss-Moreau, & Barrett, 2012), supporting the approach vs. avoid emotional theory. If approach emotions are right hemisphere based, it could also explain caregiver's bias toward left-side cradling of babies for right-hemisphere attunement (Bourne & Todd, 2004). Perhaps another way to think about the hemisphere differences comes from Ian McGilchrist and his book *The master and his emissary: The divided brain and the making of the western world* (2019). MiGilchrist outlines brain differences suggesting the right brain is designed to perceive the whole and the left brain is designed for detail-orientated tasks. The right hemisphere examines the broader picture, while the left hemisphere put things in context so it can act on them. Ideally, they work together. Sometimes you can get caught up in the details and miss the bigger picture, being overly left-brain focused, whereas in other cases you can see the full picture but fail to take effective action, being overly right-brain focused. As our knowledge of hemisphere differences continues to evolve, we might better understand the brain hemisphere differences. Anecdotal evidence of individuals that have had hemisphere-specific strokes, finds that these individuals experience a profound difference in their perceptions. Jill Bolte Taylor (2009) a neuroanatomist herself, writes about having a left-hemisphere stroke and how greatly it affected her understanding of the brain.

5.4 Childhood Maltreatment: Corpus Callosum

Childhood maltreatment affects the integrity of the corpus callosum, which transfers information across hemispheres (Lim, Howells, Radua, & Rubia, 2020; Teicher et al., 2004). One study involving Romanian orphans demonstrated that once they were placed in high-quality foster care, they no longer showed continued deficits in reduced corpus callosum volume, and showed some evidence of increased neuroplasticity (Sheridan, Fox, Zeanah,

McLaughlin, & Nelson, 2012). Teicher et al. (2003) believe that childhood maltreatment shows specific deficits in interhemispheric communication. Schiffer, Teicher, and Papanicolaou (1995) compared emotionally maltreated children with healthy controls in recalling neutral and unpleasant memories. Emotionally maltreated individuals exhibited increased activity in the left auditory cortex when recalling neutral memories, yet when recalling unpleasant memories brain activity switched to favor the right auditory cortex. Non-emotionally maltreated children exhibited equivalent hemispheric activity for both neutral and unpleasant memories. Authors take these findings to suggest maltreated children struggle to integrate information across brain hemispheres. Teicher, Samson, Anderson, and Ohashi (2016) believe that this lack of inter-hemisphere communication is what is responsible for the "black and white thinking" seen in borderline personality disorder and "splitting," two conditions associated with a childhood abuse background (see section 10.1). In referencing the approach vs. avoid hemisphere dichotomy (see section 9.10; Harmon-Jones & Gable, 2018), authors note that individuals with these disorders categorize people as good/ approach or bad/avoid, without the ability to see the nuance, because they lack the capacity for hemispheric transfer of information. Not all studies of borderline personality disorder and the corpus callosum show significant findings (Walterfang et al., 2010; Zanetti et al., 2007), though some do (Rüsch et al., 2007, 2010). Even the role of the corpus callosum is still a matter of debate as to whether it acts as more of an inhibitory or excitatory structure between the two hemispheres (van der Knaap & van der Ham, 2011). Much more understanding of the corpus callosum is needed before we can fully determine its role in psychopathology. Interestingly though, eye movement desensitization and reprocessing (EMDR) a treatment for trauma, has been thought to be an effective treatment method because it increases communication between the two brain hemispheres through bilateral eye movement (Christman, Garvey, Propper, & Phaneuf, 2003). Some work also suggests that the rapid eye movement in sleep may be particularly important for the storage of emotional memories (Diekelmann, Wilhelm, & Born, 2009).

5.5 Childhood Maltreatment: Brain Areas

Childhood maltreatment appears to disrupt the brain's stress response as well as its normal ability to respond to a threat. In previous chapters, the role of the amygdala and its response to fear and threat were discussed. Given that maltreatment is threatening by nature, it's not surprising that these areas are affected by childhood trauma too. The whole fear circuitry, starting from the amygdala which signals to the dACC, rACC, and vmPFC, works together in regulating emotional responses and has been shown to be disrupted in childhood maltreatment, with changes in volume, function, and connectivity (McCrory, Gerin, & Viding, 2017;

Teicher, Samson, Anderson, & Ohashi, 2016). This is consistent with psychological findings showing maltreated children have impaired emotional regulation skills (Kim & Cicchetti, 2010). However, neurobiological differences within this fear/ emotional regulation circuit are not always consistent, perhaps due to the large varieties and inconsistencies of childhood maltreatment (McCrory et al., 2017). Some specific findings do emerge, such as individuals who were subjected to childhood maltreatment show an exaggerated amygdala response (Dannlowski et al., 2013). The theory here is that during maltreatment, the brain become hypersensitive in detecting threat as means of self-protection, and the excessive amygdala activity helps identify these potential threats. Some research shows enlarged amygdala volumes from childhood maltreatment (Tottenham et al., 2010). Childhood maltreatment shows consistent decreased hippocampus volume (Dannlowski et al., 2012) and deficits in areas of the vmPFC (Gorka, Hanson, Radtke, & Hariri, 2014; van Harmelen et al., 2010). Researchers believe these changes over time contribute to a maladaptive stress response and increased risk for PTSD. Recently attention had paid to fornix in child maltreatment. The fornix is involved in episodic memory and fear conditioning (Phillips & LeDoux, 1995; Douet & Chang, 2015), and damage to the fornix has been shown to affect episodic memory (Zhuang et al., 2012). The fornix is a major afferent and efferent neural track going from the hippocampus to the hypothalamus. The hypothalamus regulates the endocrine system and is very involved in the brain's stress response, making the fornix part of a key pathway in managing the brain stress response. Lim et al. (2020) find childhood maltreatment to be marked by reduced fractional anisotropy (a complex calculation used to measure the integrity of the region's white brain matter) in the fornix. A finding corroborated by Yu, Lee, and Lee, (2017) shows an association between early trauma and fornix integrity. Consistent with these findings, individuals with childhood maltreatment show a diminished cortisol response to stress (Carpenter, Shattuck, Tyrka, Geracioti, & Price, 2011; MacMillan et al., 2009). Most all of these studies are completed in adults who experienced childhood maltreatment, indicating that the neurobiological effects of trauma on the brain and endocrine system are long lasting.

5.6 Childhood Maltreatment: Brain Networks

Individuals with childhood maltreatment also show a diminished response to reward, marked by lower activity of VS, an important component of the MCL (reward circuit) (Hanson et al., 2016). Researchers have suggested that early maltreatment leads to brain changes in reward processing, which could create a susceptibility to depression (Hanson, Hariri, & Williamson, 2015) or substance abuse (Luijten, Schellekens, Kühn, Machielse, & Sescousse, 2017).

The default mode network (DMN) is also affected by childhood maltreatment (Bluhm et al., 2009; Philip et al., 2013; Sripada, Swain, Evans, Welsh, & Liberzon, 2014). Further disruption is seen between the DMN and the SN in youth exposed to trauma (Marusak, Etkin, & Thomason, 2015). Some research indicates these connectivity deficits between the SN and DMN are related to the dissociative symptoms of PTSD (Tursich et al., 2015). Lanius, Frewen, Tursich, Jetly, and McKinnon (2015) looked at trauma and its associations between the DMN, SN, and CEN, and found evidence that trauma disrupts multiple brain networks. Some research also suggests childhood maltreatment leads to disruption between the DMN and EMN networks (Allen et al., 2019). Given the large effects of trauma on the developing brain, it is hard to draw a precise connection to how childhood maltreatment affects individual brain networks or areas. Childhood maltreatment appears to have global effects causing disruption in function, connectivity, and structure in multiple regions, making it harder to apply targeted clinical affective neuroscience treatments.

5.7 Emotional Validation and Childhood Trauma

Childhood maltreatment appears to disrupt the whole notion of the self, so emotional validation will be primary in reconnecting patients to their experience. Teicher et al. (2016) define emotional maltreatment as "intentionally eliciting feelings of guilt, shame or fear to serve the emotional needs of the perpetrator, persuading children to perform inappropriate acts, denigrating or destroying things they value, or placing them in harmful situations, such as witnessing interparental violence." The first part of the definition notes that the caregiver is putting their emotional needs in front of the child. They are manipulating the child's feelings for their benefit. I have recently heard this referred to as "gaslighting," trying to change someone's experience of the world for a perpetrator's benefit. I have seen many patients whose caregivers have manipulated the patients' beliefs out of their own emotional immaturity. This can take on many forms, but a simple example is a child struggling at school; instead of listening to the child's experience, caregivers are quick to say, "It's not that bad," or "You've got nothing to complain about." This invalidates the child's experience. There are instances where children do overreact to events; however, this still would not warrant emotional invalidation. The caregiver would still want to validate the feelings, while offering some perspective-taking. Additionally, the child's overreaction often stems from fear of being invalidated or not receiving concern from a caregiver to begin with, so they overreact in order to make themselves heard. However, it's most important that caregivers recognize that their children will not react to events the same way they will. This seems obvious but it can easily be missed by caregivers. When caregivers say "Oh, you'll make more friends" or "Nobody will care about your first-grade science project," often they are reacting from their perspective and not the child's perspective. For a child, at this place and time in life, these events feel really important. So regardless of the caregiver's perspective, they need to validate the child's experience. The effects of this invalidation may seem subtle but can have larger consequences when continually repeated. When invalidated over time, these children lose touch with their experience, which makes them lose touch with themselves. This then causes the child to rely on external mechanisms of value. If a child is not able to validate their own experience, this prevents them from valuing their feelings. Then in absence of self-knowledge, the child starts to construct their sense of self, based upon what the world around them values and not on what they value. They end up living a life motivated by what they think will bring them value, but not necessarily what they value, and in the process of doing this, they continue to invalidate themselves. Emotional maltreatment trains the child to live for someone else's needs and not their own. In clinical practice I see it all the time, in excessive people pleasing, trying to be the perfect student, letting others take advantage of them, conspicuous consumption, and workaholics. What all of these problems have in common is that the individual is living for someone else's needs and values and not their own. Helping patients see through these problems can be difficult at times but it starts with emotional validation. Childhood maltreatment and trauma interferes with your ability to listen to yourself and make good decisions based on your interests. Let me give one example of how trauma interferes with our ability for self-validation. I saw an intelligent woman who was a survivor of sexual assault as an adult. She recognizes the trauma and can talk about it, but in moving forward she struggles to trust men. She's apprehensive about dating and recognizes her own apprehension. Now knowing that she has this apprehension toward men, she stops paying attention to her feelings because she believes the feelings are interfering with her goal of dating again. She would say to herself "I know I'm scared, but if I'm going to date again, I have to ignore those feelings." In ignoring those feelings, she is also letting go of her intuition, which can help inform her which guys might be sketchy and pass on them. In this example, the patient is invalidating her feelings because they can cause her to overreact in her behavior, but in doing so her decision-making process around men becomes even more confusing. This is an insightful woman with a lot of psychological strengths; for a child growing up in an environment of emotional maltreatment, the process is even more insidious. The goal for this woman would be not to ignore her feelings, but to accept her feelings and make a decision to act on them or let them go. Then she still would be able to utilize her intuition when dating. Often with these self-invalidating patients, I know what they should do: stop living for your parents; don't let your kids take advantage of you; or tell your boss you're overworked. The solution is easy; it is getting to the solution that is hard. Patients have to recognize the value of listening to their feelings; this can be a new process for many. These patients can be frustrating at times because they get in their own way. I find for me it is helpful to recognize they are not actively choosing to sabotage themselves; they have just learned to invalidate their own experience. I have to hold back my desire to just tell them what to do and help them recognize and validate their feelings so they can make good decisions for themselves going forward.

5.8 Mirror Neurons

It has been suggested that emotional attunement, recognizing and feeling another's emotions, may be part of the mirror neuron system (Likowski et al., 2012; Schmidt, Sojer, Hass, Kirsch, & Mier, 2020). Mirror neurons are neurons that react the same when watching someone do a task as they do when doing the task itself. Originally conceptualized as part of a motor response process, mirror neurons have been increasingly thought to be involved in other brain processes like empathy (Bastiaansen, Thioux, & Keysers, 2009; Carr, Iacoboni, Dubeau, Mazziotta, & Lenzi, 2003; Jahangard et al., 2019). When we process facial information from others, it appears mirror neurons are activated (Enticott, Johnston, Herring, Hoy, & Fitzgerald, 2008). However, the recording of single neurons is needed to fully demonstrate the effect of mirror neurons fully, and this is difficult to do in humans (Lamm & Majdandžić, 2015). fMRI studies of emotions do show functional overlap when someone is observing and experiencing the same emotion; however, this does mean the same exact neurons are activated (Stevens & Taber, 2021). The inferior frontal gyrus (IFG), commonly known as Broca's area, known for its role in language processing and speech production, has been increasingly shown to be involved in human empathy, and this particular area is noteworthy for having mirror neurons in humans (Chong, Cunnington, Williams, Kanwisher, & Mattingley, 2008; Kilner, Neal, Weiskopf, Friston, & Frith, 2009). While the science of how our brain perceives emotion from others (which may change through human development, see Ch. 6, Self-Compassion) is unsettled, we do know that children regulate their emotion through attunement with their caregiver (Crugnola, Ierardi, Gazzotti, & Albizzati, 2014; Crugnola, Ierardi, Bottini, Verganti, & Albizzati, 2019).

5.9 Responding to Emotions

You may have seen this common occurrence play out while observing children on the playground. A child falls off the swing set, mildly hurt. The child immediately looks over to their caregiver. Now the caregiver can respond in several ways. In scenario one, an anxious caregiver will overreact, expressing high levels of concern, upon which the child then starts reacting more extreme. In a second scenario, the caregiver looks over at the child, and seeing no major physical trauma waves it off and tells the child to go back to playing. In an even worse second scenario, sometimes the caregiver does not react at all, albeit this is rarer. Lastly, in a third scenario, a more moderated response from the caregiver may be employed. This third scenario would look something like this, the caregiver goes over to the child, asks the child "Are you okay?," attunes to the child's experience, provides emotional or physical reassurance, and then encourages the child to keep playing. While the child has incurred no major physical damage, each response can greatly shape the child's approach to their emotions. In scenario one, the child will learn that any emotional discomfort is distressing. Through vicarious learning, they may learn to start to panic in response to their own feelings; therefore, emotional struggles of any kind will be difficult. With scenario two, the child learns to disregard their feelings; they won't become emotionally distressed by upsetting feelings, but they may start to invalidate or avoid their own emotions (see section 4.3). The third scenario helps the child to recognize and validate their feelings. The caregiver acknowledges the child's feelings, then expresses the feelings back with their own facial expression, an act of emotional validation, and then helps the child to regulate the feeling by expressing a warm smile or offering a hug, and finally, the caregiver encourages the child to keep playing and not let the emotional scare inhibit their fun on the swings. These may seem like subtle differences, but they have a large effect on shaping the child's emotional development and attachment style (see section 10.2). This is also the basis for the growing research field of implicit emotional regulation (Braunstein, Gross, & Ochsner, 2017), where emotions are regulated in the absence of direct cognitive intervention. When children have their emotions validated and regulated from infancy, they learn to self-regulate and validate their emotions without conscious thought. Once when I was teaching developmental psychology, I was asked by a student what is the best thing you can do for your children. There are a lot of ways to answer this question, and probably no correct answer, but I responded from a psychological perspective that the most important thing you can do is to overcome your emotional problems. Otherwise, you will implicitly teach these problems to your children. The caregiver that panics in response to their child falling off a swing set tends to have their own anxiety and fears that are difficult to regulate, making it hard for the caregiver to manage their child's stress or anxiety. The caregiver that pays little attention to their child's feelings when they fall off the swing likely struggles to recognize and provide validation for their own feelings. Treating your child's emotions effectively starts with treating your own feelings effectively. What builds successful implicit emotional regulation for your children is role modeling strong emotional skills in yourself. Yet not every parent does this and not everyone gets ideal emotional attunement from his or her caregiver, which makes providing validation and teaching our patients how to validate their emotions so important. Not everyone automatically validates their own feelings and when they don't it causes distress, confusion, and an inability to make good action choices. Individuals unable to validate their feelings often assume something is wrong with themselves for feeling the way that they do, which leads to shame and self-blame, two things which make psychological problems much worse. Emotional validation like mindfulness still does not fix the upsetting emotion, but it helps stop the bleeding, so to speak. If patients can learn to validate their own emotions, they start to feel more grounded and stop getting frustrated with themselves for the way that they feel. This allows the clinician to work more directly with feelings, and the patient can next start to provide self-compassion for his or her feelings.

In practicing therapy, validating feelings is paramount. Yet this process also happens through mimicry. I might mimic a patient's emotional physical expression and slowly work to a place of contentment; in this sense, I am modeling to the patient a form of implicit emotional regulation. Just like the child that fell of the swing, you feel upset with them and for them, while slowly expressing through your emotions that it will be okay. Teaching this to a new therapist is a difficult process because of its abstract sense. It's hard to provide direction for non-verbal attunement; it's largely a non-conscious process. It's not impossible though. Paying close attention allows you to deepen your emotional engagement. This is not a process that comes naturally to me; sometimes I apologize to the patients in advance for staring at them, letting them know it takes effort for me to identify their feeling states. I continue to try and build these abilities. Another method I find to be very effective is breaking group therapy sessions into dyads and having the patients practice on each other, not only does this allow them to experience much-needed validation from someone else, it helps each patient tune into the emotions of another, which normalizes their own distress, and builds their own emotional attunement skills. Individuals with depression show a particularly impaired ability in identifying the emotions of others (Mattern et al., 2015), referred to as affective theory of mind. Practicing emotional validation in group settings helps build group cohesion and allows for more individual emotional attention than I can provide as a group leader. I find it is also valuable to build these skills within the group before going on to address more distressful emotions of patients. This allows group members training in how to support one another's emotions and to develop individual emotional tolerance for when more difficult emotions typically arise in later group sessions.

5.10 Masculinity and Emotion Validation

Often when I talk with patients about emotional validation, the subjective of toughness or masculinity arises. There seems to be a societal assumption that if you're tough, especially toxic masculinity tough, then taking time to validate your emotions only slows you down from doing the hard tasks and makes you weak. In these cases (and it's not just with men),

I explain to patients I think their definition of toughness is a misnomer. I agree that toughness involves doing the hard task, even when it's emotionally painful. However, I point out that if you have to deny your emotional experience to do the hard task, you're actually in a position of weakness. Real toughness is knowing something is going to be painful and doing it anyway; having to suppress or avoid your emotional experience to get something done is a sign of weakness. If you're not aware of your emotions, you're not necessarily aware of how they could be affecting you. Suppressing your feelings only to have the emotions take you by surprise later when you don't expect it, makes you susceptible to the unknown effects of these emotions on your behavior. In identifying with your feelings by validating and accepting difficult emotions, you are in a greater position of power. I find this often helps patients reevaluate a common social norm they may have been indoctrinated with. However, even with this knowledge, accepting feelings is not always easy, so it is important when doing so to develop self-compassion for your feelings.

References

Allen, P., Sommer, I. E., Jardri, R., Eysenck, M. W., & Hugdahl, K. (2019). Extrinsic and default mode networks in psychiatric conditions: Relationship to excitatory-inhibitory transmitter balance and early trauma. *Neuroscience & Biobehavioral Reviews*, *99*, 90–100.

Alpers, G. W. (2008). Eye-catching: Right hemisphere attentional bias for emotional pictures. *Laterality*, *13*(2), 158–178.

Anders, S., Heinzle, J., Weiskopf, N., Ethofer, T., & Haynes, J. D. (2011). Flow of affective information between communicating brains. *Neuroimage*, *54*(1), 439–446.

Bastiaansen, J. A., Thioux, M., & Keysers, C. (2009). Evidence for mirror systems in emotions. *Philosophical Transactions of the Royal Society B: Biological Sciences*, *364*(1528), 2391–2404.

Beblo, T., Fernando, S., Klocke, S., Griepenstroh, J., Aschenbrenner, S., & Driessen, M. (2012). Increased suppression of negative and positive emotions in major depression. *Journal of Affective Disorders*, *141*(2–3), 474–479.

Bluhm, R. L., Williamson, P. C., Osuch, E. A., Frewen, P. A., Stevens, T. K., Boksman, K., ... & Lanius, R. A. (2009). Alterations in default network connectivity in posttraumatic stress disorder related to early-life trauma. *Journal of Psychiatry & Neuroscience: JPN*, *34*(3), 187.

Borod, J. C., Bloom, R. L., Brickman, A. M., Nakhutina, L., & Curko, E. A. (2002). Emotional processing deficits in individuals with unilateral brain damage. *Applied Neuropsychology*, *9*(1), 23–36.

Borod, J. C., Cicero, B. A., Obler, L. K., Welkowitz, J., Erhan, H. M., Santschi, C., ... & Whalen, J. R. (1998). Right hemisphere emotional perception: Evidence across multiple channels. *Neuropsychology*, *12*(3), 446.

Bourne, V. J., & Todd, B. K. (2004). When left means right: An explanation of the left cradling bias in terms of right hemisphere specializations. *Developmental Science*, *7*(1), 19–24.

Braunstein, L. M., Gross, J. J., & Ochsner, K. N. (2017). Explicit and implicit emotion regulation: A multi-level framework. *Social Cognitive and Affective Neuroscience*, *12*(10), 1545–1557.

Carpenter, L. L., Shattuck, T. T., Tyrka, A. R., Geracioti, T. D., & Price, L. H. (2011). Effect of childhood physical abuse on cortisol stress response. *Psychopharmacology*, *214*(1), 367–375.

Carr, L., Iacoboni, M., Dubeau, M. C., Mazziotta, J. C., & Lenzi, G. L. (2003). Neural mechanisms of empathy in humans: A relay from neural systems for imitation to limbic areas. *Proceedings of the National Academy of Sciences*, *100*(9), 5497–5502.

Chong, T. T. J., Cunnington, R., Williams, M. A., Kanwisher, N., & Mattingley, J. B. (2008). fMRI adaptation reveals mirror neurons in human inferior parietal cortex. *Current biology*, *18*(20), 1576–1580.

Christman, S. D., Garvey, K. J., Propper, R. E., & Phaneuf, K. A. (2003). Bilateral eye movements enhance the retrieval of episodic memories. *Neuropsychology*, *17*(2), 221.

Costafreda, S. G., Brammer, M. J., David, A. S., & Fu, C. H. (2008). Predictors of amygdala activation during the processing of emotional stimuli: A meta-analysis of 385 PET and fMRI studies. *Brain Research Reviews*, *58*(1), 57–70.

Crugnola, C. R., Ierardi, E., Bottini, M., Verganti, C., & Albizzati, A. (2019). Childhood experiences of maltreatment, reflective functioning and attachment in adolescent and young adult mothers: Effects on mother-infant interaction and emotion regulation. *Child Abuse & Neglect*, *93*, 277–290.

Crugnola, C. R., Ierardi, E., Gazzotti, S., & Albizzati, A. (2014). Motherhood in adolescent mothers: Maternal attachment, mother–infant styles of interaction and emotion regulation at three months. *Infant Behavior and Development*, *37*(1), 44–56.

Dannlowski, U., Kugel, H., Huber, F., Stuhrmann, A., Redlich, R., Grotegerd, D., ... & Arolt, V. (2013). Childhood maltreatment is associated with an automatic negative emotion processing bias in the amygdala. *Human Brain Mapping*, *34*(11), 2899–2909.

Dannlowski, U., Stuhrmann, A., Beutelmann, V., Zwanzger, P., Lenzen, T., Grotegerd, D., ... & Lindner, C. (2012). Limbic scars: Long-term consequences of childhood maltreatment revealed by functional and structural magnetic resonance imaging. *Biological Psychiatry*, *71*(4), 286–293.

Diekelmann, S., Wilhelm, I., & Born, J. (2009). The whats and whens of sleep-dependent memory consolidation. *Sleep Medicine Reviews*, *13*(5), 309–321.

Dimberg, U., Thunberg, M., & Elmehed, K. (2000). Unconscious facial reactions to emotional facial expressions. *Psychological Science*, *11*(1), 86–89.

Douet, V., & Chang, L. (2015). Fornix as an imaging marker for episodic memory deficits in healthy aging and in various neurological disorders. *Frontiers in Aging Neuroscience*, *6*, 343.

Enticott, P. G., Johnston, P. J., Herring, S. E., Hoy, K. E., & Fitzgerald, P. B. (2008). Mirror neuron activation is associated with facial emotion processing. *Neuropsychologia*, *46*(11), 2851–2854.

Erikson, E. H. (1993). *Childhood and society*. New York: WW Norton & Company.

Farroni, T., Massaccesi, S., Pividori, D., & Johnson, M. H. (2004). Gaze following in newborns. *Infancy*, *5*(1), 39–60.

Forgas, J. P. (1998). On being happy and mistaken: Mood effects on the fundamental attribution error. *Journal of Personality and Social Psychology*, *75*(2), 318.

Fox, S. E., Levitt, P., & Nelson III, C. A. (2010). How the timing and quality of early experiences influence the development of brain architecture. *Child Development*, *81*(1), 28–40.

Franchow, E.I., & Suchy, Y. (2015). Naturally-occurring expressive suppression in daily life depletes executive functioning. *Emotion*, *15*(1), 78–89

Gainotti, G. (2012). Unconscious processing of emotions and the right hemisphere. *Neuropsychologia*, *50*(2), 205–218.

Geraerts, E., Merckelbach, H., Jelicic, M., & Smeets, E. (2006). Long term consequences of suppression of intrusive anxious thoughts and repressive coping. *Behaviour Research and Therapy*, *44*(10), 1451–1460.

Gorka, A. X., Hanson, J. L., Radtke, S. R., & Hariri, A. R. (2014). Reduced hippocampal and medial prefrontal gray matter mediate the association between reported childhood maltreatment and trait anxiety in adulthood and predict sensitivity to future life stress. *Biology of Mood & Anxiety Disorders*, *4*(1), 1–10.

Hains, S. M., & Muir, D. W. (1996). Infant sensitivity to adult eye direction. *Child Development*, *67*(5), 1940–1951.

Hanson, J. L., Albert, D., Iselin, A. M. R., Carre, J. M., Dodge, K. A., & Hariri, A. R. (2016). Cumulative stress in childhood is associated with blunted reward-related brain activity in adulthood. *Social Cognitive and Affective Neuroscience*, *11*(3), 405–412.

Hanson, J. L., Hariri, A. R., & Williamson, D. E. (2015). Blunted ventral striatum development in adolescence reflects emotional neglect and predicts depressive symptoms. *Biological Psychiatry*, *78*(9), 598–605.

Harmon-Jones, E., & Gable, P. A. (2018). On the role of asymmetric frontal cortical activity in approach and withdrawal motivation: An updated review of the evidence. *Psychophysiology*, *55*(1), e12879.

Harmon-Jones, E., Gable, P. A., & Peterson, C. K. (2010). The role of asymmetric frontal cortical activity in emotion-related phenomena: A review and update. *Biological Psychology*, *84*(3), 451–462.

Hu, T., Zhang, D., Wang, J., Mistry, R., Ran, G., & Wang, X. (2014). Relation between emotion regulation and mental health: A meta-analysis review. *Psychological Reports*, *114*(2), 341–362.

Jahangard, L., Tayebi, M., Haghighi, M., Ahmadpanah, M., Holsboer-Trachsler, E., Bahmani, D. S., & Brand, S. (2019). Does rTMS on brain areas of mirror neurons lead to higher improvements on symptom severity and empathy compared to the rTMS standard procedure?–Results from a double-blind interventional study in individuals with major depressive disorders. *Journal of Affective Disorders*, *257*, 527–535.

Kilner, J. M., Neal, A., Weiskopf, N., Friston, K. J., & Frith, C. D. (2009). Evidence of mirror neurons in human inferior frontal gyrus. *Journal of Neuroscience*, *29*(32), 10153–10159.

Kim, J., & Cicchetti, D. (2010). Longitudinal pathways linking child maltreatment, emotion regulation, peer relations, and psychopathology. *Journal of Child Psychology and Psychiatry*, *51*(6), 706–716.

Krautheim, J. T., Dannlowski, U., Steines, M., Neziroğlu, G., Acosta, H., Sommer, J., … & Kircher, T. (2019). Intergroup empathy: Enhanced neural resonance for ingroup facial emotion in a shared neural production-perception network. *Neuroimage*, *194*, 182–190.

Lakin, J. L., & Chartrand, T. L. (2003). Using nonconscious behavioral mimicry to create affiliation and rapport. *Psychological Science*, *14*(4), 334–339.

Lamm, C., & Majdandžić, J. (2015). The role of shared neural activations, mirror neurons, and morality in empathy–A critical comment. *Neuroscience Research, 90,* 15–24.

Lanius, R. A., Frewen, P. A., Tursich, M., Jetly, R., & McKinnon, M. C. (2015). Restoring large-scale brain networks in PTSD and related disorders: A proposal for neuroscientifically-informed treatment interventions. *European Journal of Psychotraumatology, 6*(1), 27313.

Likowski, K. U., Mühlberger, A., Gerdes, A., Wieser, M. J., Pauli, P., & Weyers, P. (2012). Facial mimicry and the mirror neuron system: Simultaneous acquisition of facial electromyography and functional magnetic resonance imaging. *Frontiers in Human Neuroscience, 6,* 214.

Lim, L., Howells, H., Radua, J., & Rubia, K. (2020). Aberrant structural connectivity in childhood maltreatment: A meta-analysis. *Neuroscience & Biobehavioral Reviews, 116,* 406–414.

Lindquist, K. A., Wager, T. D., Kober, H., Bliss-Moreau, E., & Barrett, L. F. (2012). The brain basis of emotion: A meta-analytic review. *The Behavioral and Brain Sciences, 35*(3), 121.

Luijten, M., Schellekens, A. F., Kühn, S., Machielse, M. W., & Sescousse, G. (2017). Disruption of reward processing in addiction: An image-based meta-analysis of functional magnetic resonance imaging studies. *JAMA Psychiatry, 74*(4), 387–398.

MacMillan, H. L., Georgiades, K., Duku, E. K., Shea, A., Steiner, M., Niec, A., ... & Walsh, C. A. (2009). Cortisol response to stress in female youths exposed to childhood maltreatment: Results of the youth mood project. *Biological Psychiatry, 66*(1), 62–68.

Malle, B. F. (2006). The actor-observer asymmetry in attribution: A (surprising) meta-analysis. *Psychological Bulletin, 132*(6), 895.

Marusak, H. A., Etkin, A., & Thomason, M. E. (2015). Disrupted insula-based neural circuit organization and conflict interference in trauma-exposed youth. *NeuroImage: Clinical, 8,* 516–525.

Mattern, M., Walter, H., Hentze, C., Schramm, E., Drost, S., Schoepf, D., ... & Schnell, K. (2015). Behavioral evidence for an impairment of affective theory of mind capabilities in chronic depression. *Psychopathology, 48*(4), 240–250.

McCrory, E. J., Gerin, M. I., & Viding, E. (2017). Annual research review: Childhood maltreatment, latent vulnerability and the shift to preventative psychiatry–the contribution of functional brain imaging. *Journal of Child Psychology and Psychiatry, 58*(4), 338–357.

McGilchrist, I. (2019). *The master and his emissary: The divided brain and the making of the western world.* New Haven, CT: Yale University Press.

Mesman, J., van IJzendoorn, M. H., & Bakermans-Kranenburg, M. J. (2009). The many faces of the still-face paradigm: A review and meta-analysis. *Developmental Review, 29*(2), 120–162.

Monk, C. S., Webb, S. J., & Nelson, C. A. (2001). Prenatal neurobiological development: Molecular mechanisms and anatomical change. *Developmental Neuropsychology, 19*(2), 211–236.

Moore, G. A., Cohn, J. F., & Campbell, S. B. (2001). Infant affective responses to mother's still face at 6 months differentially predict externalizing and internalizing behaviors at 18 months. *Developmental Psychology, 37*(5), 706.

Myers, D. G., & Smith, S. M. (2015). *Exploring social psychology*. New York, NY: McGraw-Hill.

Najt, P., Bayer, U., & Hausmann, M. (2013). Models of hemispheric specialization in facial emotion perception—a reevaluation. *Emotion, 13*(1), 159.

Niedenthal, P. M., & Brauer, M. (2012). Social functionality of human emotion. *Annual Review of Psychology, 63*, 259–285.

Oberman, L. M., Winkielman, P., & Ramachandran, V. S. (2007). Face to face: Blocking facial mimicry can selectively impair recognition of emotional expressions. *Social Neuroscience, 2*(3–4), 167–178.

Patel, S., Oishi, K., Wright, A., Sutherland-Foggio, H., Saxena, S., Sheppard, S. M., & Hillis, A. E. (2018). Right hemisphere regions critical for expression of emotion through prosody. *Frontiers in Neurology, 9*, 224.

Philip, N. S., Sweet, L. H., Tyrka, A. R., Price, L. H., Carpenter, L. L., Kuras, Y. I., ... & Niaura, R. S. (2013). Early life stress is associated with greater default network deactivation during working memory in healthy controls: A preliminary report. *Brain Imaging and Behavior, 7*(2), 204–212.

Phillips, R. G., & LeDoux, J. E. (1995). Lesions of the fornix but not the entorhinal or perirhinal cortex interfere with contextual fear conditioning. *Journal of Neuroscience, 15*(7), 5308–5315.

Prochazkova, E., & Kret, M. E. (2017). Connecting minds and sharing emotions through mimicry: A neurocognitive model of emotional contagion. *Neuroscience & Biobehavioral Reviews, 80*, 99–114.

Ross, E. D., & Monnot, M. (2008). Neurology of affective prosody and its functional–anatomic organization in right hemisphere. *Brain and Language, 104*(1), 51–74.

Rüsch, N., Bracht, T., Kreher, B. W., Schnell, S., Glauche, V., Il'yasov, K. A., ... & van Elst, L. T. (2010). Reduced interhemispheric structural connectivity between anterior cingulate cortices in borderline personality disorder. *Psychiatry Research: Neuroimaging, 181*(2), 151–154.

Rüsch, N., Luders, E., Lieb, K., Zahn, R., Ebert, D., Thompson, P. M., ... & van Elst, L. T. (2007). Corpus callosum abnormalities in women with borderline personality disorder and comorbid attention-deficit hyperactivity disorder. *Journal of Psychiatry & Neuroscience, 32*(6), 417.

Schiffer, F., Teicher, M. H., & Papanicolaou, A. C. (1995). Evoked potential evidence for right brain activity during the recall of traumatic memories. *The Journal of Neuropsychiatry and Clinical Neurosciences, 7*(2), 169–175.

Schmidt, S. N., Sojer, C. A., Hass, J., Kirsch, P., & Mier, D. (2020). fMRI adaptation reveals: The human mirror neuron system discriminates emotional valence. *Cortex, 128*, 270–280.

Schore, A. N. (2001). Effects of a secure attachment relationship on right brain development, affect regulation, and infant mental health. *Infant Mental Health Journal, 22*(1–2), 7–66.

Shenk, C. E., & Fruzzetti, A. E. (2011). The impact of validating and invalidating responses on emotional reactivity. *Journal of Social and Clinical Psychology, 30*(2), 163–183.

Sheridan, M. A., Fox, N. A., Zeanah, C. H., McLaughlin, K. A., & Nelson, C. A. (2012). Variation in neural development as a result of exposure to institutionalization early in childhood. *Proceedings of the National Academy of Sciences, 109*(32), 12927–12932.

Smith, S. D., & Bulman-Fleming, M. B. (2005). An examination of the right-hemisphere hypothesis of the lateralization of emotion. *Brain and Cognition, 57*(2), 210–213.

Sripada, R. K., Swain, J. E., Evans, G. W., Welsh, R. C., & Liberzon, I. (2014). Childhood poverty and stress reactivity are associated with aberrant functional connectivity in default mode network. *Neuropsychopharmacology, 39*(9), 2244–2251.

Stevens, F. L., & Taber, K. H. (2021). The neuroscience of empathy and compassion in pro-social behavior. *Neuropsychologia, 107925.*

Taylor, J. B. (2009). *My stroke of insight.* London: Hachette UK.

Teicher, M. H., Andersen, S. L., Polcari, A., Anderson, C. M., Navalta, C. P., & Kim, D. M. (2003). The neurobiological consequences of early stress and childhood maltreatment. *Neuroscience & Biobehavioral Reviews, 27*(1–2), 33–44.

Teicher, M. H., Dumont, N. L., Ito, Y., Vaituzis, C., Giedd, J. N., & Andersen, S. L. (2004). Childhood neglect is associated with reduced corpus callosum area. *Biological Psychiatry, 56*(2), 80–85.

Teicher, M. H., Samson, J. A., Anderson, C. M., & Ohashi, K. (2016). The effects of childhood maltreatment on brain structure, function and connectivity. *Nature Reviews Neuroscience, 17*(10), 652.

Tottenham, N., Hare, T. A., Quinn, B. T., McCarry, T. W., Nurse, M., Gilhooly, T., … & Thomas, K. M. (2010). Prolonged institutional rearing is associated with atypically large amygdala volume and difficulties in emotion regulation. *Developmental Science, 13*(1), 46–61.

Trevarthen, C. (1996). Lateral asymmetries in infancy: Implications for the development of the hemispheres. *Neuroscience & Biobehavioral Reviews, 20*(4), 571–586.

Tursich, M., Ros, T., Frewen, P. A., Kluetsch, R. C., Calhoun, V. D., & Lanius, R. A. (2015). Distinct intrinsic network connectivity patterns of post-traumatic stress disorder symptom clusters. *Acta Psychiatrica Scandinavica, 132*(1), 29–38.

van der Knaap, L. J., & van der Ham, I. J. (2011). How does the corpus callosum mediate interhemispheric transfer? A review. *Behavioural Brain Research, 223*(1), 211–221.

van Harmelen, A. L., van Tol, M. J., van der Wee, N. J., Veltman, D. J., Aleman, A., Spinhoven, P., … & Elzinga, B. M. (2010). Reduced medial prefrontal cortex volume in adults reporting childhood emotional maltreatment. *Biological Psychiatry, 68*(9), 832–838.

Wallez, C., & Vauclair, J. (2011). Right hemisphere dominance for emotion processing in baboons. *Brain and Cognition, 75*(2), 164–169.

Walterfang, M., Chanen, A. M., Barton, S., Wood, A. G., Jones, S., Reutens, D. C., … & Pantelis, C. (2010). Corpus callosum morphology and relationship to orbitofrontal and lateral ventricular volume in teenagers with first-presentation borderline personality disorder. *Psychiatry Research: Neuroimaging, 183*(1), 30–37.

Weinberg, M. K., & Tronick, E. Z. (1996). Infant affective reactions to the resumption of maternal interaction after the still-face. *Child Development, 67*(3), 905–914.

Wood, A., Rychlowska, M., Korb, S., & Niedenthal, P. (2016). Fashioning the face: Sensorimotor simulation contributes to facial expression recognition. *Trends in Cognitive Sciences, 20*(3), 227–240.

Yu, S. T., Lee, K. S., & Lee, S. H. (2017). Fornix microalterations associated with early trauma in panic disorder. *Journal of Affective Disorders, 220,* 139–146.

Zanetti, M. V., Soloff, P. H., Nicoletti, M. A., Hatch, J. P., Brambilla, P., Keshavan, M. S., & Soares, J. C. (2007). MRI study of corpus callosum in patients with borderline personality disorder: A pilot study. *Progress in Neuro-Psychopharmacology and Biological Psychiatry, 31*(7), 1519–1525.

Zhuang, L., Wen, W., Trollor, J. N., Kochan, N. A., Reppermund, S., Brodaty, H., & Sachdev, P. (2012). Abnormalities of the fornix in mild cognitive impairment are related to episodic memory loss. *Journal of Alzheimer's Disease, 29*(3), 629–639.

6 Self-Compassion

Self-compassion is the next skill I work on with patients after they can validate their emotions. Neff and Germer (2017) define self-compassion as "being touched by and open to one's own suffering, not avoiding or disconnecting from it, generating the desire to alleviate one's suffering and to heal oneself with kindness. Self-compassion also involves offering non-judgmental understanding to one's pain, inadequacies, and failures, so that one's experience is seen as part of the larger human experience." I'm not exactly sure how emotional awareness, emotional validation, or self-compassion all affect one another. There seems to be an interaction effect, where increasing one seems to increase the others. Too often though, individuals with psychopathology push away their emotional pain instead of accepting it, while research shows that acceptance of one's emotions with compassion can be transformative.

6.1 Primary and Secondary Emotions

Greenberg and Pascual-Leone (2006) make an important distinction between primary and secondary emotions. Secondary emotions are symptomatic emotions that result from the avoidance of a primary emotion. Individuals can also have tertiary emotions, resulting from the secondary emotions. For example, an individual may be ashamed (secondary emotion) by their sadness (primary emotion), and anytime a topic is broached that could potentially evoke the individual's shame, they get anxiety (tertiary emotion). In this example, avoiding one's anxiety also results in an avoidance of their shame and subsequence sadness. Enacting self-compassion for one's anxiety may help them recognize their shame, further self-compassion for shame could help them accept their sadness, and self-compassion for their sadness may result in self-acceptance and amelioration of their sadness. Once this sadness is accepted, the shame and anxiety that resulted from avoiding the sadness disappear. So, for some psychological disorders, just providing self-compassion, which can increase emotional acceptance, can be the solution. Occasionally I have helped patients with this in a session or two, but often it takes time in an

DOI: 10.4324/9781003150893-6

example like this to accept and regulate the anxiety, then the shame, and finally the sadness.

Self-compassion is inversely related to psychopathology (MacBeth & Gumley, 2012), and has been shown to be an effective intervention across many types of psychopathology (Ferrari et al., 2019). An fMRI study even demonstrated that compassion from a health care professional results in reduced feelings of distress, marked by a reduction in left AI activity (Sarinopoulos et al., 2013). Self-compassion is considered to have three components, the first being mindfulness, which was discussed earlier and creates an openness to our feelings. The second is common humanity, to recognize that we are all imperfect. This helps to normalize our feelings and not to assume that we are the first and only individuals to struggle with these emotions. The last component is self-kindness, which takes a non-judgmental stance towards the self. Here again, similar to when we validate our feelings, it is important not to judge our feelings, especially in a negative way. Common humanity helps with this as well, as we are often much more accepting of other's behaviors and feelings than we are of our own. By taking a non-judgmental stance towards our feelings, there is no shame in experiencing whatever feeling may arise. Letting go of shame creates the self-acceptance necessary to reconsolidate feelings and change stuck states of negative emotion to a place of neutral acceptance.

6.2 Empathy and Self-Compassion

Reviewing the literature on self-compassion, it seems hard to find anything negative about self-compassion. Yet, given all the benefits of self-compassion, why might it be such a struggle to utilize? I think the bottom line here is, it's difficult to be with our feelings. To understand this better, let's start with examining compassion. Looking at etymology, compassion comes from the Latin "com" meaning "with" and "pati" meaning "to suffer." So, compassion involves suffering with someone, which initially does not sound like much fun. Psychological research shows that when we see someone else in a state of distress, depending upon how we respond to that distress, we can experience empathetic concern or personal distress (Batson, Fultz, & Schoenrade, 1987). Empathetic concern has been referred to as compassion (Singer & Klimecki, 2014), while personal distress results in feeling alarmed, worried, disturbed, and so on. Ashar, Andrews-Hanna, Dimidjian, and Wager (2017) examine the brain's response to empathetic concern and personal distress, which they call empathetic care and empathetic distress. Empathetic care resulted in a mixed feelings state marked by areas of mOFC, vmPFC, NA, and the VS. The mOFC, VS, and NA are part of the MCL, which reinforces rewarding behaviors (Taber, Black, Porrino, & Hurley, 2012). While empathetic distress, marked by feelings of distress, preferentially activated the PreMC and somatosensory cortex (S1 & S2). These regions are involved in the representation of self and others' body states. The authors suggest since no motor tasks were performed in the experiment, the PreMC, S1, and S2 might aid in sharing the experience of others. The researchers also found empathetic care and empathetic distress predicted charitable donations, with empathetic care being a stronger predictor of increased donations.

So, seeing someone in distress and empathizing with them can invoke differing responses: empathic concern or personal distress. Recently the value of empathy, which has typically been considered to be a positive quality, has become debated (Da Loba, 2016). With some like Paul Bloom (2017) arguing in his book *Against Empathy* that empathy is actually harmful to morality. One of the challenges in this work is understanding what exactly empathy is. According to the neuroscience research, empathy is not one single process. Empathy can be divided into two basic components: cognitive empathy, which is the ability to understand another's experience through perspective-taking; and affective empathy, which is feeling someone's emotion. Cognitive empathy and affective empathy are both functionally and regionally specific in the brain (Shamay-Tsoory, Tomer, Goldsher, Berger, & Aharon-Peretz, 2004; Stietz, Jauk, Krach, & Kanske, 2019). Cognitive empathy involves the use of TP, TPJ, and the STS, regions involved in mentalizing and theory of mind, along with dmPFC, and vmPFC, which are involved in judgment and decision making (Bzdok et al., 2012; Fan, Duncan, de Greck, & Northoff, 2011; Schnell, Bluschke, Konradt, & Walter, 2011). These more neocortical brain regions allow us to understand another better, to put ourselves in someone else's shoes. Affective empathy involves the AI and dACC areas, which are related to the experience and evaluative of emotion (Corradi-Dell'Acqua, Tusche, Vuilleumier, & Singer, 2016; Jauniaux, Khatibi, Rainville, & Jackson, 2019). It is also important to distinguish affective empathy from emotional contagion. With affective empathy, you recognize the emotion is coming from outside yourself, whereas with emotional contagion you don't know the source of the emotion (Walter, 2012). We might assume that when feeling affective empathy for someone, we would be inclined to help him or her. However, that is not necessarily the case, and little evidence exists to demonstrate that empathy leads to pro-social behavior (Eisenberg & Miller, 1987; Vachon, Lynam, & Johnson, 2014). In fact, some evidence exists demonstrating that empathy actually makes us less pro-social (Decety & Yoder, 2016). This is often referred as to as the collapse of compassion, illustrated by the common phrase, "One death is a tragedy, a million deaths are a statistic." This phenomenon has been demonstrated empirically (Cameron & Payne, 2011; Västfjäll, Slovic, Mayorga, & Peters, 2014) and supports the idea that although affective empathy may increase our concern for someone else, at a certain point we are too overwhelmed to care anymore. Cameron et al. (2019) even tried paying individuals to care more and found that participants would rather avoid feeling affective empathy. So, is Paul Bloom correct in labeling empathy as bad? Well, not all studies agree, and some do show a relationship between affective empathy and pro-social behavior (Ashar et al., 2017). Eisenberg and Fabes (1990) suggest that there may be an optimal level for affective empathy: too little and there is no motivation to help; too much and the individual is overwhelmed by feelings rendering them unable to direct resources to others in need. Some support for this theory comes from a study with a rodent population, which manipulated stress levels in rats and observed helping. Results showed that a moderate stress response was most related to helping behavior (Ben-Ami Bartal et al., 2016). FeldmanHall, Dalgleish, Evans, and Mobbs (2015) also find that if individuals can respond to their affective empathy with empathetic concern as opposed to personal distress, individuals are more likely to engage in altruistic behavior. So, it may be that affective empathy itself is not the problem, but how we respond to and manage our affective empathy that makes the difference in whether we can engage in pro-social behavior, or have to leave and take care of ourselves.

There seem to be some definitive parallels here to being a therapist. Too little emotional investment in your patients and there may be a lack of motivation in seeing your patients succeed. Alternatively, too much emotional investment seems like a recipe for compassion fatigue or burnout. What determines whether we respond with empathetic concern or personal distress when seeing our patients suffer? Research is increasingly demonstrating the power of compassion in calming the central nervous system, regulating emotion, and subsequent increases in pro-social behavior (Kemeny et al., 2012; Stellar, Cohen, Oveis, & Keltner, 2015). Moreover, individuals trained in compassion show unique connectivity patterns within the brain when compared to novices, suggesting they are processing their emotions differently (Lutz, Brefczynski-Lewis, Johnstone, & Davidson, 2008). Engen and Singer (2015) found that compassion training helps to regulate emotion through the activation of mOFC, NA, and VS, which is the same reward network that we see activated during empathetic concern (Ashar et al., 2017). Perhaps it is the act of compassion that determines whether our affective empathy response results in empathetic concern or personal distress. Weisz and Zaki (2018) break down empathy into three brain processes. First is experience sharing, or affective empathy, which involves the dACC and AI. The second is empathetic concern, which involves reward circuits including VS, VTA, NA, and mOFC. The third is mentalizing, or cognitive empathy, which involves dmPFC, TJP, and TP. Interestingly, de Waal and Preston's (2017) work on empathy in primates shows a very similar empathic process. First, there is a transfer of feelings from one animal to another, much like emotional contagion or affective empathy. Secondly, the empathizing animal self-regulates that emotion and helps soothe the original animal in distress. Then thirdly, the empathizing animal engages in perspective-taking through which they can help solve the distressed animal's concern and they experience an intrinsic self-reward (de Waal & Preston, 2017). It seems it is compassion that can allow us to adapt our initial affective empathy response from a feeling of distress into a feeling of care for another. It's always distressful to experience another's suffering, yet compassion helps us to manage that distress, allowing us to then engage in altruistic behavior toward the other in need. Finally, cognitive empathy is utilized to understand how to best help the distressed individual (Stevens & Taber, 2021).

Unfortunately, affective empathy and compassion appear to be somewhat of a reflexive brain response; it's not necessarily a conscious choice between empathic concern or personal distress. Even trained therapists can struggle to be present with a patient's difficult emotions without falling into personal distress. Given such, I believe there are three important things to recognize about compassion. First, compassion, like most brain processes, takes effort, which means it's a limited resource (Inzlicht & Friese, 2019). In the short run, therapists might very well get burned out. This is okay if as a therapist you feel it's happening to you, then take care of yourself. Secondly, compassion is a skill and can be increased over time with training. Even if you're burned out now as a therapist, it doesn't mean it has to be a career-ender you for. Lastly, through practicing self-compassion, you will not only lower your own stress level, preventing burnout, you will also increase your emotional capacity for compassion with your patients.

6.3 Applying Self-Compassion

So far up to this chapter, we've covered being aware of emotions and validating emotions. Next, we need to provide compassion for emotions. One technique I use with patients is asking them how they would talk to a five-year-old who had a bad day at school. It seems for many people it is easier to practice compassion in this context. It seems relative to ourselves, we can be kinder to a five-year-old, it's easier not to judge a five-year-old for feeling down, and we can express to them that it is normal and okay to have bad days. Sometimes in this exercise patients will say, "Come on let's go outside and play tag," and I have to remind them to be sure to validate the child's experience. Once the patient acknowledges the child is feeling bad it is hard not to express care for that feeling. Usually, this is not too difficult. When I next ask the patient to try and express that same compassion to themselves, it often becomes much more difficult. Here patients struggle with self-judgment, self-criticism, and shame: all the opposite of self-compassion. I work with each of these reactions, being careful not to judge, shame, or even criticize the patient's self-judgments. I will not say it's irrational to think that way (even though it is). I try to help recognize the past benefits they may have gained from being so self-critical or judgmental. I might say something like, "Your self-criticism has pushed you to work hard and be successful, so it may be hard to let go of." This validates the patient's self-criticism and acknowledges the benefits that past harshness of self may have produced. Next, I work with the patients to see that there could be an alternative way where life can be smoother for them. I want the patient to think, "Could I still be successful without being so self-critical?" I might now say, "We know self-criticism has helped you be successful, but perhaps we can try a small experiment where we don't use self-criticism and see if we can still be successful. If it doesn't work out, you can always revert back to your old habits." I don't try to convince the patient with reason that his or her self-criticism is probably harming them; I ask them to try out self-compassion and see for themselves. I find a positive experience with self-compassion goes a lot farther than any reasoning. When I practice self-compassion with patients, I have the patient speak out loud to themselves, and if they can't do that, I provide the compassionate statement and then ask them to repeat it in their own words. This is important in intervention, as it helps patients take ownership over the process. I find the less psychoeducation I do and the more experiential learning the patient does in session, the better the outcomes. You learn more from doing than listening.

When practicing self-compassion, perfectionistic patients will often start chiding their ability to be self-compassionate. I find our response patterns to our emotions can be very ingrained and it takes a slow deliberate effort to undo them. Sometimes patients are surprised to recognize how mean they can be to themselves, recognizing they would never talk to a friend the way they talk to themselves. I sometimes point out how unfair it is of the patient that they are willing to let go of other's mistakes, but not their own. I use myself as an example to illustrate this saying, "Should I blame myself that you still have this disorder? The fact I haven't fixed it by now must mean I made a mistake." Patients will sometimes assure me it's not my fault. I point out that, "Me blaming myself for your problems could be just as arbitrary as you blaming yourself." Sometimes this humor and logic help, but more often it's just about caring for one's self. It sounds simple, but it's hard. Sometimes we try to find past instances of self-care and apply them to current emotions. If all else fails, I will say, "Part of you made this appointment for therapy; that's an act of self-care. We need to tap into that part, expanding it to apply to the rest of yourself." This can often result in a state of cognitive dissonance, where the patient simultaneously feels compelled to both care and criticize themselves. Somewhere along the way, the patient learned that being hard on themselves gets results. Maybe it's an internalized voice from a parent who withheld love as an expectation for high performance. I find it important to honor these past experiences. Noting to the patient you did what you needed to do to get love at the time. Some patients will hold on to the negative emotions, like a scarlet letter, a penance for past mistakes. It may take self-forgiveness to undo this self-punishment (see section 9.2). But once patients learn self-compassion, they will see themselves as deserving of feeling better.

Another tool I use for helping patients practice self-compassion is having patient video or audiotape themselves talking to themselves. Many different forms of therapy like internal family systems and self psychology have made reference to parts of the self. I often hear individuals refer to part of their self as the inner child. There are times when we feel strong and other times when we feel vulnerable and need support. As a therapist, I try to provide this support, but I know that I am not always able to be there for my patients, nor is it a viable long-term solution. So, I have patients' record video or audio messages offering supportive and self-compassion to themselves. The patients are then able to play these messages back to themselves as needed. This helps them practice skills to support and care for themselves, as well as integrate the different parts of themselves if you take that approach. Additionally, I have been told it can be helpful for patients to record themselves when they are distraught or panicking to review later and take a compassionate stance towards themselves. Like any skill when you are emotionally overwhelmed it is the hardest time to practice that skill. But through practicing self-compassion regularly and creating content like videos or writing supportive messages on the mirror, the patient develops a blueprint for how to respond to him or herself when they become emotionally upset. They then start being able to take care of themselves during an emotional crisis.

These first three steps I find are important for managing the challenging emotions that come up in therapy. Sometimes patients' problems can be solved during this initial process. But for patients with trauma or challenging emotional histories, more work will need to be done. Chapters 7 and 8 can help additionally prepare the patients for the difficult emotions that may arise in psychotherapy. The next chapter Understanding Emotion provides a way to help clinicians translate affective science to patients that may be wary of the process. Chapter 8 will be familiar to many clinicians as these are more traditional therapeutic techniques, however, the topic will be examined from an emotional and affective neuroscience perspective.

References

Ashar, Y. K., Andrews-Hanna, J. R., Dimidjian, S., & Wager, T. D. (2017). Empathic care and distress: Predictive brain markers and dissociable brain systems. *Neuron*, *94*(6), 1263–1273.

Batson, C. D., Fultz, J., & Schoenrade, P. A. (1987). Distress and empathy: Two qualitatively distinct vicarious emotions with different motivational consequences. *Journal of Personality*, *55*(1), 19–39.

Ben-Ami Bartal, I., Shan, H., Molasky, N. M., Murray, T. M., Williams, J. Z., Decety, J., & Mason, P. (2016). Anxiolytic treatment impairs helping behavior in rats. *Frontiers in Psychology*, *7*, 850.

Bloom, P. (2017). *Against empathy: The case for rational compassion*. London, UK: Random House.

Bzdok, D., Schilbach, L., Vogeley, K., Schneider, K., Laird, A. R., Langner, R., & Eickhoff, S. B. (2012). Parsing the neural correlates of moral cognition: ALE meta-analysis on morality, theory of mind, and empathy. *Brain Structure and Function*, *217*(4), 783–796.

Cameron, C. D., Hutcherson, C. A., Ferguson, A. M., Scheffer, J. A., Hadjiandreou, E., & Inzlicht, M. (2019). Empathy is hard work: People choose to avoid empathy because of its cognitive costs. *Journal of Experimental Psychology: General, 148*(6), 962.

Cameron, C. D., & Payne, B. K. (2011). Escaping affect: How motivated emotion regulation creates insensitivity to mass suffering. *Journal of Personality and Social Psychology, 100*(1), 1.

Corradi-Dell'Acqua, C., Tusche, A., Vuilleumier, P., & Singer, T. (2016). Cross-modal representations of first-hand and vicarious pain, disgust and fairness in insular and cingulate cortex. *Nature Communications, 7*(1), 1–12.

Da Loba, A. (2016, December 16). Does Empathy Guide or Hinder Moral Action? *The New York Times*. Retrieved from http://www.nytimes.com.

de Waal, F. B., & Preston, S. D. (2017). Mammalian empathy: Behavioural manifestations and neural basis. *Nature Reviews Neuroscience, 18*(8), 498–509.

Decety, J., & Yoder, K. J. (2016). Empathy and motivation for justice: Cognitive empathy and concern, but not emotional empathy, predict sensitivity to injustice for others. *Social Neuroscience, 11*(1), 1–14.

Eisenberg, N., & Fabes, R. A. (1990). Empathy: Conceptualization, measurement, and relation to prosocial behavior. *Motivation and Emotion, 14*(2), 131–149.

Eisenberg, N., & Miller, P. A. (1987). The relation of empathy to prosocial and related behaviors. *Psychological Bulletin, 101*(1), 91.

Engen, H. G., & Singer, T. (2015). Compassion-based emotion regulation up-regulates experienced positive affect and associated neural networks. *Social Cognitive and Affective Neuroscience, 10*(9), 1291–1301.

Fan, Y., Duncan, N. W., de Greck, M., & Northoff, G. (2011). Is there a core neural network in empathy? An fMRI based quantitative meta-analysis. *Neuroscience & Biobehavioral Reviews, 35*(3), 903–911.

FeldmanHall, O., Dalgleish, T., Evans, D., & Mobbs, D. (2015). Empathic concern drives costly altruism. *Neuroimage, 105*, 347–356.

Ferrari, M., Hunt, C., Harrysunker, A., Abbott, M. J., Beath, A. P., & Einstein, D. A. (2019). Self-compassion interventions and psychosocial outcomes: A meta-analysis of RCTs. *Mindfulness, 10*(8), 1455–1473.

Greenberg, L. S., & Pascual-Leone, A. (2006). Emotion in psychotherapy: A practice-friendly research review. *Journal of Clinical Psychology, 62*(5), 611–630.

Inzlicht, M., & Friese, M. (2019). The past, present, and future of ego depletion. *Social Psychology, 50*(5–6), 370–378.

Jauniaux, J., Khatibi, A., Rainville, P., & Jackson, P. L. (2019). A meta-analysis of neuroimaging studies on pain empathy: Investigating the role of visual information and observers' perspective. *Social Cognitive and Affective Neuroscience, 14*(8), 789–813.

Kemeny, M. E., Foltz, C., Cavanagh, J. F., Cullen, M., Giese-Davis, J., Jennings, P.,... & Ekman, P. (2012). Contemplative/emotion training reduces negative emotional behavior and promotes prosocial responses. *Emotion, 12*(2), 338.

Lutz, A., Brefczynski-Lewis, J., Johnstone, T., & Davidson, R. J. (2008). Regulation of the neural circuitry of emotion by compassion meditation: Effects of meditative expertise. *PloS One, 3*(3), e1897.

MacBeth, A., & Gumley, A. (2012). Exploring compassion: A meta-analysis of the association between self-compassion and psychopathology. *Clinical Psychology Review, 32*(6), 545–552.

Neff, K., & Germer, C. (2017). Self-compassion and psychological well-being. In Emma M. Seppälä et al., *The Oxford handbook of compassion science* (pp. 371–386). New York: Oxford University Press.

Sarinopoulos, I., Hesson, A. M., Gordon, C., Lee, S. A., Wang, L., Dwamena, F., & Smith, R. C. (2013). Patient-centered interviewing is associated with decreased responses to painful stimuli: An initial fMRI study. *Patient Education and Counseling, 90*(2), 220–225.

Schnell, K., Bluschke, S., Konradt, B., & Walter, H. (2011). Functional relations of empathy and mentalizing: An fMRI study on the neural basis of cognitive empathy. *Neuroimage, 54*(2), 1743–1754.

Shamay-Tsoory, S. G., Tomer, R., Goldsher, D., Berger, B. D., & Aharon-Peretz, J. (2004). Impairment in cognitive and affective empathy in patients with brain lesions: Anatomical and cognitive correlates. *Journal of Clinical and Experimental Neuropsychology, 26*(8), 1113–1127.

Singer, T., & Klimecki, O. M. (2014). Empathy and compassion. *Current Biology, 24*(18), R875–R878.

Stellar, J. E., Cohen, A., Oveis, C., & Keltner, D. (2015). Affective and physiological responses to the suffering of others: Compassion and vagal activity. *Journal of Personality and Social Psychology, 108*(4), 572.

Stevens, F. L., & Taber, K. H. (2021). The neuroscience of empathy and compassion in pro-social behavior. *Neuropsychologia, 107925*.

Stietz, J., Jauk, E., Krach, S., & Kanske, P. (2019). Dissociating empathy from perspective-taking: Evidence from intra-and inter-individual differences research. *Frontiers in Psychiatry, 10*, 126.

Taber, K. H., Black, D. N., Porrino, L. J., & Hurley, R. A. (2012). Neuroanatomy of dopamine: Reward and addiction. *The Journal of Neuropsychiatry and Clinical Neurosciences, 24*(1), 1–4.

Vachon, D. D., Lynam, D. R., & Johnson, J. A. (2014). The (non) relation between empathy and aggression: Surprising results from a meta-analysis. *Psychological Bulletin, 140*(3), 751.

Västfjäll, D., Slovic, P., Mayorga, M., & Peters, E. (2014). Compassion fade: Affect and charity are greatest for a single child in need. *PloS One, 9*(6), e100115.

Walter, H. (2012). Social cognitive neuroscience of empathy: Concepts, circuits, and genes. *Emotion Review, 4*(1), 9–17.

Weisz, E., & Zaki, J. (2018). Motivated empathy: A social neuroscience perspective. *Current Opinion in Psychology, 24*, 67–71.

7 Understanding Emotion

Once we have recognized, validated, and provided self-compassion for our feelings, the next step is to try and understand them. For if we can understand our feelings, we might be able to prevent negative feeling states in the future. Prior, it was discussed how we sometimes feel "crazy" when our feelings don't match the current situation. Emotional memories can get triggered, which causes us to react differently in situations than we would expect. So, our feelings sometimes are inconsistent with the environmental situation. Another problem can arise too when our feelings and thoughts influence us towards different behavioral choices. This is because the way we feel and think about something doesn't always match. I think we carry around an assumption that our brains should be coherent, but that is not always the case.

Sometimes we can think one way about a situation and feel another. Remember dual systems theory (see section 3.1); sometimes the intuitive response and rational response come into conflict. I used to give this example to my students: say you have an exam tomorrow and a friend asks you to go out for pizza. In this situation, you might be conflicted, thinking you should stay home and study, while also really desiring to go out and have fun. This is a basic example of very mild mental distress, which results in feelings of stress and discomfort. Deciding what to do is stressful here. If we stay home we will be disappointed that we did not go out, while if we go out, we will feel guilty for not studying. It is seemingly a no-win situation, leaving one in a state of mental discomfort no matter which option is chosen. Our thoughts push us to behave one way, our feelings in a different way. Deciding what to do is not easy and we could be upset by either choice. In simple terms, this could be understood as two brain systems coming into conflict. In our brain there exists an older subcortical limbic system and a newer prefrontal cortex region, both of which influence our behavior. The limbic system is often referred to as the "feeling" brain, whereas the prefrontal cortex is considered the "thinking" brain. Between the regions is the ACC, which as discussed earlier, is where conflict often occurs, and the conflict is between thoughts and feelings.

First, if we accept that our thoughts and feelings don't have to match

DOI: 10.4324/9781003150893-7

it's easier to accept conflict within the self. By allowing ourselves to have conflicting interests, it helps us to understand our thoughts and emotions. In reference to the prior example, if we don't accept our contradictory thoughts and feelings, we might assume that we don't care about our exam if we go out, or we don't care about friends if we stay in. Accepting the conflict helps us recognize we can have competing interests within ourselves. Accepting this conflict may be difficult because the brain does not like contradictory states (see cognitive dissonance theory, Festinger, 1957). Yet if we can accept this conflict, it allows us to recognize more thoughts and feelings, and in doing so a decision can be made. For in either going out for pizza with friends or staying home and studying, thoughts and feelings exist for both choices. One can recognize that in addition to thinking they should stay home and study; there also exists a feeling about wanting to do well on the exam or passing the course and graduating. Furthermore, in addition to feeling like going out, a thought exists around that choice too. One might consider, "I don't get many opportunities to go out and see my friends," or "I recognize that I can call and make plans to go out later in the week." When the individual can recognize their thoughts and feelings for both choices, then they can make a sound decision to stay home or go out, without suffering from anxiety or regret. Taking time to understand our thoughts and our feelings helps us to make good decisions, along with preventing stress and discomfort when the brain is in contradiction.

I think as therapists we can often make a mistake here. When the brain is in conflict, we treat the conflict as the problem. Offering skills like deep breathing and relaxation with the goal of reducing the symptoms the conflict creates. This is not directly harmful, but it can have the unintended consequence of trying to mitigate the conflict as the goal of treatment, instead of trying to understand what is causing the conflict. If therapists just help the patient lower the discomfort caused by the conflict they might feel better, but they would still be uncertain about what to choose: "Should I go out for pizza or stay home and study?" It is only when you access and listen to your thoughts and feelings that you can make a balanced decision without regret. If therapists just treat the conflict, they only treat the symptom and miss the problem causing the conflict. If someone is depressed, we can treat the symptoms of depression, but we if just treat the symptoms we miss what is causing the depression. Through understanding emotions better, we can understand the problem behind the symptoms. I think we need to reconceptualize psychopathology as a reaction to problems and not the problem itself. I used to think that when I got sick, having a headache, sore throat, and fatigue were the problem. Recently I have started to reconceptualize that assumption. Now I think that getting sick is my body's way of taking over to help me change my behavior. Typically, before I get sick, I have not been treating my body all that well; I'm not eating well, not sleeping, probably not washing my hands. At this point, germs are building up in my body because I'm doing a bad job running things. My body, looking out for my or its own best interests, produces symptoms of headache, sore throat, and fatigue to get me to slow down and take care of myself. The headache, sore throat, fatigue are not the problem: the germs are. I think those symptoms are there to change my behavior, so my body can fight the germs. If I don't change my behavior to take better care of my body, no amount of aspirin, throat lozenges, or cough drops is going to prevent me from getting sick again. So, helping patients manage difficult emotions is only part of what is needed; patients also need to understand what that emotion is telling them so they can fix the problem.

7.1 Misattribution of Emotion

Taking time to understand our emotions also keeps us from misattributing our feelings. Sometimes when we have a strong feeling, we can misattribute it to something in our immediate environment. Again, this is illustrated in the famous Dutton and Aron (1974) experiment where study participants were more likely to rate a female confederate as more attractive if they had just crossed a shaky bridge. The theory is that the feeling of increased arousal was attributed to the female, when actually it was the result of crossing a dangerous bridge. In recognizing that our emotions are not always germane to the situation, it's important to be aware of the feelings, so we don't misattribute them. For example, in couples therapy, I've seen that one partner often interprets the other partner's behavior as hurtful to them. The first partner's hurt is real; however, the assumption that their spouse is intentionally trying to hurt them may be false. Because the hurt feeling is so strong, they are quick to attribute it to what is most apparent in the environment, the spouse. The spouse's behavior may have triggered an emotional memory from the past which activated the strong feeling of hurt (see section 5.1). Even in situations where the spouse's behavior did actually hurt, it may not have been their intention. Strong feelings can be easily misattributed and it's hard to convince the person otherwise, especially if there is little to no trust. This is true for marriages and psychotherapy relationships. I had a patient who was convinced that their inability to orgasm during sex was because their partner did not care about them, even though there were obvious physical explanations. I had a patient who was convinced that his job was causing his depression, even though he had been depressed since childhood and held multiple jobs before his current one. These are all examples of misattribution of emotion, and I've learned that trying to change these patients' minds to what seems obvious to me is waste of time. Often there is an emotional incentive to not knowing the truth. If the partner can be blamed for the lack of orgasm, that patient doesn't have to accept their physical limitations, or if work can be blamed for depression, then the patient's feelings and past trauma don't need to be addressed.

I encourage therapists not to spend time trying to convince their patients of what may be obvious, but instead to help patients to recognize feelings, validate them, and build self-compassion. In doing so, the emotions start to untangle and the patient is no longer emotionally afraid to recognize these obvious truths. Support and care go a lot farther than reason.

In understanding our emotions, it's important to recognize that all of our feelings are valid but our attributions for them are not always correct. A common example of this I see is with patients who have an anxiety disorder and continually want help to fix problems in their environment. They attribute their anxiety to an external cause when the cause is really internal. These patients have anxiety, and they will always find something to be anxious about; addressing the external sources never fixes the problem. Here I try to get the patient to focus more on themselves and their feelings and less on the external environment. Once they start seeing results, they will often recognize that they are misattributing internal anxiety to external sources. One way to prevent the misattribution of emotion is to slow down and be with your feelings before rushing to assume what is causing them. This can often help individuals who too often attribute their internal emotions to others around them, and they consequently have a lot of tumultuous relationships. Judging our feelings too quickly can lead one to dismiss them without full consideration. I encourage patients to be curious about their feelings and take a moment before reacting to a strong feeling. This extra time allows for further processing of the emotion to take place in the brain and recognizing alternative interpretations. This can be especially important for negative emotions. Since negative feelings feel bad by definition, we often want to get rid of these feelings quickly, either by attributing them to someone or something else, or by dismissing them. I think not only do we not want to feel the negative emotion, we worry that by experiencing the negative feeling we'll engage in negative behavior. Remember that the feelings don't directly cause negative behavior, only our reactions to them. If we can accept our feelings to understand them before reacting, we can learn from the feelings. This, of course, is the original purpose of feelings and will ultimately help us solve the problem.

7.2 Emotional Arousal

It's important to monitor your patient's level of emotional arousal. Research has shown that a moderate level of arousal is best for therapeutic outcomes (Carryer & Greenberg, 2010; Corrigan, Fisher, & Nutt, 2011). This is similar to the historical Yerkes and Dodson (1908) inverted U theory for task performance. The research demonstrates that performance is maximized when physiological or mental arousal is at a moderate level. Too low and the participant is bored and not engaged in the task, too high and the participant is too overwhelmed to perform at their best. This is why we like to play sports against someone around our own level; if it's too easy, there is no challenge and if too hard, we give up. This same principle can be applied to therapy, which is why clinicians should be cognizant of the level of emotion the patient is experiencing. Too little emotion in therapy could mean the patient is not engaged or avoiding something. Too much emotion and the patient is too overwhelmed, unable to apply new coping mechanisms or take time to learn from their feelings. A strong therapist should be up-regulating and down-regulating a patient's emotion to maintain a moderate level of arousal. One of the common debates in psychotherapy is which treatment modality is best for patients. Often this debate arises between those from a psychodynamic background and those from a CBT background. While each modality has a different theoretical understanding of the mind, the primary difference in treatment styles is whether the goal of therapy is up-regulating or down-regulating emotion (Stevens, 2019). Psychodynamic clinicians see their job as activating unconscious affect-laden memories, usually from childhood, while CBT clinicians often understand their role as someone who helps patients to down-regulate their feelings. In my experience, good clinicians both help increase feelings when a patient is dissociated from emotions and down-regulate feelings when a patient becomes overwhelmed. It is in this moderate stage of arousal, where a patient is activating new emotions but not overwhelmed, where the greatest therapeutic change can happen.

Sometimes we can start working with our feelings right away as we notice them. Other times our feelings may be too overwhelming to work with productively. In this case, we need to build coping or emotion regulation skills before moving on. Next, we will talk about emotion regulation skills. If the emotion currently is at a moderate arousal level, clinicians can then move on to working with specific emotions. However, it can be beneficial for patients to have some of these skills should they become overwhelmed with feelings.

References

Carryer, J. R., & Greenberg, L. S. (2010). Optimal levels of emotional arousal in experiential therapy of depression. *Journal of Consulting and Clinical Psychology, 78*, 190–199. doi:10.1037/a0018401.

Corrigan, F. M., Fisher, J. J., & Nutt, D. J. (2011). Autonomic dysregulation and the window of tolerance model of the effects of complex emotional trauma. *Journal of Psychopharmacology, 25*, 17–25. doi:10.1177/0269881109354930.

Dutton, D. G., & Aron, A. P. (1974). Some evidence for heightened sexual attraction under conditions of high anxiety. *Journal of Personality and Social Psychology, 30*(4), 510.

Festinger, L. (1957). *A theory of cognitive dissonance* (Vol. 2). California: Stanford University Press.

Stevens, F. L. (2019). Affect regulation and affect reconsolidation as organizing principles in psychotherapy. *Journal of Psychotherapy Integration, 29*(3), 277.

Yerkes, R. M., & Dodson, J. D. (1908). The relation of strength of stimulus to rapidity of habit-formation. *Journal of Comparative Neurology and Psychology, 18*(5), 459–482.

8 Emotional Regulation/Coping with Emotion

This section will address ways to down-regulate emotion. These are skills therapists can use with patients in session when they might be feeling too much emotion. They are also skills that ideally should be practiced when a patient is not emotionally overwhelmed. Just like a musician will practice getting things down before the pressure of a big performance, patients benefit most when they practice emotional regulation skills before they actually need them. When emotionally overwhelmed it is hard to master a new skill. Just like any skill too, regular practice improves ability.

One comment I find myself repeating to my patients is: "**You can't change your feelings, you can only change how you respond to your feelings**." This means that once you have a feeling, you can't wish it away, and doing that invalidates one's emotional experience. Sometimes when I tell this to other clinicians there is some confusion. I don't mean to say you can't mitigate or prevent future feelings through therapeutic interventions. Depending upon how you respond to your anxiety, you can make it better or worse in the future. Deep breathing, as opposed to cycling through anxious thoughts, will prevent anxiety from escalating. Yet, there are limits to what emotional regulation skills can do. For example, in borderline personality disorder where a patient often holds highly negative views of themselves, emotional regulation skills can minimize the extreme feelings of self-hate by learning to manage and control the feelings. They don't eliminate them, because you cannot change one's self-image through emotion regulation. These feelings need to be accepted and potentially reconsolidated (see Chapter 11). So, for many feelings like sadness, if you're sad; you're sad. You can try and distract yourself or avoid the feeling, but it does not just go away (for a good example of this watch the children's film *Inside Out* [Docter & Del Carmen, 2015]). What individuals can do and where they do have power and control is in how they respond to their feelings. As discussed earlier accepting, validating, and providing self-compassion for your feelings is an important first step. Next, applying coping skills will help in regulating emotion. This helps the patient get confident in having mastery over their feelings. If patients don't feel comfortable in their ability to

DOI: 10.4324/9781003150893-8

regulate their feelings, they often won't continue in the therapeutic process to ameliorate fully their psychological disorder. Typically, in these situations, once the patient has gotten past the original emotional stressor, they discontinue therapy, not wanting to explore the basis of the emotional stressor, because they don't feel confident in managing these feelings as they arise.

Many therapy modalities start by teaching coping skills. I will do this too if the patient presents in an acute state of overwhelming distress. In these cases, raising emotional awareness, validating emotions, or self-compassion is not as important as mitigating the overwhelming feeling to help the patient get through the acute distress. Moreover, if these feelings are not effectively regulated individuals may resort to more drastic measures like suicide or drug use to alleviate their emotional distress. **For patients in acute emotional distress, regulate emotions as the first step** (see section 8.3). However, most patients do not present in an acute state of distress, and for these individuals it is just as important to accept their emotions as it is to regulate them. It's interesting that most clinicians I see practicing from a psychodynamic orientation work with those of higher socioeconomic status in outpatient clinics, where most patients can independently down-regulate their emotions. My colleagues practicing CBT often work in inpatient and acute settings where managing emotional distress is the primary task. These patients need help down-regulating their feelings.

The challenge with psychodynamic modalities is they can at times overlook the importance of teaching emotional regulation skills to patients. I once had a supervisor who believed that he contributed to the suicidal death of one of his patients because he up-regulated emotions too quickly. Alternatively, the danger of therapeutic modalities that solely focus on teaching coping skills is that it can create an implied assumption that emotions are something to be controlled or tamed. Emotions become the villain, or something that needs to be extinguished, as opposed to listened to. Creating a therapeutic paradigm where emotions are valued allows patients to be more willing to accept their feelings and experience less shame around having difficult feelings. This next section will be an overview of coping skills. Many different types of therapies exist offering great coping skills to help individuals. Reviewing them all is beyond the scope of this book; below is a sample of skills I find effective. These skills are primarily used for individuals experiencing overwhelming levels of emotion.

8.1 Physiological Interventions

When emotionally overwhelmed, regardless of the emotion, the body will experience a sympathetic nervous response, commonly referred to as the flight or fight response. Whether the threat is real or perceived, the body will respond the same way. Typically, in a therapeutic environment, the threat is perceived, as the patient is in no real physical danger. However, regardless of the actual nature of the threat, the body can still go into shock if the sympathetic nervous response becomes too elevated. This can happen in the form of a panic attack, where an individual faints after the sympathetic nervous system can no longer adapt. This can happen in individuals with PTSD when they experience a traumatic flashback, and the nervous system becomes overwhelmed, resulting in a state of dissociation from self. Dissociative Identity Disorder is another example on the more extreme end. Sometimes these responses are referred to as maladaptive, but they are actually an adaptive coping response when your body can no longer cope with the stress of the emotion. This tonic immobility is seen through the animal species; when animals are under great duress, they will often resort to an apparent death or playing dead as a way to cope with the stressor (Humphreys & Ruxton, 2018). Tonic immobility also appears to be a last resort mechanism for humans to cope with a stressor when the sympathetic nervous system can no longer effectively respond. When patients are overwhelmed, clinicians want to decrease the sympathetic nervous response to prevent a state of tonic immobility or dissociation. One typical way to down-regulate the sympathetic nervous system is to regulate breathing. Breathing exercises are part of many therapy interventions for this reason. Deep breathing encourages slower breaths and helps restore oxygen to the body, which is quickly being used by the active sympathetic nervous system; this extra oxygen will decrease the likelihood of the patient fainting too. It can also be helpful to breathe with your patient, not only does this offer a live model, but it also creates a mirroring effect. Individuals tend to match the behavior of those around them; if the therapist offers a relaxed demeanor exhibiting deep breathing, often the patient will unconsciously match it (Chartrand & Bargh, 1999; Ramseyer & Tschacher, 2011). Regular practice of being aware of one's breathing and regulating breathing to a consistent rate will prevent future instances of an exaggerated sympathetic nervous response when the patient feels excessive emotion.

Physiology of the body and mind want to match; it's hard to be in a state of panic if your body is relaxed. So, any coping skills that can help regulate the body's physiology are also effective tools for managing mental distress. Muscle relaxation exercises where the patient learns to recognize and control the tightness or looseness of their muscles can be helpful. Stress is often associated with muscle tension and learning how to relax muscles helps regulate the sympathetic nervous response. To help a patient learn mastery over the tension in their muscles. I often have patients tense and relax different muscles within the body. This focus on a single muscle or group of muscles helps bring recognition to where certain tension may lie in the body. Additionally, through tensing and relaxing muscles patients gain a sense of agency in controlling the physiological tension in their bodies. Often individuals do not think to control the resting state of their body. We tend to restore back to our default posture unless conscious intention is paid. By focusing on a single muscle or group of muscles by tensing and releasing the tension, clinicians can help the patient recognize chronic tension they may hold and that they have the ability to let go of that tension.

In the flight or fight response, the body is on high alert, any methods that can be employed to mitigate the response can be helpful. For example, lying down is a physical position not associated with the flight or fight response, by having a patient lie on a couch can send a counter signal to the brain that they are safe. Playing relaxing music might be another example, anything that can reverse the sympathetic nervous response could be a useful tool in helping patients cope with overwhelming emotions. Some individuals can notice their heart rate and adjust to slow their pulse down. I've used biofeedback mechanisms with athletes in sports psychology training to help them become more attuned with their physiology and make adjustments as needed. These tools can be applied to clinical practice as well.

8.2 Cognitive Interventions

While the focus of this book is on emotions, it also valuable to recognize how our thoughts can affect emotions. While I don't believe thoughts can cause a primary or original emotion, thoughts can contribute to the reinforcement of secondary emotions (see section 6.1). One of the major assumptions of cognitive therapy is by changing cognitions you will then change affect. This rests on a cognitive primacy hypothesis that cognitive precedes emotion. On its face validity assuming the cognitive primacy hypothesis can be troubling. The premise assumes if we get bad news, we can always re-contextual this bad news to make ourselves feel better. For example, if we break our arm, we can examine the positives of the situation and our arm will feel better, or somehow the situation of having a broken arm will turn into a positive thing. However, where cognitive therapy can be helpful is not reinforcing negative feelings and not personalizing things. If you feel anxious because you are worried about losing a job and you think of all the bad things that will happen as a result, you will have more negative feelings, reinforcing the anxiety. Perhaps some things might be worthy of consideration, but for the most part that excessive thinking is called rumination and it's not good. Replaying bad events in your head only makes you feel worse, accepting the experience, validating it, and providing compassion for yourself is a much better use of your brain, instead of trying to go back and undo the past.

Cognitive reappraisal is also very useful for not overly personalizing events. If something goes wrong it can be practical to take some time and think about how you potentially contributed to the problem. However, many patients obsess over mistakes they made or assume that other's people poor behavior is about them. Now I cannot prove to my patients that when their colleague didn't ask them to lunch it wasn't personal. What we can do is examine the situation and see if there is a pattern. Perhaps the patient is doing something that offends others. If so, let's make changing that a therapeutic goal, otherwise we have to let it go. We'll never know the true intention of the colleague, but if the patient is acting in a way that is congruent to whom they want to be, we have to let go of other's actions. Maybe, that colleague has their own personal hang-ups or just doesn't like the color of our hair. Either way, I quickly examine the situation with the patient, make a judgment, and let it go. Ruminating on events that we have no control of serves no purpose. We have to accept that we can't please everyone in the world.

Neuroimaging research demonstrates that cognitive reappraisal can be a useful tool in regulating emotion (Wolgast, Lundh, & Viborg, 2011). Cognitive reappraisal involves the dlPFC, vlPFC, dmPFC, and posterior partial cortex (Buhle et al., 2014) the same areas the make up the central executive network (CEN). CEN is involved in executive function and carrying out goal-directed tasks, and the above research shows that the CEN can be activated in reducing amygdala activation often associated with emotional distress. A growing body of research is identifying the differences between explicit emotional regulation, largely defined as cognitive reappraisal, and implicit emotional regulation, largely defined as extinction learning (Braunstein, Gross, & Ochsner, 2017). The vmPFC and rACC areas involved in the inhibition and extinction of fear, are not active in cognitive reappraisal, and these areas are important for implicit emotional regulation (Etkin et al., 2015). Further studies support this dichotomy with some overlap in activity in the dACC and AI; it also has been suggested that the dACC and AI (see section 3.4) may not be part of an emotion regulation strategy, but rather an enduring emotional response (Picó-Pérez et al., 2019). Both explicit and implicit emotional regulation are considered effective strategies for managing emotion because they dampen amygdala activity (Ochsner et al., 2004; Buhle et al., 2014). However, with this explicit/implicit labeling distinction, implicit processes that involve more emotional areas of the brain are by definition not consciously recognized. Insinuating that for clinical practitioners we don't have the ability to intervene in changing these implicit processes. This may also create a bias in the field toward for clinicians to solely use explicit/cognitive interventions. Affective interventions may be harder to quantify because they often involve more implicit processes.

8.3 Suicidal Patients

Just as a moderate level of arousal is optimal for psychotherapy, so is a balance of cognition and affect. Previously we discussed the importance of up-regulating emotion when emotional awareness is low. Alternatively, it is just as important to recognize when a patient is overly emotionally focused and to help them to activate cognitive brain areas. This is most apparent to me when

I see suicidal patients. Typically, these patients are flooded with affect and want to escape the world. Once I've validated their feelings, I find it is extremely important to engage cognitions, to help patients remember that emotions are ephemeral, and these feelings will not last. I encourage them to remember how they do not always feel like this. I encourage them to see this experience as an episode, like a bad car accident that nobody would want to go through, but something that you can recover from. It is paramount for these patients to use cognitions to understand their emotional experience, that while they are currently overwhelmed this is a temporary state and will pass. Furthermore, with the right treatment, they can get better and not have to continue to experience these distressing episodes. Some suicidal patients do not present with overwhelming affect, and these patients worry me because they've been so emotionally troubled suicide is a relief. This is a delicate matter, I try to instill hope, talking about patients that have improved and with the right therapy and how things can change. I try to get the patient to see me as an ally, not someone who is trying to take away their escape option of suicide, but someone with a better plan. Don't up-regulate emotion with these patients until you feel safe.

References

Braunstein, L. M., Gross, J. J., & Ochsner, K. N. (2017). Explicit and implicit emotion regulation: A multi-level framework. *Social Cognitive and Affective Neuroscience, 12*(10), 1545–1557.

Buhle, J. T., Silvers, J. A., Wager, T. D., Lopez, R., Onyemekwu, C., Kober, H., ... & Ochsner, K. N. (2014). Cognitive reappraisal of emotion: A meta-analysis of human neuroimaging studies. *Cerebral Cortex, 24*(11), 2981–2990.

Chartrand, T. L., & Bargh, J. A. (1999). The chameleon effect: The perception–behavior link and social interaction. *Journal of Personality and Social Psychology, 76*(6), 893.

Docter, P., & Del Carmne, R. (2015). *Inside out [Film]*. Pixar.

Etkin, A., Büchel, C., & Gross, J. J. (2015). The neural bases of emotion regulation. *Nature Reviews Neuroscience, 16*(11), 693–700.

Humphreys, R. K., & Ruxton, G. D. (2018). A review of thanatosis (death feigning) as an anti-predator behaviour. *Behavioral Ecology and Sociobiology, 72*(2), 22.

Ochsner, K. N., Ray, R. D., Cooper, J. C., Robertson, E. R., Chopra, S., Gabrieli, J. D., & Gross, J. J. (2004). For better or for worse: Neural systems supporting the cognitive down-and up-regulation of negative emotion. *Neuroimage, 23*(2), 483–499.

Picó-Pérez, M., Alemany-Navarro, M., Dunsmoor, J. E., Radua, J., Albajes-Eizagirre, A., Vervliet, B., ... & Fullana, M. A. (2019). Common and distinct neural correlates of fear extinction and cognitive reappraisal: A meta-analysis of fMRI studies. *Neuroscience & Biobehavioral Reviews, 104*, 102–115.

Ramseyer, F., & Tschacher, W. (2011). Nonverbal synchrony in psychotherapy: Coordinated body movement reflects relationship quality and outcome. *Journal of Consulting and Clinical Psychology, 79*(3), 284.

Wolgast, M., Lundh, L. G., & Viborg, G. (2011). Cognitive reappraisal and acceptance: An experimental comparison of two emotion regulation strategies. *Behaviour Research and Therapy, 49*(12), 858–866.

9 Working with Specific Emotions

An emotion can be the result of an external or internal stimulus. A strong feeling can indicate we need to change something externally in our environment or it could indicate we need to change something internally within the individual. Given that emotions can often be misattributed, it's important to try and understand the emotion. Sometimes emotional can have multiple sources. In this chapter, we look at how to work with individual emotions and interventions for both externally and internally driven emotions.

9.1 Anger

Panksepp (2004) identifies areas of the amygdala, hypothalamus, and periaqueductal gray for being involved in the anger response. Panksepp finds that the anger circuit is hierarchically arranged; higher regions are dependent upon the lower regions. Thus, the amygdala is dependent upon the hypothalamus and periaqueductal gray, the hypothalamus is dependent upon periaqueductal gray, but the periaqueductal gray can operate independent of these areas, indicating that anger is a very primitive emotion. The OFC appears to be important in the regulation of the anger response, in both calculating reward expectations based on actions and in social response monitoring (Blair, 2004). If one were to think of Freud's id, the instinctual drive, as the periaqueductal gray, the OFC would be the equivalent of Freud's superego, monitoring the social costs of behavior.

Anger can be a difficult emotion for us to embrace due to some of the cultural norms around anger. Since the feeling of anger is often intertwined with maladaptive behaviors, the feeling of anger is often seen as pejorative. As a culture, we have chastised the feelings of anger, which should be considered separate from the behaviors that result from anger. We encourage others to not feel angry, assuming angry feelings will lead to bad behaviors. This invalidates individual's emotional experiences, often causing them to feel shame for their feelings. We can feel angry without having to act out in a negative way. We as a culture should see the feeling of anger separately from any behavior that might result from it. Therapists

DOI: 10.4324/9781003150893-9

should work with the feeling of anger in one capacity and the behavioral expression of the anger in another. For example, when a child's lunch is taken by another child at school, feeling angry is a natural response, but attacking the perpetrator with violence is a poor choice in how to respond. As caregivers, we want to validate the child's anger and think about the most adaptive behavioral responses. Assuming that the feeling of anger causes the maladaptive behavior confuses things and makes us believe our feeling is wrong. Therapists should work with the child in making smart behavioral choices, while at the same time trying better to understand the child's anger. Was the anger a normal reaction to being teased or could it have been an exaggerated response from built-up feelings of anger and resentment from the child's past? In the latter case, these feelings need to be addressed to prevent future episodes of excessive anger.

Anger is a feeling we get when something is not as we expect it to be, and we typically want to act on upon it. Anger is an approach emotion (Carver & Harmon-Jones, 2009), meaning that our natural inclination is to act when feeling angry. However, due to concerns about maladaptive behavior that result from anger, individuals often inhibit their anger, which leads to conflict within the brain. I have had many patients complain about their wife or boyfriend, and when I ask them why they don't address this complaint with their partner they say, "I don't want to start a fight or an argument:" a legitimate concern. However, by inhibiting their anger they are building resentment toward their partner over time, which is not good for any relationship. This also leads to confusion in many of my patients, because they are simultaneously angry at themselves for ignoring their concerns and angry at their partner for their difficult behavior, which makes sorting out the anger a challenge. Yet knowing where our anger is coming from (self vs. other) and not misattributing will be important in deciding how to act. Often, we develop habits throughout our lives where we tend to blame others or ourselves when something goes wrong. These habits can start early, and it can be helpful to know your habits when trying to understand anger. If we are too quick to blame others, we can miss opportunities to make personal changes. If we are too quick to blame ourselves, we can become overly critical, sometimes even self-loathing. Sometimes our anger is just a normal response. When someone hurts us, it's natural to feel anger. This often signals to us that we need to set a stronger boundary. Telling someone is it not okay to call you hurtful names would be an example of setting a boundary. It can be helpful for others to know your limits; for example, when friendly teasing is taken too far. However, when boundaries get repeatedly crossed, it is also important to set a consequence for when the boundary is not respected. An example of a consequence would be I refused to speak with you after you call me hurtful names.

Situations could also result in feelings of anger towards one's self. People who are not asserting themselves and letting others hurt them may feel angry with themselves too for not doing enough to protect themselves.

Anger toward self doesn't always have to be the result of hurt with another. People can be angry with themselves for not taking advantage of an opportunity or not performing their best. This type of anger, if left unresolved, can become self-destructive. In this case, individuals can start hurting themselves through unhealthy behaviors or negative self-talk. Individuals with built-up anger towards themselves or others, often need to engage in self-forgiveness and/or forgiveness.

9.2 Forgiveness and Self-Forgiveness

To let go of anger, the person who did the harm must be forgiven. Forgive means to give back; it literally means to take the anger someone has given you and give it back to them. Ostensibly this sounds easy, but it's often more complicated, and individuals are reluctant to forgive others. This is because holding on to one's anger can act as a useful form of self-protection. If someone tries to hurt us again, holding on to that anger gives us an immediate means through which to protect ourselves. When my anger gets activated, I can use that to protect myself or hurt someone else before they hurt me. We can react with that stored anger as a way to protect ourselves. Yet, carrying around that stored anger is also a burden. We need a better way to protect ourselves from hurt if we are going to let go of our anger. This can be done by changing ourselves, setting better boundaries, and not leaving ourselves vulnerable to hurt. If we can change ourselves to keep from getting hurt again, then we no longer need to hold on to that anger as a form of self-protection against this other person. An example in therapy would be a patient who is holding onto anger towards a parent for hurting them. They may carry around that anger toward the parent and be ready to unleash it should the parent try and hurt them again. Helping that patient grow to set boundaries as an adult around their parents, allows them to forgive the parent without the risk of being hurt again. So, often we have to change as individuals before we can forgive others.

This is true for self-forgiveness too. Often, we hold on to anger towards ourselves. This anger serves a purpose, acting as a reminder not to make the same mistakes that caused problems before. By holding on to this anger towards ourselves, we suffer continuously as we punish ourselves for our past mistakes. In self-forgiveness too, we need to change as individuals to help forgive ourselves. We need to recognize what caused those mistakes and understand that we are not the same person we were in the past. By making necessary personal changes we are no longer vulnerable to make those same mistakes again. We can then forgive ourselves, giving our anger (or any other emotion) back to our old selves. We no longer need anger as a reminder to manage our behavior. Letting go of difficult emotions like anger allows us to live more freely and less inhibited. Through forgiveness and self-forgiveness, we no longer need to be overly self-conscious or worry that we will engage in behaviors that will leave us hurt again.

We can trust that as a new more mature person, we can protect ourselves from others hurting us, and from self-inflicted hurt. Other emotions, like shame and guilt, can be lessened by forgiveness and self-forgiveness as well.

9.3 Abandonment and Loneliness

I've noticed as a group therapist when I ask the group what emotion(s) they like would like to cover, abandonment is a common request. Abandonment occurs when we've been neglected in some way. We feel left by others. Sometimes this can be an overwhelming feeling, often when this is the case it is the result of past feelings of abandonment being activated in connection with current feelings of abandonment. Some individuals are neglected as children, creating a feeling of abandonment, and when that feeling becomes too overwhelming, the child dissociates from the feeling, creating what you might call a stored trauma response. Then often small events happen in adulthood (e.g., a boyfriend forget to call you) which activate these overwhelming stored feelings of abandonment. Typically, the individual can be surprised and left feeling "crazy," because the feeling doesn't seem germane to the current situation. In this case, the best thing the individual can do is get support from someone else, the opposite of the neglected experience they had as a child. However, this may be more difficult than it ostensibly seems. Many individuals that have experienced abandonment try to protect themselves by shutting others out, which acts as a protection mechanism against being abandoned again. They are reluctant to reach out to others, because if they reach out and it's not returned, once again they are flooded with abandonment feelings. Since the feelings of abandonment are so overwhelming, individuals become afraid to trust others and isolate as a way of not putting themselves at risk for being abandoned again. This isolation over time leads to loneliness.

Loneliness is often a feeling we experience when we are afraid to express vulnerability around others. Individuals with abandonment history who choose to isolate naturally feel lonely. Loneliness can also result from a fear of social losses. I have seen patients who have lost spouses and were afraid to develop new relationships, out of fear they would be left feeling a deep loss again. The loneliness is a signal that individuals lack social connection. Some psychologists believe this is a built-in evolutionary mechanism to improve the survival of the organism; if left alone they are more vulnerable to environmental hazards (Cacioppo & Hawkley, 2009). Loneliness is not a positive feeling; research shows that the brain responds similarly to the pain of social loss as it does to physical pain, both activating dACC, and AI regions (Eisenberger, 2015). In overcoming loneliness, one may have to face fears of vulnerability and abandonment around others, for one cannot experience connection with others without the vulnerability of loss. In this sense, we cannot avoid feelings of abandonment or loneliness. In choosing to be with others we will inevitably feel loss when others leave us; it's an unavoidable existential dilemma. Here again, it is important to accept and work with our feelings rather than avoid them. Individuals who have experienced childhood neglect may need to reconsolidate those past feelings of trauma. Both individuals who have experienced the death of loved ones or had caregivers who didn't care have gone through a great loss, which results in sadness.

9.4 Sadness

Feeling sad is often the result of loss, such as a close relationship, and sadness is a normal healthy response. Of course, ongoing states of despair like loneliness can lead to chronic sadness. Panksepp (2010) identifies a distress circuit running from the periaqueductal gray, through areas of thalamus, and on to the ACC; interestingly, this circuit is inhibited by neuropeptides like oxytocin. Oxytocin is released during social bonding and helps to regulate stress levels (Heinrichs, Baumgartner, Kirschbaum, & Ehlert, 2003). Research shows that children who experienced early neglect subsequently showed a diminished oxytocin release in response to caregivers even after multiple years of nurturing in a stable environment (Fries, Ziegler, Kurian, Jacoris, & Pollak, 2005). This suggests that early life experiences like childhood maltreatment can have long-term effects on the brain's ability to manage emotions like sadness (see sections 5.4–5.6). Panksepp (2010) identifies the sadness circuit as a separation-distress system. He believes that secure attachment is so closely tied to mental health because separation from loved ones quickly results in distressful emotions. Pair-bonding neuropeptides like oxytocin regulate this circuit, and chronic sadness or depression could be our brain's signal that we need increased social connection. Sadness can also activate multiple brain networks like SN, DMN, and CEN. However, sadness is uniquely different from other emotions for its confinement between regions, especially for significantly reduced co-activation between cortical and subcortical regions (Arias et al., 2020). This could provide some insight as to why we often struggle to accept sadness. Whether intentional or not, there is a gap in connecting subcortical emotional areas with more conscious thinking areas.

Sometimes patients question the purpose or usefulness of feeling sad. I tell my patients that acknowledging sadness prevents suffering. Sometimes individuals encourage each other to get over or move on past their sadness, but this is not always healthy because it can lead to avoiding grief or even worse, shame about the feeling of sadness. As discussed earlier, not accepting or acknowledging the primary emotion of sadness leads to a secondary emotion, which is often depression or melancholy. By not accepting sadness (primary emotion) we are pushing away a feeling that wants to arise (see section 6.1). This tension between wanting to feel sad and pushing down the feeling results in depression. In Buddhism, this is referred to as suffering. We cannot avoid sadness as individuals, but we can avoid suffering by accepting our feelings. An example of this is Elisabeth Kubler-Ross's model on loss and grief. At first, we experience denial: not wanting to accept the loss. This leads to anger and depression. Only when we move through the stage of depression by accepting our loss, do we move on past the loss. This is not to say we have to experience depression, but we do have to accept our sadness. We do have to grieve, which is a less pejorative word than Kubler-Ross's depression. Furthermore, if we can see our sadness as part of honoring our loss, it makes it easier to accept than if we judge it as something bad. Substituting the word grief as a natural honorable reaction to loss makes the sadness easier, rather than depression which indicates a stuck steady state. How we think about our sadness can play a large role in how we respond to it.

Grief, although commonly associated with the loss of something that one had before, can also be related to the loss of a future that never occurred. Some individuals may feel grief about never having gotten married, having children, or any expectation that never came to fruition. Sometimes it can be perplexing to a therapist when a patient has much sadness, but no tangible loss. Loss can occur for things that never existed, as long the mind conceives of the possibility.

9.5 Fear and Anxiety

Anxiety involves a worry about the future and fear is concern about what could happen to you. Individuals that have experienced being over-whelmed by emotion, such as being bitten by a dog, often avoid future experiences associated with that event. Fear associations or memories have been shown to be the strongest and most stable of conditioned associations, which from a survival standpoint have obvious benefits (Öhman & Mineka, 2001) (for the neuroscience of fear see section 11.1). Unfortunately, these negative emotional memories exert a large influence on our future behavior regardless of objective reasoning. Many people know that an airplane is the safest way to travel, yet still avoid getting on a plane. If we know the airplane is so unlikely to crash, why do we go to such great lengths to avoid the experience?

Patients will often report to me that they are still afraid of the airplane crashing despite contrary knowledge. However, I often find this to be an attribution error. Often what patients are really afraid of is their own emotional reaction. In this sense, they are afraid of being afraid. In this fear of the fear, they are not so much concerned with the outside environment, but with having to go through their own unpleasant experience. They are not afraid of the plane crashing, so much as they are of experiencing their fear and anxiety. People are often afraid of their feelings. Patients will often express concerns of fear around events that are in no way physically threatening, such as public speaking or asking someone on a date. Raj, a character on *Big Bang Theory,* has caligynephobia, which is a fear of attractive women. Women are actually something the character desires, but he avoids women because of his fears. There is no traditional source of fear in these concerns, like something from the environment that can harm you. Yet, individuals are still afraid because they don't want to experience their own anxiety when having to speak in public or experience potential romantic rejection. Our fears and anxieties more typically involve a fear of our own experience and the more we avoid that experience the more that fear can grow. Individuals will go to great lengths to avoid their feelings. It is important to know, in working with fear and anxiety, that this is most often a feeling we need to work with internally, than something in our environment that we need to change. Accepting and working with these feelings is difficult, but recognizing the feelings come from within also allows individuals to understand they have more control over these feelings than they may realize.

It is often important to explore this internal fear. When individuals fear things like rejection or public speaking, what they are actually afraid of is something more closely related to themselves. For example, someone fearing rejection might be afraid that if they are rejected then they are un-datable, perhaps even unlovable. This is much more frightening than the loss of a prospective date. I had a patient that had anxiety around potentially having a terminal illness. If I just tried to alleviate his fears through rea-soning with him about diseases, I would have missed that what he is really afraid is of dying before raising his children, a fear that goes back to his childhood. Whenever a patient expresses high levels of anxiety at seemingly benign environmental factors, I try to help the patient recognize what else might be driving that fear. These patients typically have deeper more personal fears, but attribute their anxiety or avoidance behavior to more superficial rationale, because acknowledging these deeper fears is extremely scary.

9.6 Desire and Compulsion

Emily Dickinson once wrote "the heart wants what it wants," indicating that one can't change desire and perhaps should just accept it. However, many situations exist where following desire or what we are compelled to do hurts us, such as drug use, gambling, or any behavior taken to the extreme. Ostensibly it seems odd that desires would lead us astray when they are often very good at letting us know when we are hungry, tired, or need to go the bathroom. Essentially, the question is, "Why would we desire something harmful to us?" This is because wanting (desire) and liking are separate brain systems (Berridge & Robinson, 2016). The wanting system does not accurately predict the current value, utility, or enjoyment for a given behavior. The wanting system involves the brain's MCL/do-pamine circuit, that reinforces choice behaviors, whereas the liking system is a hedonic response system, modulated by opioid or endocannabinoid neurotransmitters. Both wanting and liking active the NA, albeit different regions (Smith & Berridge, 2007). Dopamine influences our brain to make choices that have been rewarding in the past, even if they are no longer currently rewarding. The MCL/ dopamine circuit reinforces us to seek out that same object or experience that was previously rewarding; this occurs regardless of whether that object or experience still provides a beneficial value. The most obvious example is drug use, which can be initially pleasurable but after repetitive use no longer provides a feeling of liking. Even those of us that can't relate to drug use can recall having had that extra slice of pizza that was delicious early on, but no longer provides that same value once we are full. It is ironic that as individuals we would seek out objects or experiences even when they hurt us. The MCL is not designed to maximize pleasure; it seeks dopamine. Perhaps this is an evolutionary leftover in our brain designed to reinforce behaviors that would contribute to our survival. In prehistoric times, high sugar content foods were in rare supply, so engaging in behaviors that led towards consumption or even excessive consumption helped maintain the survival of the organism. Of course, in current times high sugar foods are much easier to obtain and excessive consumption leads to other problems like diabetes, yet our brains have not evolved to adapt to the current environment. Anselme and Robinson (2016), citing the presence of dopamine pathways in invertebrates, suggest that the subcortical MCL operates below conscious awareness, which helps explain why it can be so difficult to control our desires.

The wanting and liking distinction is commonly referred to in pathologies like drug use or pornography addiction, yet it is apparent in many other types of psychopathology as well. Obsessive-Compulsive Disorder occurs also as an inability to regulate compulsive behaviors, which come in tandem with obsessive thoughts. These thoughts influence the MCL, which then rewards obsessive behaviors with a dopamine response. Individuals with OCD typically recognize the irrationality of their behavior but feel compelled to act. In doing so they receive dopamine, which in turn lowers anxiety, and the individuals feel a temporary relief (Wood & Ahmari, 2015). However, this is only momentary until the next obsessive thought quickly enters the mind and the process starts all over again. In treating OCD the goal is to regulate the desire to engage in the compulsive behavior. Once the patient can manage the desire without engaging in the compulsion, the dopamine reinforcement loop ceases. The desire to engage in compulsive behavior is similar to the desire to take an unnecessary drug.

When working with patients that engage in unhealthy behaviors like smoking or eating excessive junk food, I try to help patients recognize the wanting or craving desire that occurs in relation to these substances. Often the individual experiences an immediate stress relief when they use the unhealthy substance, which reinforces the habitual behavior, in the same way that OCD behaviors momentarily lower anxiety. Individuals that don't have a dependence on these substances will often assume that users should be able to make a calculated cost-benefit analysis, see the damage they are causing themselves, and just stop. However, our brains don't always respond to rational thinking and the immediate desire trumps the long-term costs. With these patients too, stopping immediately can be overwhelming and often will set the patient up for failure. Each additional failure makes the patient feel more hopeless about quitting. I explain to these patients the goal is more about managing the desire or cravings than changing the behavior; the stronger we can get at managing the desire, the more likely we are not to engage in the unhealthy behavior. For example, with quitting smoking I ask patients to wait one minute from the time of the onset of the desire till they smoke. During this minute their goal is to cope with their feelings of desire, by accepting the feeling without smoking. After a minute they can then smoke. After a week or two, we double the time two minutes, then five minutes, and so on, before the patient can smoke. During each period, the patient is learning how to regulate their desire without giving into the behavior of smoking.

Another common pathology related to dopamine is engaging in unhealthy or abusive relationships. These relationships often start as enjoyable in the beginning, then over time become destructive. The individual is no longer experiencing a benefit from the relationship but still desires the relationship. The wanting of the past love or whatever previous value existed from the relationship prevents them from terminating the relationship. Here individuals are stuck and unable to act in their own best interest. Others looking objectively from the outside can see that the relationship is hurting the individual, but the individual cannot mitigate the desire. They may even understand the negative effects the relationship is having on them but feel trapped by their desire. The psychodynamic literature would refer to this as repetition compulsion, and the wanting or desire can begin in the original caregiver relationship. Something about this original relationship was rewarding and individuals will seek that same rewarding experience again in future relationships even if it stops being beneficial. Patients that speak of being in relationships where they are constantly let down are stuck in this dopamine loop, wanting something they don't necessarily like. I had a friend once say that he dated the same guy in three different bodies, which I thought was an insightful recognition of this desire and the inability to stop yourself. Helping patients to recognize and regulate their desires can help them overcome compulsive behaviors that no longer produce value.

Lastly, letting go past desires or wants can also involve an additional component of grief, as was discussed in the sadness section previously. Letting go of childhood desires can often involve an acceptance that one will never achieve desired objects or experiences they once had or longed for as a child. This acceptance and letting go of the past can often be a challenge with elderly patients too, who sometimes express excessive nostalgia. With the losses one experiences as an adult, there can be a desire to go back in time to a more enjoyable past. Helping these patients let go of their desire and grieve the past, will be important for continued psychological health and in creating new meaning as one ages.

9.7 Disgust

Disgust is considered one of the basic primary emotions. The emotion of disgust helps individuals recognize pathogens and avoid them (Rozin & Fallon, 1987). The insula (AI & PI) which recognize sensory information in the body may be particularly involved in the experience of disgust (Calder, Keane, Manes, Antoun, & Young, 2000; Wicker et al., 2003), and often when people say "I feel disgusting" they are referring to the presence of their whole body versus feeling disappointed or happy, which may be less of a full-body sensation. Yet, other studies have demonstrated that the insula is no more activated in disgust than other emotions (Schaich Borg, Lieberman, & Kiehl, 2008). Jabbi, Bastiaansen, and Keysers (2008) suggest that brain areas involved in disgust will vary based on whether the subject is experiencing, observing, or imagining disgust; however, they find the AI active in all three conditions. More recent research indicates that the PI is involved more with the primary disgust response, while the AI is activated on a more secondary level, considering the context of the situation (Ying et al., 2018). This suggests certain brain areas like the AI may have evolved in reference to moral disgust, modulating the emotional response based on the context of the immoral act.

Disgust has roots in avoidance of toxins like spoiled food or feces, but it has come to be associated with lapses in morality. References of disgust are often made towards aspects of sex. Even off-color jokes about race, religion, or sexuality are often said to be disgusting. In one interesting study when subjects were asked to recall unethical behaviors from their past, they then went on to purchase more cleaning products (Zhong & Liljenquist, 2006), indicating people associate moral transgressions with dirtiness. When we say that guy is pretty "dirty" we may not be referring to his hygiene. Disgust is also related to shame. Research shows that when participants are shown angry faces, they feel more guilt, and when they are shown disgusting faces, they feel more shame (Giner-Sorolla & Espinosa, 2011).

The whole concept of morality, disgust, and shame hearkens back to the beginning of the foundations of psychotherapy under Freud. Freud discovered the mental cure by hypnotizing patients with conversion disorders and recognizing that under hypnosis the patients could move. Freud eventually had the patient verbalize past memories, typically of sexual assault, and found that expressing these memories/feelings would then dissipate the patient's conversion disorder (Herman, 1992). Herman (1992) suggests that patients felt shame and disgust from their sexual trauma, which caused them to repress memories of the abuse, resulting in the conversion disorder. Disgust, like shame, leads to a denial of the self, resulting in psychopathology. Looking at sexual taboos across societies, a correlation exists between levels of psychopathology and the degree to which society deems sexual behaviors disgusting (Munroe & Gauvain, 2001). It may be no coincidence that the Victorian Era in which Freud laid the foundation of psychotherapy was also one of sexual repression, where women's sexuality was immoral.

In working with patients experiencing disgust, it's important to help patients normalize, de-stigmatize, and not shame behavioral choices, especially those that are congruent with the patient's true sense of self. It wasn't until 1973 that homosexuality was removed from the DSM (Drescher, 2015). In this sense, our social norms determined what was psychopathology and disgusting. Sexuality minorities still experience a great deal of stigma that negatively impacts their mental health (Hatzenbuehler, 2009). It's also important to try and recognize when we as therapists may be expressing disgust at a patient's choices. I'm a therapist but I'm also a human, so I try and recognize when I do have moral judgments or experience disgust at a patient's behavior and own them. For example, I might say, "That's really different from my lifestyle," or "I could never imagine myself doing that," followed by "So what's that like for you?". I try to recognize that my morality and experience of a situation may be very different from someone else's. This usually helps patients feel less judged and allows us to explore the cost/benefits of the patient's behavior.

9.8 Gratitude

Often in psychotherapy, we focus on bad feelings. Of course, it is important to ameliorate the negative feelings, but focusing solely on bad feelings can be exhausting and may prevent the patient from staying invested in therapy. Research shows that depressed individuals have a biased worldview, overly focused on the negative (Marsh, Hammond, & Crawford, 2019). Having gratitude can help balance negative perspectives and help patients finding meaning in their negative feelings. For example, when a patient feels sad about a loss, I will sometimes point out that their investment in an object or relationship had value. As much as the loss hurts, it's important to honor the meaning and value of what was lost. I point out that we can have gratitude for having had the experience with the object or relationship. This helps patients find meaning in their negative feelings and gratitude for past experiences. If a patient feels anxious about an upcoming performance, the anxiety is also about wanting to perform well. In this sense, the individual cares about themselves and their performance. Wanting to do well is natural, and because they care about themselves, they have anxiety around the performance. Once the anxiety has meaning, gratitude can be practiced for this meaning. Often bad feelings are related to concerns about self, and ideally, we should practice gratitude that we care enough about ourselves we attend to these bad feelings.

9.9 Self-Consciousness Emotions/Shame

Self-conscious emotions are emotions that do not exist at birth but develop around the age of two, when children start to recognize themselves as independent beings. These emotions involve a cognitive appraisal of self: pride being a positive view of self; shame being a negative view of self. Since self-conscious emotions involve a cognitive judgment, they involve more thinking areas associated with PFC and mentalizing areas like the TPJ, IFG, and STS (Beer, 2007). These emotions are important in examining behavior in the social context and can help regulate social behavior. For example, feelings of embarrassment or guilt may help to regulate future behavior, especially for adhesion to social norms.

Shame is a difficult emotion because it defines the self as bad (see also section 10.1). Shame is different from guilt: in guilt, people judge their behavior; in shame, people judge themselves as bad. When individuals experience shame as opposed to guilt, they feel less empathetic and struggle more with taking the perspective of other individuals (Yang, Yang, & Chiou, 2010). Guilt motivates one towards behavior change, whereas shame results in a denial of self and reduced action for behavior change (Stevens & Abernethy, 2018). This makes shame a uniquely challenging emotion to work with. Individuals are often reluctant to accept or acknowledge feelings of shame because they are directly related to a negative evaluation of the self that one may feel powerless to change. Individuals don't want to feel bad about themselves, so it is often easier to deny the existence of the feeling. Yet the denial of one's emotional experience prevents the ability to reconsolidate the emotions denied, rendering an individual in a permanent state of suffering. Self-compassion is especially important when experiencing shame to access the primary emotional state for affect reconsolidation.

9.10 Jealousy and Envy

Jealousy and envy are similar; both are unpleasant feelings of wanting what someone else has. Envy typically involves wanting what someone else has, while jealously is more likely to involve another person who is a potential threat to an existing relationship (Smith, Kim, & Parrott, 1988). For example, an individual may become jealous of a sibling when that sibling receives praise from a parent; the jealous individual fears the praise because it could be a threat to the relationship with that parent. Hart, Carrington, Tronick, and Carroll (2004) found that infants display jealousy behaviors when their mothers pay attention to a lifelike doll instead of the infant.

Envy is considered to be either benign or malicious in nature (Van de Ven, Zeelenberg, & Pieters, 2009). Benign envy would involve admiration, looking up to someone, or having great respect for another. The more typical malicious envy is wanting something from someone which you cannot have, and this is associated with resentment toward another. The distinction may rest on how we respond to our desire. Do we see ourselves as capable of achieving the desire? If so, then the envy is benign. We may then look up to the successful/envied individual as a model for our own behavior. However, if we see ourselves as incapable of obtaining the desired object or situation, then the envy is malicious. In this case, it may seem unfair that someone has more than we do, and this typically results in anger or discontentment. With malicious envy, there is a desire to sabotage or damage the envied individual (Van de Ven et al., 2009).

In this context, if a patient is envious of a colleague taking a vacation, it may be worth exploring why the patient struggles to have such things for him or herself. In benign envy, the patient recognizes their need for a vacation, and envy can help direct a patient towards meeting their desired needs. In malicious envy, the patient may not be allowed to take a vacation, and the anger surrounding this could result in the patient wanting to ruin their colleague's vacation. In psychotherapy it's important to explore these emotions. In malicious envy, what barriers get in the way of the patient's need for a vacation? Are there barriers that the patient creates or external barriers that might be hard for the patient to accept? Patients that feel they have little control or agency are likely to have higher levels of envy (Smith, Parrott, Ozer, & Moniz, 1994). This could be both a psychological and social problem. Empowering patients to help expand their locus of control may help lower envy (see Chapter 10). In addition, removing social barriers that prevent advancement could decrease envy as well. From a clinical standpoint, it may also be beneficial to help patients accept that there are desires they may never achieve. It is also important to recognize that envy doesn't always have to be related to external objects. Often times I see patients' enviousness of another's lack of anxiety, self-judgment, or calm demeanor. I often use a metaphor of chronic illness or disability here to help patients. They never asked for this psychological disorder, just as others are born into disability or ill health that they never asked for. In order to move forward, we must accept our conditions as opposed to dwelling on what could have been. Noticing patients' envies can additionally help to establish treatment goals for patients to have better mental health. If they are envious of their friend's happiness this likely means the patient lacks fulfillment.

Jealousy often is tied to social exclusion (Leary, 1990), even when individuals claim to be jealous of someone else's status, qualities, or achievements, the underlying fear may be that if they don't possess such things and they will be less desirable and socially isolated because of this insufficiency. Jealousy appears to be related to and mediated by self-esteem (Salovey & Rodin, 1991; DeSteno, Valdesolo, & Bartlett, 2006), indicating that if an individual has a strong sense of self-esteem, events that might evoke jealousy may not result in a strong jealous feeling. The theory is that if individual feels confident in himself or herself, events that may threaten their self-worth don't lead to fears of exclusion. Essentially: "Others can be successful, and I won't be socially excluded."

There are very few brain imaging studies associated with the emotion of jealousy. One study by Kelley, Eastwick, Harmon-Jones, and Schmeichel (2015) finds that jealousy increases left frontal cortical activity. Authors were also able to manipulate jealousy by increasing activity in the left or right hemisphere of the brain through transcranial magnetic stimulation, which would then increase or decrease jealousy levels respectively. While more brain research needs to be done on jealousy, this finding does offer some clinical insight. Many emotions display an approach/avoid dimension. Some emotions want us to approach the stimuli, while other emotions implore us to avoid the stimuli. Anger and fear are two emotions that are similar in that they have a negative valence and are high on arousal, but anger invokes an approach to the stimuli, while fear motivates one to move away from the stimuli. A review of studies on emotion and left vs. right frontal cortical activity finds increased left activity compared with right frontal cortical activity leads us to approach motivation, while greater right than left activity leads towards withdrawal (Harmon-Jones, Gable, & Peterson, 2010; Fetterman, Ode, & Robinson, 2013; Harmon-Jones & Gable, 2018). For clinicians this means that when a patient feels jealousy, they may want to act out, potentially trying to correct the felt injustice of the jealousy. However, if jealousy is a threat to being socially excluded, it could be related to the patient's self-esteem, and solutions to jealousy should be more internally than externally focused. Buying a fancy new car out of jealousy likely won't solve the problem if an individual fears that he or she is inadequate to receive love, care, and respect from others. This may also explain why jealousy is considered to be a more intense emotion than envy (Smith & Kim, 2007). Jealousy seems to be based more on one's sense of self-worth, rather than just a desire for something someone else has. Addressing problems in self-worth might involve deeper emotional change, which will be discussed in the next chapters.

References

Anselme, P., & Robinson, M. J. (2016). "Wanting," "liking," and their relation to consciousness. *Journal of Experimental Psychology: Animal Learning and Cognition*, 42(2), 123.

Arias, J. A., Williams, C., Raghvani, R., Aghajani, M., Baez, S., Belzung, C., ... & Kemp, A. H. (2020). The neuroscience of sadness: A multidisciplinary synthesis and collaborative review. *Neuroscience & Biobehavioral Reviews, 111*, 199–228.

Beer, J. S. (2007). Neural systems for self-conscious emotions and their underlying appraisals. *The Self-conscious Emotions: Theory and Research*, 53–67.

Berridge, K. C., & Robinson, T. E. (2016). Liking, wanting, and the incentive-sensitization theory of addiction. *American Psychologist, 71*(8), 670.

Blair, R. J. R. (2004). The roles of orbital frontal cortex in the modulation of antisocial behavior. *Brain and Cognition, 55*(1), 198–208.

Cacioppo, J. T., & Hawkley, L. C. (2009). Loneliness. In M. R. Leary & R. H. Hoyle (Eds.), *Handbook of individual differences in social behavior* (pp. 227–240). New York, NY: The Guilford Press.

Calder, A. J., Keane, J., Manes, F., Antoun, N., & Young, A. W. (2000). Impaired recognition and experience of disgust following brain injury. *Nature Neuroscience, 3*(11), 1077–1078.

Carver, C. S., & Harmon-Jones, E. (2009). Anger is an approach-related affect: Evidence and implications. *Psychological Bulletin, 135*(2), 183.

DeSteno, D., Valdesolo, P., & Bartlett, M. Y. (2006). Jealousy and the threatened self: Getting to the heart of the green-eyed monster. *Journal of Personality and Social Psychology, 91*, 626–641. doi:10.1037/0022-3514.91.4.626.

Drescher, J. (2015). Out of DSM: Depathologizing homosexuality. *Behavioral Sciences, 5*(4), 565–575.

Eisenberger, N. I. (2015). Social pain and the brain: Controversies, questions, and where to go from here. *Annual Review of Psychology, 66*, 601–629.

Fetterman, A. K., Ode, S., & Robinson, M. D. (2013). For which side the bell tolls: The laterality of approach-avoidance associative networks. *Motivation and Emotion, 37*(1), 33–38.

Fries, A. B. W., Ziegler, T. E., Kurian, J. R., Jacoris, S., & Pollak, S. D. (2005). Early experience in humans is associated with changes in neuropeptides critical for regulating social behavior. *Proceedings of the National Academy of Sciences, 102*(47), 17237–17240.

Giner-Sorolla, R., & Espinosa, P. (2011). Social cuing of guilt by anger and of shame by disgust. *Psychological Science, 22*(1), 49–53.

Harmon-Jones, E., & Gable, P. A. (2018). On the role of asymmetric frontal cortical activity in approach and withdrawal motivation: An updated review of the evidence. *Psychophysiology, 55*(1), e12879.

Harmon-Jones, E., Gable, P. A., & Peterson, C. K. (2010). The role of asymmetric frontal cortical activity in emotion-related phenomena: A review and update. *Biological Psychology, 84*(3), 451–462.

Hart, S. L., Carrington, H. A., Tronick, E. Z., & Carroll, S. R. (2004). When infants lose exclusive maternal attention: Is it jealousy? *Infancy, 6*(1), 57–78.

Hatzenbuehler, M. L. (2009). How does sexual minority stigma "get under the skin"? A psychological mediation framework. *Psychological Bulletin, 135*(5), 707.

Heinrichs, M., Baumgartner, T., Kirschbaum, C., & Ehlert, U. (2003). Social support and oxytocin interact to suppress cortisol and subjective responses to psychosocial stress. *Biological Psychiatry, 54*(12), 1389–1398.

Herman, J. (1992). *Trauma and recovery*. New York: Basic Books.

Jabbi, M., Bastiaansen, J., & Keysers, C. (2008). A common anterior insula representation of disgust observation, experience and imagination shows divergent functional connectivity pathways. *PloS One, 3*(8), e2939.

Kelley, N. J., Eastwick, P. W., Harmon-Jones, E., & Schmeichel, B. J. (2015). Jealousy increased by induced relative left frontal cortical activity. *Emotion, 15*(5), 550.

Leary, M. R. (1990). Responses to social exclusion: Social anxiety, jealousy, loneliness, depression, and low self-esteem. *Journal of Social and Clinical Psychology, 9,* 221–229. doi:10.1521/jscp.1990.9.2.221.

Marsh, C., Hammond, M. D., & Crawford, M. T. (2019). Thinking about negative life events as a mediator between depression and fading affect bias. *Plos One, 14*(1), e0211147.

Munroe, R. L., & Gauvain, M. (2001). Why the paraphilias? Domesticating strange sex. *Cross-Cultural Research, 35*(1), 44–64.

Öhman, A., & Mineka, S. (2001). Fears, phobias, and preparedness: Toward an evolved module of fear and fear learning. *Psychological Review, 108*(3), 483.

Panksepp, J. (2004). *Affective neuroscience: The foundations of human and animal emotions.* Oxford: Oxford University Press.

Panksepp, J. (2010). Affective neuroscience of the emotional BrainMind: Evolutionary perspectives and implications for understanding depression. *Dialogues in Clinical Neuroscience, 12*(4), 533.

Rozin, P., & Fallon, A. E. (1987). A perspective on disgust. *Psychological Review, 94*(1), 23.

Salovey, P., & Rodin, J. (1991). Provoking jealousy and envy: Domain relevance and self-esteem threat. *Journal of Social and Clinical Psychology, 10*(4), 395–413.

Schaich Borg, J., Lieberman, D., & Kiehl, K. A. (2008). Infection, incest, and iniquity: Investigating the neural correlates of disgust and morality. *Journal of Cognitive Neuroscience, 20*(9), 1529–1546.

Smith, K. S., & Berridge, K. C. (2007). Opioid limbic circuit for reward: Interaction between hedonic hotspots of nucleus accumbens and ventral pallidum. *Journal of Neuroscience, 27*(7), 1594–1605.

Smith, R. H., & Kim, S. H. (2007). Comprehending envy. *Psychological Bulletin, 133*(1), 46.

Smith, R. H., Kim, S. H., & Parrott, W. G. (1988). Envy and jealousy: Semantic problems and experiential distinctions. *Personality and Social Psychology Bulletin, 14*(2), 401–409.

Smith, R. H., Parrott, W. G., Ozer, D., & Moniz, A. (1994). Subjective injustice and inferiority as predictors of hostile and depressive feelings in envy. *Personality and Social Psychology Bulletin, 20*(6), 705–711.

Stevens, F. L., & Abernethy, A. D. (2018). Neuroscience and racism: The power of groups for overcoming implicit bias. *International Journal of Group Psychotherapy, 68*(4), 561–584.

Van de Ven, N., Zeelenberg, M., & Pieters, R. (2009). Leveling up and down: The experiences of benign and malicious envy. *Emotion, 9*(3), 419.

Wicker, B., Keysers, C., Plailly, J., Royet, J. P., Gallese, V., & Rizzolatti, G. (2003). Both of us disgusted in My insula: The common neural basis of seeing and feeling disgust. *Neuron, 40*(3), 655–664.

Wood, J., & Ahmari, S. E. (2015). A framework for understanding the emerging role of corticolimbic-ventral striatal networks in OCD-associated repetitive behaviors. *Frontiers in Systems Neuroscience, 9*, 171.

Yang, M.-L., Yang, C.-C., & Chiou, W.-B. (2010). When guilt leads to other orientation and shame leads to egocentric self-focus: Effects of differential priming of negative affects on perspective taking. *Social Behavior and Personality: An International Journal, 38*(5), 605–614. doi:10.2224/sbp.2010.38.5.605.

Ying, X., Luo, J., Chiu, C. Y., Wu, Y., Xu, Y., & Fan, J. (2018). Functional dissociation of the posterior and anterior insula in moral disgust. *Frontiers in Psychology, 9*, 860.

Zhong, C. B., & Liljenquist, K. (2006). Washing away your sins: Threatened morality and physical cleansing. *Science, 313*(5792), 1451–1452.

10 Notions of Self

Life experiences, especially early life experiences, shape our personality and sense of self. Much of psychology is devoted to how individuals become who they are. This next section will touch on a few examples investigating how early life events affect an individual's adult coping style with emotion. This is important for only for its theoretical value in understanding how different patients respond to their feelings, but also in its practical value in building coping strategies and changing the patient's self-concept.

10.1 Shame/Splitting

A friend once said to me when talking about psychology, "What purpose does the emotion of shame serve?" We could recognize the value of all the other emotions, but at that time couldn't understand what value or purpose shame had. Why would having an overall negative view of the self serve any purpose for an individual? Years later, upon further reflection, I realized the benefit shame has in providing a delusional sense of control when one has no control. I see this most pronounced in victims of childhood abuse; these patients consistently have a negative view of themselves. Ostensibly, why would they have such views when they haven't done anything wrong; only their abuser has. As a child, the world is a very precarious place, and it is scary to be in a world in which you have such little control over your environment. Living in an environment as a child where you are continually abused is overwhelming; there is no way out. So, these patients as children create a delusion where they can control the abuse. They falsely believe that they are bad and if they can be good, then they will not get abused. This creates a basic notion that the self is bad. These patients feel shame about themselves and often don't know why. The patient struggles in life because at a baseline they are bad and have an internal self-hate. Through shaming part of themselves as a child they created a false sense of control. This false sense of control allowed the child not to feel helpless in their abuse. This is also seen to a lesser extent in adult victims of sexual assault or rape. These are typically women that blame themselves for the assault. Ostensibly it doesn't make any sense because no one would

DOI: 10.4324/9781003150893-10

knowingly choose to be sexually assaulted, but the delusion does create a false sense of control, that perhaps the victim can prevent future assaults by changing her behavior. It appears our need for security is so strong that we will falsely blame ourselves for wrongdoing if it can provide a feeling of security. In working with these patients, we have to accept and love the part of the self that is hated. It often takes multiple sessions to access and reconsolidate these emotions. I do find explaining this process of splitting to patients helps normalize their feelings and recognize why accessing these extremely uncomfortable emotions is principal.

10.2 Attachment's Effects on Emotion

Around 1970, Mary Ainsworth designed a now famous psychological study in infant attachment referred to as The Strange Situation (Ainsworth & Bell, 1970). Ainsworth removed an infant from their mother for a period of time and then watched the infant's behavior when they reunited with the caregiver. She discovered three unique styles, which are now referred to as secure attachment, anxious attachment, and avoidant attachment. A fourth attachment style, fearful attachment, was later added as a mix of anxious and avoidant attachment (Bartholomew, 1990). Infants with secure attachment experience distress when the mother leaves and are happy upon reuniting with the mother, while infants in the anxious category exhibit an intense distress when the mother leaves, then skeptically return to the mother when she comes back. Infants in the avoidant category show little distress when the mother leaves and little interest in reuniting with the mother when she returns. Initially, the work was important to child psychology; later it was found that our attachment styles extended into our adult relationships (Hazan & Shaver, 1987). At this point, clinical psychologists took note of how attachment styles could be related to psychopathology; for example, avoidant personality disorder (Crittenden, 1995). Mikulincer, Shaver, and Pereg (2003) later hypothesized that insecure attachment evolves when the attachment figure is not available or attentive, at which point the child will first hyper-activate their emotions to get the caregiver's attention. If this strategy does not work the child will next deactivate their feeling, perhaps dissociating from their experience to cope with the distressing emotions around a lack of an attachment figure. In my own research, I have examined these attachment styles in relation to how individuals perceive and cope with emotion. Individuals with avoidant attachment style are less aware of their feelings, while individuals with an anxious attachment style tend to be more aware of their feelings; they also tend to be more impulsive and let the feelings interfere with their goals (Stevens, 2014). Some neuroimaging research supports this, finding high activity in the dACC and AI (areas involved in emotional recognition) in anxiously attached compared to avoidantly attached individuals (DeWall et al., 2012). Recognizing a patient's attachment style could be useful for clinicians. Individuals with avoidant attachment may be less aware of feelings. Helping these individuals to recognize their emotions will be important in overcoming their pathology. Individuals with an anxious attachment style may need more help in regulating their emotions so they do not engage in unhealthy coping strategies. This pattern of hyper-emotionality and hypo-emotionality also displays itself across psychological disorders; someone with an anxious attachment style could be much more likely to develop or be diagnosed with generalized anxiety disorder, being more expressive with their emotional concerns. Alternately, someone with an avoidant attachment style is less likely to express his or her feelings, consistent with PSTD or a dissociative disorder diagnosis. This again hearkens back to the importance of maintaining a moderate level of arousal in psychotherapy. Anxious individuals will more likely need help down-regulating their feelings, while avoidant individuals need the opposite, help to up-regulate their feelings.

In examining attachment styles, Bartholomew (1990) created a two-dimensional chart for attachment disorders with anxious and avoidant attachment each representing a separate axis. Being low on both the anxious and avoidant dimensions indicates secure attachment. Being low on the anxious dimension and high on avoidant indicates avoidant attachment (world bad/self good). Being high on the anxious dimension and low on avoidant indicates anxious attachment (world good/self bad). Being high on both anxious and avoidant dimensions indicates fearful attachment. Bartholomew theorizes that the anxious dimension represents how one views the world, as a continuum between safe and unsafe. The second avoidant dimension represents how one views the self, ranging from positive self-image to negative self-image. If Bartholomew's theory is correct, people's attachment has a large effect on their worldview and the view of themselves. Increasingly, evidence is amounting that early attachment has large effects on the development of psychopathology (Hart, 2010; Schore, 2015; Siegel, 2020).

One theory for why attachment could affect psychopathology later in life is that these early schema patterns set expectations for future relationships. Lane, Smith, and Nadel (2020) suggest that early learning experiences influence how new stimuli are perceived. For example, an individual with an anxious attachment style will expect unstable relationships from others, so ambiguous feedback may be interpreted as a rejection. Furthermore, that individual may see these unstable relationships as normal. This can be true not just for attachment style, but any notions of self. Just like the self-fulfilling prophecy (Madon, Jussim, & Eccles, 1997), whatever people believe about themselves, they will find evidence in their environment to support it. Individuals are going to try and find consistency between their identity and feedback from the environment. We have an autobiographical memory of ourselves and we look for information consistent with the ideas we have about ourselves (Bengtsson & Penny, 2013). This self-reinforcing system helps build negative schemas that individuals have about themselves and the world, shaping their personalities.

10.3 Personality Disorders

One way to conceptualize personality disorders is an adaptive response to the environment, which is no longer adaptive. A histrionic personality disorder where one acts in an overly dramatic fashion can be seen as the anxiously attached child expressing an intense distress to get the attention of another. As a child, this dramatic behavior could have been adaptive to maintain the attention of the caregiver, yet as an adult causes interpersonal problems. Avoidant personality disorder would be a manifestation of an avoidant attachment style, having to cope without the support of a caregiver. Now as an adult the avoidant personality sees little benefit in reaching out to others. Narcissistic personality disorder could be seen as an adaptive reaction for a child trying to please parents that have conditional love for the child based on his or her achievements. Borderline personality disorder, marked by black and white thinking, an unstable self-image, and self-harm, would be an adaptive reaction for a child who engaged in splitting to cope with childhood abuse. Instead of labeling these personalities as dysfunctional and untreatable (Kersting, 2004), they can be seen as a past coping response that is no longer adaptive. Helping patients to recognize their strengths in adapting to difficult environments can help them to feel more empowered and less stigmatized by their psychological disorder.

10.4 Applications to Practice

Individuals don't like to access feelings of self-hate. In working with these more difficult states of emotion, therapeutic rapport and trust will be of high importance. With less intense emotions, the therapeutic relationship is not as important to develop before fixing the problem. However, with emotions like shame and self-hate, the patient has to trust that the clinician will be able to help them to regulate their emotions through these overwhelming feeling states. If the trust is not established, the patient will typically avoid these feeling states, and rightfully so, because if the patient is unable to regulate such strong feelings effectively, they can often resort to harmful behaviors like substance abuse, self-harm, or even suicide as a mechanism to cope with the overwhelming feelings of shame and self-hate. Once the therapist feels confident in the patient's coping skills, they should then plan to up-regulate emotion for affect reconsolidation.

References

Ainsworth, M. D. S., & Bell, S. M. (1970). Attachment, exploration, and separation: Illustrated by the behavior of one-year-olds in a strange situation. *Child Development*, 49–67.

Bartholomew, K. (1990). Avoidance of intimacy: An attachment perspective. *Journal of Social and Personal relationships*, 7(2), 147–178.

Bengtsson, S. L., & Penny, W. D. (2013). Self-associations influence task-performance through Bayesian inference. *Frontiers in Human Neuroscience*, 7, 490.

Crittenden, P. M. (1995). Attachment and psychopathology. In S. Goldberg, R. Muir, & J. Kerr (Eds.), *Attachment theory: Social, developmental, and clinical perspectives* (pp. 367–406). Hillsdale, NJ: Analytic Press, Inc.

DeWall, C. N., Masten, C. L., Powell, C., Combs, D., Schurtz, D. R., & Eisenberger, N. I. (2012). Do neural responses to rejection depend on attachment style? An fMRI study. *Social Cognitive and Affective Neuroscience*, 7(2), 184–192.

Hart, S. (2010). *The impact of attachment (Norton series on interpersonal neurobiology)*. New York: WW Norton & Company.

Hazan, C., & Shaver, P. (1987). Romantic love conceptualized as an attachment process. *Journal of Personality and Social Psychology*, 52(3), 511.

Kersting, K. (2004). Axis II gets short shrift. *Monitor on Psychology*, 35, 50.

Lane, R. D., Smith, R., & Nadel, L. (2020). Neuroscience of enduring change and psychotherapy: Summary, conclusions, and future directions. In *Neuroscience of enduring change* (pp. 433–468). Oxford: Oxford University Press.

Madon, S., Jussim, L., & Eccles, J. (1997). In search of the powerful self-fulfilling prophecy. *Journal of Personality and Social Psychology*, 72(4), 791.

Mikulincer, M., Shaver, P. R., & Pereg, D. (2003). Attachment theory and affect regulation: The dynamics, development, and cognitive consequences of attachment-related strategies. *Motivation and Emotion*, 27(2), 77–102.

Schore, A. N. (2015). *Affect regulation and the origin of the self: The neurobiology of emotional development*. New York, NY: Routledge.

Siegel, D. J. (2020). *The developing mind: How relationships and the brain interact to shape who we are*. New York, NY: Guilford Press.

Stevens, F. L. (2014). Affect regulation styles in avoidant and anxious attachment. *Individual Differences Research*, 12(3), 123–130.

11 Affect Reconsolidation

A friend of mine recently told me about the Mandela effect, the strange phenomenon where people remember something different from how it actually occurred. You should google the Mandela effect if you're not familiar with it for some good examples. I was surprised myself at how off my memory is. I don't remember logos and symbols as they actually are, but something different. It's not that my memory failed me, that I couldn't remember them, it's that I actually remembered these artifacts differently from what they really are. My experience tells me that the world is not as it is. At first, I felt a little delusional, but the more I thought about memory, it made sense to me. These are common pop culture artifacts that I have experienced seeing multiple times in my environment or recalled from my own memory. Upon each re-experiencing of these artifacts, my memory reconsolidates so the original memory is no longer there. It's not an additional memory; my actual memory of the artifact changes, and keeps changing upon each reconsolidation of that memory, so what I think is obvious because I've seen it so many times is just a reconsolidation of my last memory and not always accurate (see also section 3.3). My memory feels real to me, like the first time I saw the artifact, even though it's not recalling that, it's just recalling the way I last remembered it. The Mandela effect has helped convince me of the power of affect (memory) reconsolidation.

Memory reconsolidation is the process of updating and changing memories when they are recollected. Memory reconsolidation is the term you will find in the scientific literature; I use the term affect reconsolidation because in the practice of psychotherapy, it's not the nature of the memory that is changing but the emotions surrounding the memory. When participants undergo affect reconsolidation, they don't forget they had a fear or the previous emotion, and the memory of the event may not change, but visceral emotion(s) experienced when the event is recollected change (Soeter & Kindt, 2015a). The facts of the episodic memory remain intact, but how the patient feels about the experience becomes very different. Memory reconsolidation was first identified in the rodent population and demonstrated that when a memory became reactivated it could become subject to change.

DOI: 10.4324/9781003150893-11

Increasingly memory reconsolidation is being studied in humans (Elsey, Van Ast, & Kindt, 2018). When I first came across it in the literature, it didn't seem too different to me than extinction training. I had learned about classical conditioning early in my training and the concept was widely understood and accepted within psychology. However, upon further study, there are some marked differences between memory reconsolidation and extinction learning (Merlo, Milton, Goozée, Theobald, & Everitt, 2014). Most importantly, memory reconsolidation rewrites the original memory, whereas in extinction a new memory is formed, and no change to the original memory occurs. Memory reconsolidation results in ongoing enduring changes, and while extinction can change behavior, extinction learning can also result in a spontaneous recovery of the original memory (Monfils, Cowansage, Klann, & LeDoux, 2009; Vervliet, Craske, & Hermans, 2013). This does not happen with memory reconsolidation because the original memory is changed or reconsolidated. With extinction, however, the new memory competes with the old memory, and the old memory may prevail. In order for affect reconsolidation to occur, the old memory needs to be reactivated. This is an important point to consider and perhaps why many psychodynamic clinicians focus on past memories. For enduring change to occur, the old memory, often associated with negative emotions, needs to be reactivated. So, therapists that are encouraging their patients to go back and experience their bad feelings, are on to something. However, we must also be aware of the concerns around retraumatizing patients when activating these old bad memories. This is why the second step of affect reconsolidation is so crucial. Clinicians must then provide a new healthy experience within which to recode the old memory. Without this, the old memory can just be reinforced (see Figure 11.1). When recalling an event, the hippocampus interacts with neocortical areas, creating a spider web of linkages associated with that memory (Kumaran, Hassabis, & McClelland, 2016), and we have a prediction or predictions of what will happen based on that memory. These

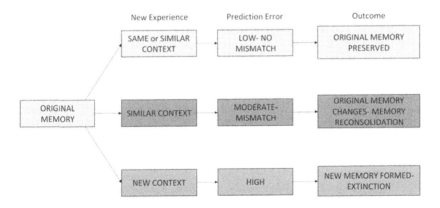

Figure 11.1 Memory reconsolidation.

predictions represent what is likely to happen given past experiences. Sometimes the predicted outcome of the choice doesn't match the actual outcome, and this is called prediction error. For example, I once had a friend named Dave, but I kept wanting to call him Chad. Perhaps he looked like a Chad I used to know. The memory of Dave's face was associated with the name Chad, and I kept predicting that Chad was this face's name. Because of this, when I saw Dave, I called him Chad. When doing so, I received an uncomfortable puzzled look from Dave. This mismatch between the expected response (smile) from Dave and the actual response (puzzled look) resulted in a prediction error. After a few repeated prediction errors, I learned to reconsolidate or re-associate the memory of Dave's face with the name Dave, and the problem stopped. Prediction error in reference to affect reconsolidation occurs along an inverted U function of change (Nadel, 2020). If there is too little prediction error, no memory change occurs. Dave politely smiles when I call him Chad, and I continue to associate Dave's face with the name Chad. On the other end, if there is too great a prediction error, a new distinct memory takes form. With too great a prediction error, the context changes. It would be something like this: "I used to associate that face with my old friend Chad, but now that face looks like my new friend Dave." I would have new memory my new friend Dave and old memory my old friend Chad. Since I have no memory of an old friend with Dave's face, the prediction error is moderate, and I've effectively reconsolidated the memory (Should I actually have an old friend Chad that looks like Dave's face, I would probably start calling that Chad, Dave).

Here is another example, because it's tricky. If I were to go back and visit my old high school, it would activate old memories. I might think, this is where I used to eat lunch, use the library, etc. I would be surprised to learn that my old math classroom has been reorganized and is now the art room. My prediction was for this to be the math room, and now a prediction error or mismatch occurs. With too little a prediction error, my memory doesn't get updated, the math room stays the math room. Maybe the art supplies in the room don't reach a threshold of uniqueness or prediction error to change my memory. With too much prediction error, I create a new memory. I might think, "This room is vastly different from my memory, so remodeling must have occurred; this was the math room before remodeling and it's now the art room:" a new additional memory. I have my old memory of it being the math room when I was a student and my new memory that the room was remodeled into an art room. With a moderate amount of prediction error, the old/original memory becomes updated. The math room is now the art room stored in my memory. My memory changes to this room being where I took art classes, not math classes, when I was in high school. This is valuable to think about in terms of psychotherapy. The prediction error must be large enough that it creates a new neural pairing and does not reinforce the old memory. Someone that felt unloved by their parents must experience a felt sense of love when the old memory is reactivated; otherwise, the felt sense of being unloved can just be reinforced. Also, the prediction error cannot be too great. A therapist telling the patient, "You are loved: think of your friend, your dog, or your romantic partner," could be too much of a mismatch. The patient might say, "Oh they don't count," or "That's not real love." In these circumstances, the patient has created a new separate memory, which doesn't allow for reconsolidation of the old memory. The patient has decided that the love they experienced from this other person represents a different context and does not change their previous experience. To prevent this increased prediction error, I try to match the conditions better. I help the patient to understand the lack of love they feel is a lack of self-love. Maybe their parents didn't love them, which is bad, but worse is now that patient doesn't love themselves. I match the feelings of the patient not loving themselves when their parents didn't love them (old memory) with the patient currently loving themselves. This seems to create the optimal prediction error for therapeutic change. Matching self-love with no self-love reduces the mismatch. Some therapists believe the therapist should provide the love or whatever unmet need exists for the patient in creating the mismatch experience. While I'm all for caring for patients, this can sometimes lead to too great of a prediction error. The patient might say, "You're only doing this because it's your job" or "I'm paying you." Also, it can create a dependency on the therapist, which can cause further issues. I find that the patient providing self-love while reactivating the old memory of when they didn't love themselves as a child to be optimal here. Another challenge you see here is a longing for an unmet need from the parent. Having patients trying to get this need met as an adult, is almost always a waste of time because the parent will never meet that need. The patient has to grieve the love they never got and recognize the real problem now is that they struggle to love themselves. Empowering the patient to meet their own needs is a much more successful therapeutic practice than plotting with the patient on how to achieve that unmet need from the parent.

11.1 The Neurobiology of Extinction and Affect Reconsolidation

Memory is most associated with the hippocampus brain area, but it's more complex than just sitting in one area like a file cabinet; even different areas of the hippocampus are active in encoding, compared with retrieval (Eldridge, Engel, Zeineh, Bookheimer, & Knowlton, 2005). Although memory is an area of brain research that is still being developed, it appears that during memory retrieval, the hippocampus acts as a conductor, interacting with other neocortical areas in recreating that memory experience. For example, a song comes on the radio. It activates an old memory, including visuals, smells; even tactile stimuli may be recalled about the event, along with information related to the event, and the hippocampus coordinates among all of the brain areas where this information resides in recreating the event. Different types of memory too will activate different brain regions. Procedural memories, like playing tennis, activate motor areas of the brain, while declarative memories, like those for events or facts, activate areas of the MTL and PFC respectively (Moscovitch et al., 2005). Memory for facts is referred to as semantic memory, while memory for events is referred to as episodic. It appears semantic memory draws even more on the PFC in remembering dates or historical information; however, episodic memory also draws upon the PFC (Moscovitch et al., 2005). Some researchers consider that episodic and semantic information exist on a continuum, starting with single occasions on the far episodic end and more rehearsed informed experiences resting on the far semantic end (Ryan, Hoscheidt, & Nadel, 2008; Kumaran et al., 2016). As experiences repeat or become more rehearsed, storage of the memory moves from hippocampus-based areas to more involvement of the vmPFC (Takashima et al., 2006; Bonnici & Maguire, 2018). It seems as memory is repeated, it takes on a more cognitive representation of the past (this is marked by increased vmPFC activity), and less of an experiential recall of the past, (marked by hippocampus activity accessing more sensory brain areas).

Psychotherapy mostly involves working with emotionally charged episodic memories; these memories not only involve the hippocampus, PFC, and MTL, but also the amygdala (Dahlgren, Ferris, & Hamann, 2020). The entire network of the amygdala, hippocampus, and vmPFC is more active for emotional memories (Nawa & Ando, 2019). Amygdala activity specifically is associated with stronger encoding (consolidation) and retrieval of memories (Kensinger & Schacter, 2006). In fact, damage to the amygdala, like the lesions typically found in Urbach-Wiethe disease cause disruptions in the emotional enhancement of declarative memory (Adolphs, Cahill, Schul, & Babinsky, 1997). Further research finds that direct electrical stimulation of the amygdala can increase memory recall (Inman et al., 2018). This network of brain regions is important in understanding the context of emotional memories. Seeing a tiger should cause heightened emotion, probably marked by amygdala activation, but if the vmPFC is co-activated, ascertaining the situational context (zoo or in the wild) together these brain regions contribute to the final emotional response: excitement or fear. These same brain regions are noteworthy in that they are commonly coactivated in disorders of psychopathology, like anxiety (Adhikari, 2014), PTSD (Hughes & Shin, 2011), and depression (Heinz et al., 2005). One theory is that deficits in contextual processing contribute to the maladaptive emotional response of feeling, for example, anxious in a benign context (Maren, Phan, & Liberzon, 2013). Interventions to disrupt or change interactions within this network of brain regions could help establish common targeted treatments for psychopathology.

Classical conditioning uses this same brain network (Sotres-Bayon, Cain,

& LeDoux, 2006). Extinction training is just the reversal of classical conditioning and has long been a principal treatment in behavior therapy. Extinction works through forming a new conditioned response or memory, allowing the vmPFC to inhibit the prior learned response. It appears that the hippocampus signals the vmPFC when to institute this new response, resulting in an inhibitory response to the amygdala (Vervliet et al., 2013). Electrical stimulation of the vmPFC appears to strengthen the new memories in extinction (Milad & Quirk, 2002). Further studies also show that greater cortical thickness and increased activation of the vmPFC are related to improved extinction training (Milad et al., 2005; Milad et al., 2007).

While affect reconsolidation and extinction involves the same brain regions, they are uniquely distinct neurobiological processes. Schiller, Kanen, LeDoux, Monfils, and Phelps (2013) compared brain changes after an extinction versus reconsolidation intervention. When the memory was reconsolidated, functional coupling between the amygdala and vmPFC was decreased. It appears with extinction, that the vmPFC inhibits the emotional response, but the neural connections to the amygdala still exist, allowing for spontaneous recovery. Reconsolidation, though, actually changes the neural connectivity between the vmPFC and amygdala. This permanent change in neural connectivity results in a lasting change of the memory (Björkstrand et al., 2015).

11.2 Applying Affect Reconsolidation vs. Extinction

Research shows that just activating the old memory can result in extinction training or reconsolidation. For reconsolidation to occur, a mismatch (prediction error) between the reactivated old memory and the new experience must exist (Pedreira, Pérez-Cuesta, & Maldonado, 2004). Affect reconsolidation involves the following steps:

1. Activate old memory
2. Provide a mismatch in the emotional experience
3. Reinforce and repeat

1. Step one is necessary because the old emotional memory needs to be activated for change to occur. How a clinician reactivates the old memory could have different approaches; some research suggests that fear memory can be reactivated and reconsolidated indirectly (Soeter & Kindt, 2015b). On the other hand, therapeutic approaches like EMDR, have people specifically recall trauma memories. I find that talking with patients about their experience, whether in the present or past, evokes these challenging old memories. If the patient feels safe, I find that the therapy naturally accesses these memories, because they have such a strong effect on the patient's everyday experience. This is often marked in therapy by the patient having a strong emotional

reaction. When this occurs, I try to identify the emotion/emotional memory. Many times, it is not a memory in a traditional sense, but rather a deep feeling of sadness, because it's not a single event experience, but a lifetime of negative feelings. At this moment, I then try to offer a new emotion or experience (step two). Some clinicians, like Ecker and Bridges (2020), believe emotion need not be activated for memory reconsolidation to occur. This may be true for non-affective laden memories. In terms of psychotherapy, you are almost always working with difficult emotions. In my experience, I have had patients talk about emotional or traumatic memories absent of emotion. However, they are dissociated from their feelings, and this does not result in affect reconsolidation. I find in this condition I am unable to change the patient's emotional experience of the memory because the emotional experience is not activated (step one). Evidence also seems to support the necessity of experiencing emotion for effective psychotherapy (Goldman, Greenberg, & Pos, 2005; Pascual-Leone & Greenberg, 2007; Pos, Greenberg, & Warwar, 2009).

Most CBT practitioners use an extinction approach in the treatment of anxiety disorders, which often results in a return of symptoms over time (Craske et al., 2017). This happens because during exposure treatment, the old memory is not always activated, thus step one is never completed. For example, a patient with a phobia of dogs is exposed to a dog and manages the anxiety response to the dog. This will likely result in an improvement of the phobia, because the patient may be able to experience a dog and remain calm. However, the original phobia (old memory) still exists; the only difference is a new memory for dogs co-exists with the old memory. If the patient were to have another new experience with a dog, the original phobia could re-occur, or the new calming memory could occur. This would likely depend upon the context and factors such as the type of dog, the environment surrounding the dog, or other individuals present. These contextual cues would likely signal the brain to experience the original phobic memory or the new calming memory. This would cause an improvement in the patient's phobia, but not a full remission. For reconsolidation to occur and a greater likelihood of full remission of symptoms, the patient would need to be exposed to the original phobic memory (step one), not just the experience with a new dog. This is why reconsolidation is often considered to be an internal process, as opposed to extinction, which is an external treatment process (Welling, 2012). Internal processing involves activating old memories, external processing involves engaging in new behaviors in the environment. In this sense the feared stimuli/emotion rests within the individual, not the external environment. Reconsolidation has also been considered the historical equivalent to the corrective emotional experience, a therapeutic experience that forever changes the patient (Levenson, Angus, & Pool, 2020).

2. Step two involves providing a different emotional experience in the face of the old emotional memory, often the opposite emotion. When I work with patients on this step, I encourage them to hold both the old memory and the new memory simultaneously. Patients often report this as being a challenge to their brains. This incompatibility puts our brains in a state of cognitive dissonance, which is naturally uncomfortable. Patients will report wanting to "give in" to the old memory, letting go of the new experience we are trying to provide. Or patients will want to have the new memory/experience absence of the old memory, saying, "That's in the past; can't we just forget about it?" Clinicians doing affect reconsolidation should expect some resistance but recognize that if there is too much resistance, the patient may not be ready to experience the old memory. Don't push it. You can always revisit the old memory; err on the side of caution. In these cases, you can practice affect tolerance or emotional regulation skills, or work on experiencing and reconsolidating less intense emotions (see previous chapters).

Another important distinction between extinction and reconsolidation is that affect reconsolidation is used for multiple emotions, whereas extinction training usually just involves confronting a feared stimulus (Welling, 2012). Traditional behavioral approaches involving exposure therapy are fairly straightforward: expose the patient to the fear stimulus; lower arousal; and continue until elimination of phobic response. It becomes more complicated with a disorder like PTSD where there are no external stimuli to employ exposure therapy. The feared emotion rests within the individual, who is afraid of some past traumatic event. In treating PTSD, it's clear how affect reconsolidation would be a better approach than extinction. With affect reconsolidation, clinicians aim to re-activate the feared old memory and replace it with a mismatch condition. A clinician would not want to take an external approach, recreating the environmental conditions of the original trauma, which could potentially re-traumatize the patient. Consistent with affect reconsolidation, the clinician wants to ensure that when the old trauma memory is reactivated it will be paired with a new positive experience (the mismatch condition), which would also prevent reinforcement of the old traumatic memory. Internal emotional memories can exist for a number of difficult emotions, as discussed prior, that could be candidates for affect reconsolidation. Many patients struggle with feelings of worthlessness, abandonment, and shame. These emotions are not just fear-based and cannot be effectively treated through an exposure paradigm. Reconsolidating emotions like worthlessness, abandonment, and shame involve a different mismatch condition than relaxation in conjunction with anxiety. Shame might be paired with self-acceptance, abandonment could be paired with a recoupment of self, or worthlessness mismatched with worth. Affect reconsolidation involves changing the emotional experience of the patient from a negative to a positive valence.

3. Step three involves repetition and practice. In this step, a clinician might assign homework to reinforce the reconsolidated memory. For example, a patient that felt shame when asserting herself may practice being more assertive in her everyday environment. Patients need to be aware of their experience and emotions when doing step three homework. Just doing the homework without regard for one's internal experience might change behavior, but does not help in reconsolidating the memory. I tell my patients to stay present with their feelings to help create the emotional change. If they become emotionally overwhelmed that's okay; they should retreat from the behavior and practice self-compassion for the emotion. Then later in therapy we can reassess what went right or wrong. It's important that patients feel a sense of mastery over their emotional experience; otherwise, they will not want to continue the process of change. I try to let patients set their own step three goals, so they feel more in control.

References

Adhikari, A. (2014). Distributed circuits underlying anxiety. *Frontiers in Behavioral Neuroscience, 8*, 112.

Adolphs, R., Cahill, L., Schul, R., & Babinsky, R. (1997). Impaired declarative memory for emotional material following bilateral amygdala damage in humans. *Learning & Memory, 4*(3), 291–300.

Björkstrand, J., Agren, T., Frick, A., Engman, J., Larsson, E. M., Furmark, T., & Fredrikson, M. (2015). Disruption of memory reconsolidation erases a fear memory trace in the human amygdala: An 18-month follow-up. *PLoS One, 10*(7), e0129393.

Bonnici, H. M., & Maguire, E. A. (2018). Two years later–Revisiting autobiographical memory representations in vmPFC and hippocampus. *Neuropsychologia, 110*, 159–169.

Craske, M., Stein, M., Eley, T., Milad, M. R., Holmes, A., Rapee, R. M., & Wittchen, H. U. (2017). Anxiety disorders. *Nature Reviews Disease Primers, 3*, 17024. doi:10.1038/nrdp.2017.24.

Dahlgren, K., Ferris, C., & Hamann, S. (2020). Neural correlates of successful emotional episodic encoding and retrieval: An SDM meta-analysis of neuroimaging studies. *Neuropsychologia*, 107495.

Ecker, B., & Bridges, S. K. (2020). How the science of memory reconsolidation advances the effectiveness and unification of psychotherapy. *Clinical Social Work Journal, 48*, 287–300.

Eldridge, L. L., Engel, S. A., Zeineh, M. M., Bookheimer, S. Y., & Knowlton, B. J. (2005). A dissociation of encoding and retrieval processes in the human hippocampus. *Journal of Neuroscience, 25*(13), 3280–3286.

Elsey, J. W., Van Ast, V. A., & Kindt, M. (2018). Human memory reconsolidation: A guiding framework and critical review of the evidence. *Psychological Bulletin*, *144*(8), 797.

Goldman, R. N., Greenberg, L. S., & Pos, A. E. (2005). Depth of emotional experience and outcome. *Psychotherapy Research*, *15*(3), 248–260.

Heinz, A., Braus, D. F., Smolka, M. N., Wrase, J., Puls, I., Hermann, D., ... & Büchel, C. (2005). Amygdala-prefrontal coupling depends on a genetic variation of the serotonin transporter. *Nature Neuroscience*, *8*(1), 20–21.

Hughes, K. C., & Shin, L. M. (2011). Functional neuroimaging studies of post-traumatic stress disorder. *Expert Review of Neurotherapeutics*, *11*(2), 275–285.

Inman, C. S., Manns, J. R., Bijanki, K. R., Bass, D. I., Hamann, S., Drane, D. L., ... & Willie, J. T. (2018). Direct electrical stimulation of the amygdala enhances declarative memory in humans. *Proceedings of the National Academy of Sciences*, *115*(1), 98–103.

Kensinger, E. A., & Schacter, D. L. (2006). Amygdala activity is associated with the successful encoding of item, but not source, information for positive and negative stimuli. *Journal of Neuroscience*, *26*(9), 2564–2570.

Kumaran, D., Hassabis, D., & McClelland, J. L. (2016). What learning systems do intelligent agents need? Complementary learning systems theory updated. *Trends in Cognitive Sciences*, *20*(7), 512–534.

Levenson, H., Angus, L., & Pool, E. (2020). Viewing psychodynamic/interpersonal theory and practice through the lens of memory reconsolidation. In *Neuroscience of enduring change* (pp. 300–359). Oxford: Oxford University Press.

Maren, S., Phan, K. L., & Liberzon, I. (2013). The contextual brain: Implications for fear conditioning, extinction and psychopathology. *Nature Reviews Neuroscience*, *14*(6), 417–428.

Merlo, E., Milton, A. L., Goozée, Z. Y., Theobald, D. E., & Everitt, B. J. (2014). Reconsolidation and extinction are dissociable and mutually exclusive processes: Behavioral and molecular evidence. *Journal of Neuroscience*, *34*(7), 2422–2431.

Milad, M. R., Quinn, B. T., Pitman, R. K., Orr, S. P., Fischl, B., & Rauch, S. L. (2005). Thickness of ventromedial prefrontal cortex in humans is correlated with extinction memory. *Proceedings of the National Academy of Sciences*, *102*(30), 10706–10711.

Milad, M. R., & Quirk, G. J. (2002). Neurons in medial prefrontal cortex signal memory for fear extinction. *Nature*, *420*(6911), 70–74.

Milad, M. R., Wright, C. I., Orr, S. P., Pitman, R. K., Quirk, G. J., & Rauch, S. L. (2007). Recall of fear extinction in humans activates the ventromedial prefrontal cortex and hippocampus in concert. *Biological Psychiatry*, *62*(5), 446–454.

Monfils, M. H., Cowansage, K. K., Klann, E., & LeDoux, J. E. (2009). Extinction-reconsolidation boundaries: Key to persistent attenuation of fear memories. *Science*, *324*(5929), 951–955.

Moscovitch, M., Rosenbaum, R. S., Gilboa, A., Addis, D. R., Westmacott, R., Grady, C., ... & Nadel, L. (2005). Functional neuroanatomy of remote episodic, semantic and spatial memory: A unified account based on multiple trace theory. *Journal of Anatomy*, *207*(1), 35–66.

Nadel, L. (2020). What is a memory that it can be changed? In R. D. Lane & L. Nadel (Eds.), *Neuroscience of enduring change: Implications for psychotherapy*. Oxford: Oxford University Press.

Nawa, N. E., & Ando, H. (2019). Effective connectivity within the ventromedial prefrontal cortex-hippocampus-amygdala network during the elaboration of emotional autobiographical memories. *NeuroImage, 189*, 316–328.

Pascual-Leone, A., & Greenberg, L. S. (2007). Emotional processing in experiential therapy: Why "the only way out is through." *Journal of Consulting and Clinical Psychology, 75*(6), 875.

Pedreira, M. E., Pérez-Cuesta, L. M., & Maldonado, H. (2004). Mismatch between what is expected and what actually occurs triggers memory reconsolidation or extinction. *Learning & Memory, 11*(5), 579–585.

Pos, A. E., Greenberg, L. S., & Warwar, S. H. (2009). Testing a model of change in the experiential treatment of depression. *Journal of Consulting and Clinical Psychology, 77*(6), 1055.

Ryan, L., Hoscheidt, S., & Nadel, L. (2008). Perspectives on episodic and semantic memory retrieval. *Handbook of Behavioral Neuroscience, 18*, 5–616.

Schiller, D., Kanen, J. W., LeDoux, J. E., Monfils, M. H., & Phelps, E. A. (2013). Extinction during reconsolidation of threat memory diminishes prefrontal cortex involvement. *Proceedings of the National Academy of Sciences, 110*(50), 20040–20045.

Soeter, M., & Kindt, M. (2015a). An abrupt transformation of phobic behavior after a post-retrieval amnesic agent. *Biological Psychiatry, 78*(12), 880–886.

Soeter, M., & Kindt, M. (2015b). Retrieval cues that trigger reconsolidation of associative fear memory are not necessarily an exact replica of the original learning experience. *Frontiers in Behavioral Neuroscience, 9*, 122.

Sotres-Bayon, F., Cain, C. K., & LeDoux, J. E. (2006). Brain mechanisms of fear extinction: Historical perspectives on the contribution of prefrontal cortex. *Biological Psychiatry, 60*(4), 329–336.

Takashima, A., Petersson, K. M., Rutters, F., Tendolkar, I., Jensen, O., Zwarts, M. J., … & Fernandez, G. (2006). Declarative memory consolidation in humans: A prospective functional magnetic resonance imaging study. *Proceedings of the National Academy of Sciences, 103*(3), 756–761.

Vervliet, B., Craske, M. G., & Hermans, D. (2013). Fear extinction and relapse: State of the art. *Annual Review of Clinical Psychology, 9*.

Welling, H. (2012). Transformative emotional sequence: Towards a common principle of change. *Journal of Psychotherapy Integration, 22*(2), 109.

12 Conclusion

12.1 Shifting Paradigms

One of the tenets of CBT is challenging irrational cognitions. Many individuals with psychopathology hold irrational cognitions related to self, believing they're worthless, unlovable, or must be perfect. CBT challenges the patients' thinking that their beliefs are wrong, and the beliefs *are* wrong. The problem is, even though the cognitions are wrong, they feel right. As an early clinician practicing CBT at times, I remember patients saying to me, "Yeah, I know I'm not worthless, but that's how I feel." I felt stuck and I remember thinking, "So just change your thinking and then you will feel better." It never really worked. I felt frustrated as a clinician, like I had missed something. I asked myself, "Do I keep pressuring the patient about their thinking, give up, or try something else?" I didn't know what else to do, and I think at times I shamed patients. Saying things like "Well, if you know you are not worthless, stop telling yourself you are so you don't keep feeling down," and paying little attention to the emotional experience of the patient. What the patient told me prior was there their truth; they understood there was no logical reason for them to feel worthless, they just did. When I continued to point out their illogical nature, I just contributed to shaming their feelings. The patient probably thought, "There is something wrong with me personally; I cannot make the connection between logical thinking and my feelings." An explicit attitude can be changed through logical reasoning, but implicit attitudes don't respond to such logic; they change through experiential learning (Rydell & McConnell, 2006), affect reconsolidation being an example of such. Explicitly, depressed individuals typically know they shouldn't think poorly of themselves; it's just hard not to because it doesn't match how they actually feel. Implicit attitudes are based on an associative learning process and are more emotional in nature (see section 2.4), making them less susceptible to reason. I won't assume this has been every clinician's experience, but this is where I've seen CBT go wrong. CBT assumes patients should be able to change their feelings through thought. This can result in patients feeling shame about feelings when they are unable to change them and blaming themselves for

DOI: 10.4324/9781003150893-12

feeling bad. Therapies overly focusing on cognitions also run the risk of ignoring emotions, which misses a critical part of therapy. I had the honor of seeing Albert Ellis perform psychotherapy live as a student; his logic and reasoning were sound, but there was no attention to emotion. A skilled CBT therapist is probably better at attending to the emotional experience than I was in my formative days, but the premise of CBT still sits sets up many patients for failure. This is not solely a problem of CBT; psychodynamic and psychoanalytic approaches that take an overly cognitive approach also run the risk of ignoring a patient's emotions. When psychodynamic approaches focus only on developing insight and interpretations of the patient's pathology, they miss the emotional experience of the patient, and improvement is limited. I used to tell my students, Woody Allen has been in psychoanalysis most of his life, he knows why he struggles mentally, but his mental state still hasn't improved. It's paramount to recognize the limits of psychotherapy approaches that disregard emotion. CBT can help stop the reinforcement of negative thoughts, but it cannot change basic primary emotions. This is why a paradigm shift towards interventions utilizing emotion and affect reconsolidation is broadly needed. The good news is, this is happening. Psychodynamic-based approaches like Diana Fosha's accelerated experiential psychodynamic therapy (AEDP) and Hanna Levenson's time-limited dynamic psychotherapy (TLDP) are shifting to more experiential and emotion-based treatments. On the CBT side, David Barlow's unified protocol is expanding CBT into more affective domains. My hope is that as we better understand the brain processes in mental illness, we can develop more effective integrative approaches to psychotherapy.

12.2 An Affective Neuroscience Approach

From an affective neuroscience viewpoint, most psychological disorders can probably be organized into deficits within three or four brain networks. The fear circuit (Nair, Paré, & Vicentic, 2016), is an emotional memory network that involves the amygdala, vmPFC, hippocampus, and related hippocampal area in the MTL (Nawa & Ando, 2019) (see section 11.1), that is involved in storage and retrieval of emotional memories. Although not always considered a separate brain network, Godsil, Kiss, Spedding, and Jay (2013) find a convergence of dysfunction in this network among psychological disorders like PTSD, schizophrenia, and depression. This emotional memory network would be involved in the encoding of traumatic memories associated with PTSD and is a target network for affect reconsolidation. In order to reconsolidate emotional memories, one must first have awareness of their feelings, and this appears to be related to the SN. Alexithymia, symptoms of dissociation, and blunted affect appear to have disrupted functioning in the SN (Hogeveen, Bird, Chau, Krueger, & Grafman, 2016; Stevens, 2016). I also tend to think many dissociative and somatic disorders also involve disruption to SN, but research in this area is limited. Activating the SN will be important in increasing emotional awareness, which is a theme throughout this book, starting with the chapter on mindfulness. The MCL dysfunction is seen in faulty reward learning, where individuals struggle to discontinue behaviors that were once rewarding but are now harmful. This is when we are unable to escape our drive for dopamine and act against our best interests. Disorders of addiction would be marked by dysfunction in the MCL (see section 9.6). Other networks may not directly contribute to psychological disorders, but still play a role. Rumination, present in depression and anxiety, involves excessive self-referential thinking, which is associated with DMN. Although we didn't cover ADHD in this book because it's less emotional in nature, deficits in attention are associated with the VAN and DAN, and perhaps the SN as well. Other psychological disorders too, like neurodevelopmental and neurocognitive disorders, were not addressed in this book, as they are more cognitive and less emotional in brain dysfunction. These disorders probably should be addressed from a cognitive and not an affective neuroscience perspective. Additionally, my experience with these disorders is limited, and I would urge readers to consult elsewhere for optimal treatment strategies. Much more research needs to be completed before we can fully map the various psychological disorders onto functional brain processes. By doing so, psychology can become a more empirically-based science, and no longer will freshman shake their heads when the Oedipus complex is taught. Through affective neuroscience, we can develop more informed treatment approaches to help guide clinicians.

12.3 Reductionistic Approach

Throughout much of training, I recognized a common eye roll amongst many of my fellow therapists whenever the term manualized treatment came up. It's not that manualized treatment doesn't have any value, but the assumption was it's too reductive, treating all patients the same with no regard for nuance. Manualized treatment helps structure therapy by creating empirically-based models that anyone can apply if they follow the manual. However, many of my colleagues and mentors in training felt these manualized treatments were too stringent an approach, glossing over therapeutic rapport, and not always allowing enough time for the patient to share their experience (most manualized approaches work with eight–ten session model). Alternatively, taking a therapeutic approach with no regard to science creates other problems. Reductionistic science is always going to lose nuance by trying to create a single model for all. One of the challenges in developing emotional approaches to therapy is identifying common treatment strategies while recognizing the uniqueness of everyone's emotional experience. The emotional experience can vary greatly between individuals. One person experiences sadness as a good feeling, while another is stuck in a cycle of crying spells. Emotions are hard to quantify individually; an overly dramatic person may express anger in a very different way than the quite vindictive type. Our external and internal expression of emotion can vary; for example, women tend to be more expressive than men with their feelings (Kring & Gordon, 1998). Emotions too are often mixed; sexual masochists derive sexual pleasure from pain, while schadenfreude is a German feeling word for enjoying someone else's pain. Emotions can also be troublesome, as patients' emotions can trigger emotions in therapists, known as countertransference. I think because of these reasons, psychotherapy has disregarded emotion at times, reducing psychotherapy down to a simple equation. A bad event produces an irrational cognition, which results in a disorder, and it just takes a simple correction to fix the equation. Reductionism can be helpful but also confining. As we create treatments for emotions, we have to tease apart common change principles with individual variations in expression. An emotional approach to psychotherapy involves being open to the complexities of emotional experience. Therapists should be open to different approaches when things are not working and be willing to fail using new techniques.

12.4 Therapists Own Emotional Development

My hope is for clinicians reading this book is that understanding the neuroscience behind psychotherapy will help improve the quality of psychotherapy delivered; however, I can't tell you exactly when to use which intervention, and for which patients. Therapists must use their judgment to decide where to focus time and attention. Although the book offers a neuroscience-based framework for therapeutic change, how to best create that change will depend upon the skills and judgment of the therapist.

To maximize this approach, I do recommend therapists use an adaptive thinking strategy and pay attention to their own emotional growth. Adaptive thinking is a meta-cognitive process, where you try to become aware of your preconceptions about a theory or a patient. It is the ability to recognize that your thinking for a given situation is wrong and to change your thinking style to adapt to a new environmental context. One place I see this is in couples therapy. It goes something like this: The wife complains she is not supported by her husband. The husband trying to fix the problem, asks, "What can I do to fix this?" The wife responds, "You don't have to do anything." The husband throws up his hands in frustration. Both the husband and wife are thinking about the problem differently. The husband thinks, "There is a problem; I should take action and fix it." The wife thinks, "I am clearly in distress and need emotional support." The wife sees the problem as a lack of emotional support, while the husband sees the problem as a missing action step. Both are thinking in the way that they conceptualize problems, but to fix this they need to use adaptive thinking.

That is, they need to think about their thinking, and how they could think differently. Therapists sometimes assume what has worked as a treatment for previous patients should work as a treatment for new patients, and often it does. Although, this is not always the case, and when I get stuck like this, I ask myself, "How might the patient be thinking about this problem differently?" This is much easier to say than do. It is hard to step out of one's thinking paradigm and recognize that previously effective interventions are not working. However, I have a couple of recommendations here. Pay attention to your own feelings as a therapist; when you are feeling frustrated or stuck it's likely the same thing is happening with your patient. At times I've noticed myself feeling bored after several sessions; this indicates to me that whatever I'm doing or have done is no longer effective. I need to adapt my style for continued improvement of the patient. It is also best to assume that the patient is not intentionally trying to sabotage the treatment, but more likely has reached a point where they are scared to move forward. When stuck, I recommend asking the patient, "What are you feeling?" Be sure to get a feeling response and not an explanation of what may be happening. The question easily can be dodged by the patient with an "I don't know." Ask the patient to slow down and check-in with their experience, moving beneath their surface response. I find this can often ground and redirect the therapy from a previous pathway that wasn't working before. Perhaps this works as a way of acknowledging and moving towards a feeling that was previously avoided or ignored, whether it is intentional or not.

Therapists should try and consider emotions to be adaptive responses, even if they are not adaptive to the current situation. Therapists should ask themselves, "What might the patient's feeling represent and why might they feel this way?" I encourage patients to see that bad feelings are telling them they need something. Bad feelings are akin to physical pain in the body, as they both report that something is not right in the system, and the bad feelings are the feedback telling us we need to change things. Quelling the emotion itself won't fix the deeper problem of what is causing the emotion. It's valuable not to run away from your experience but to accept it regardless of what the experience maybe. In this regard, a therapist's own emotional development is important. If therapists struggle to accept their own feelings, they will also have trouble helping their patients who struggle with those same emotions. Clinicians can develop through practicing skills on themselves and responding effectively to their own emotions, which in turn will benefit the patient. Just as the caregiver lays the foundation for the child's emotional development through emotional attunement and reflection of feelings, so does the therapist in the response to patients' emotions (see section 5.2). The emotional dialogue in therapy is mostly a non-verbal implicit process, meaning the therapists' instincts in responding to their own emotions are often what gets taught to their patients. This book presented a lot of neuroscience to help clinicians understand how the brain works with emotion. However, this knowledge doesn't replace the hard work of caring for one's emotions. For clinicians to excel as therapists, they must also be good at caring for their own feelings.

References

Godsil, B. P., Kiss, J. P., Spedding, M., & Jay, T. M. (2013). The hippocampal–prefrontal pathway: The weak link in psychiatric disorders? *European Neuropsychopharmacology, 23*(10), 1165–1181.

Hogeveen, J., Bird, G., Chau, A., Krueger, F., & Grafman, J. (2016). Acquired alexithymia following damage to the anterior insula. *Neuropsychologia, 82*, 142–148.

Kring, A. M., & Gordon, A. H. (1998). Sex differences in emotion: Expression, experience, and physiology. *Journal of Personality and Social Psychology, 74*(3), 686.

Nair, S. S., Paré, D., & Vicentic, A. (2016). Biologically based neural circuit modelling for the study of fear learning and extinction. *NPJ Science of Learning, 1*(1), 1–7.

Nawa, N. E., & Ando, H. (2019). Effective connectivity within the ventromedial prefrontal cortex-hippocampus-amygdala network during the elaboration of emotional autobiographical memories. *NeuroImage, 189*, 316–328.

Rydell, R. J., & McConnell, A. R. (2006). Understanding implicit and explicit attitude change: A systems of reasoning analysis. *Journal of Personality and Social Psychology, 91*(6), 995.

Stevens, F. L. (2016). The anterior cingulate cortex in psychopathology and psychotherapy: Effects on awareness and repression of affect. *Neuropsychoanalysis, 18*(1), 53–68.

Index

Note the italicized "*f*" following certain page numbers refers to footnotes.

Made in the USA
Las Vegas, NV
26 September 2024